THE ALEXANDER SHAKESPEARE

General Editor

R. B. KENNEDY

PADGATE COUNTY HIGH SCHOOL

Dilemma
- makes life hard for himself co snasty to king.
  'A lit more than kin + less than kind!'
- indecisive in general - inability to do anything pos. about Claud death ever

THE ALEXANDER SHAKESPEARE

Hamlet

Edited by

B. DAVIES

Death

act	sc	line
* 1	2	129-37
1	4	65-7
3	1	56-82
*3	1	75-110
5	1	161-212
5	2	74
5	2	207-18

REVENGE.

ACT	SC	LINE
* 1	5	29-31
2	2	546-603
3	3	73-96
x 3	4	107-10
4	4	32-66
2	2	64-70

COLLINS PUBLISHERS: LONDON AND GLASGOW

First edition, 1973
Second impression, 1977
Reprint, 1984

©

Wm. Collins Sons and Co. Ltd.

000 197317 (NETT)
0 00 325246 9 (NON NETT)

Printed in Great Britain
Collins Clear-Type Press

Contents

An Elizabethan playhouse. Note the apron stage protruding into the auditorium, the space below it, the inner room at the rear of the stage, the gallery above the inner stage, the canopy over the main stage, and the absence of a roof over the audience.

PREFATORY NOTE

This series of Shakespeare's plays uses the full Alexander text which is recommended by many Examining Boards. By keeping in mind the fact that the language has changed considerably in four hundred years, as have customs, jokes, and stage conventions, the editors have aimed at helping the modern reader – whether English is his mother tongue or not – to grasp the full significance of these plays. The Notes, intended primarily for examination candidates, are presented in a simple, direct style. The needs of those unfamiliar with British culture have been specially considered.

Since quiet study of the printed word is unlikely to bring fully to life plays that were written directly for the public theatre, attention has been drawn to dramatic effects which are important in performance. The editors see Shakespeare's plays as living works of art which can be enjoyed today on stage, film and television in many parts of the world.

THE THEATRE IN SHAKESPEARE'S DAY

On the face of it, the conditions in the Elizabethan theatre were not such as to encourage great writers. The public playhouse itself was not very different from an ordinary inn-yard; it was open to the weather; among the spectators there were often louts, pickpockets and prostitutes; some of the actors played up to the rowdy elements in the audience by inserting their own jokes into the authors' lines, while others spoke their words loudly but unfeelingly; the presentation was often rough and noisy, with fireworks to represent storms and battles, and a table and a few chairs to represent a tavern; there were no actresses, so boys took the parts of women, even such subtle and mature ones as Cleopatra and Lady Macbeth; there was rarely any scenery at all in the modern sense. In fact, a quick inspection of the English theatre in the reign of Elizabeth I by a time-traveller from the twentieth century might well produce only one positive reaction: the costumes were often elaborate and beautiful.

Shakespeare himself makes frequent comments in his plays about the limitations of the playhouse and the actors of his time, often apologizing for them. At the beginning of *Henry V* the Prologue refers to the stage as 'this unworthy scaffold' and to the theatre building (the Globe, probably) as 'this wooden O', and emphasizes the urgent need for imagination in making up for all the deficiencies of presentation. In introducing Act IV the Chorus goes so far as to say:

> '. . . we shall much disgrace
> With four or five most vile and ragged foils,
> Right ill-dispos'd in brawl ridiculous,
> The name of Agincourt.' (lines 49–52)

In *A Midsummer Night's Dream* (Act V, Scene i) he seems to dismiss actors with the words:

> 'The best in this kind are but shadows.'

9

Yet Elizabeth's theatre, with all its faults, stimulated dramatists to a variety of achievement that has never been equalled and, in Shakespeare, produced one of the greatest writers in history. In spite of all his grumbles he seems to have been fascinated by the challenge that it presented him with. It is necessary to re-examine his theatre carefully in order to understand how he was able to achieve so much with the materials he chose to use. What sort of place was the Elizabethan playhouse in reality? What sort of people were these criticized actors? And what sort of audiences gave them their living?

The Development of the Theatre up to Shakespeare's Time

For centuries in England noblemen had employed groups of skilled people to entertain them when required. Under Tudor rule, as England became more secure and united, actors such as these were given more freedom, and they often performed in public, while still acknowledging their 'overlords' (in the 1570s, for example, when Shakespeare was still a schoolboy at Stratford, one famous company was called 'Lord Leicester's Men'). London was rapidly becoming larger and more important in the second half of the sixteenth century, and many of the companies of actors took the opportunities offered to establish themselves at inns on the main roads leading to the City (for example, the Boar's Head in Whitechapel and the Tabard in Southwark) or in the City itself. These groups of actors would come to an agreement with the inn-keeper which would give them the use of the yard for their performances after people had eaten and drunk well in the middle of the day. Before long, some inns were taken over completely by companies of players and thus became the first public theatres. In 1574 the officials of the City of London issued an order which shows clearly that these theatres were both popular and also offensive to some respectable people, because the order complains about 'the inordinate haunting of great multitudes of people, specially youth, to plays, interludes and shows; namely occasion of frays and quarrels, evil practices

10

of incontinency in great inns . . .' There is evidence that, on public holidays, the theatres on the banks of the Thames were crowded with noisy apprentices and tradesmen, but it would be wrong to think that audiences were always undiscriminating and loud-mouthed. In spite of the disapproval of Puritans and the more staid members of society, by the 1590s, when Shakespeare's plays were beginning to be performed, audiences consisted of a good cross-section of English society, nobility as well as workers, intellectuals as well as simple people out for a laugh; also (and in this respect English theatres were unique in Europe), it was quite normal for respectable women to attend plays. So Shakespeare had to write plays which would appeal to people of widely different kinds. He had to provide 'something for everyone' but at the same time to take care to unify the material so that it would not seem to fall into separate pieces as they watched it. A speech like that of the drunken porter in *Macbeth* could provide the 'groundlings' with a belly-laugh, but also held a deeper significance for those who could appreciate it. The audience he wrote for was one of a number of apparent drawbacks which Shakespeare was able to turn to his and our advantage.

Shakespeare's Actors

Nor were all the actors of the time mere 'rogues, vagabonds and sturdy beggars' as some were described in a Statute of 1572. It is true that many of them had a hard life and earned very little money, but leading actors could become partners in the ownership of the theatres in which they acted: Shakespeare was a shareholder in the Globe and the Blackfriars theatres when he was an actor as well as a playwright. In any case, the attacks made on Elizabethan actors were usually directed at their morals and not at their acting ability; it is clear that many of them must have been good at their trade if they were able to interpret complex works like the great tragedies in such a way as to attract enthusiastic audiences. Undoubtedly some of the boys took the women's parts with skill and confidence, since a man called Coryate, visiting Venice in 1611, expressed surprise that women could act as well as they: 'I saw women act, a thing that I never saw before . . . and they performed it with as good a grace, action, gesture . . . as ever I saw any masculine actor.' The quality of most of the actors who first presented Shakespeare's plays is probably accurately summed up by Fynes Moryson, who wrote, '. . . as there be, in my opinion, more plays in London than in all the parts of the world I have seen, so do these players or comedians excel all other in the world.'

The Structure of the Public Theatre

Although the 'purpose-built' theatres were based on the inn-yards which had been used for play-acting, most of them were circular. The walls contained galleries on three storeys from which the wealthier patrons watched; they must have been something like the 'boxes' in a modern theatre, except that they held much larger numbers – as many as 1500. The 'groundlings' stood on the floor of the building, facing a raised stage which projected from the 'stage-wall', the main features of which were:

1. a small room opening on to the back of the main stage and on the same level as it (rear stage);
2. a gallery above this inner stage (upper stage);
3. a canopy projecting from above the gallery over the main stage, to protect the actors from the weather (the 700 or 800 members of the audience who occupied the yard, or 'pit' as we call it today, had the sky above them).

In addition to these features there were dressing-rooms behind the stage and a space underneath it from which entrances could be made through trap-doors. All the acting areas – main stage, rear stage, upper stage and under stage – could be entered by actors directly from their dressing-rooms, and all of them were used in productions of Shakespeare's plays. For example, the inner stage, an almost cave-like structure, would have been where Ferdinand and Miranda are 'discovered' playing chess in the last act of *The Tempest*, while the upper stage was certainly the balcony from which Romeo climbs down in Act III of *Romeo and Juliet*.

It can be seen that such a building, simple but adaptable, was not really unsuited to the presentation of plays like Shakespeare's. On the contrary, its simplicity guaranteed the minimum of distraction, while its shape and construction must have produced a sense of involvement on the part of the audience that modern producers would envy.

Other Resources of the Elizabethan Theatre

Although there were few attempts at scenery in the public theatre (painted backcloths were occasionally used in court performances), Shakespeare and his fellow playwrights were able to make use of a fair variety of 'properties'; lists of such articles have survived: they include beds, tables, thrones, and also trees, walls, a gallows, a Trojan horse and a 'Mouth of Hell'; in a list of properties belonging to the manager, Philip Henslowe, the curious item 'two mossy banks' appears. Possibly one of them was used for the

'bank whereon the wild thyme blows,
Where oxlips and the nodding violet grows'

in *A Midsummer Night's Dream* (Act II, Scene i). Once again, imagination must have been required of the audience.

Costumes were the one aspect of stage production in which trouble and expense were hardly ever spared to obtain a magnificent effect. Only occasionally did they attempt any historical accuracy (almost all Elizabethan productions were what we should call 'modern-dress' ones), but they were appropriate to the characters who wore them: kings were seen to be kings and beggars were similarly unmistakable. It is an odd fact that there was usually no attempt at illusion in the costuming: if a costume *looked* fine and rich it probably *was*. Indeed, some of the costumes were almost unbelievably expensive. Henslowe lent his company £19 to buy a cloak, and the Alleyn brothers, well-known actors, gave £20 for a 'black velvet cloak, with sleeves embroidered all with silver and gold, lined with black satin striped with gold'.

13

With the one exception of the costumes, the 'machinery' of the playhouse was economical and uncomplicated rather than crude and rough, as we can see from this second and more leisurely look at it. This meant that playwrights were stimulated to produce the imaginative effects that they wanted from the language that they used. In the case of a really great writer like Shakespeare, when he had learned his trade in the theatre as an actor, it seems that he received quite enough assistance of a mechanical and structural kind without having irksome restrictions and conventions imposed on him; it is interesting to try to guess what he would have done with the highly complex apparatus of a modern television studio. We can see when we look back to his time that he used his instrument, the Elizabethan theatre, to the full, but placed his ultimate reliance on the communication between his imagination and that of his audience through the medium of words. It is, above all, his rich and wonderful use of language that must have made play-going at that time a memorable experience for people of widely different kinds. Fortunately, the deep satisfaction of appreciating and enjoying Shakespeare's work can be ours also, if we are willing to overcome the language difficulty produced by the passing of time.

SHAKESPEARE'S LIFE AND TIMES

Very little indeed is known about Shakespeare's private life: the facts included here are almost the only indisputable ones. The dates of Shakespeare's plays are those on which they were first produced.

*　　*　　*

1558 Queen Elizabeth crowned.
1561 Francis Bacon born.
1564 Christopher Marlowe born.

1566
1567 Mary, Queen of Scots, deposed.
James VI (later James I of England) crowned King of Scotland.
1572 Ben Jonson born.
Lord Leicester's Company (of players) licensed; later called Lord Strange's, then the Lord Chamberlain's, and finally (under James) The King's Men.
1573 John Donne born.
1574 The Common Council of London directs that all plays and playhouses in London must be licensed.
1576 James Burbage builds the first public playhouse, The Theatre, at Shoreditch, outside the walls of the City.
1577 Francis Drake begins his voyage round the world (completed 1580).
Holinshed's *Chronicles of England, Scotland and Ireland* published (which Shakespeare later used extensively).
1582

William Shakespeare born, April 23rd, baptized April 26th.
Shakespeare's brother, Gilbert, born.

Shakespeare married to Anne Hathaway.

15

1583 The Queen's Company founded by royal warrant.

Shakespeare's daughter, Susanna, born.

1585

Shakespeare's twins, Hamnet and Judith, born.

1586 Sir Philip Sidney, the Elizabethan ideal 'Christian knight', poet, patron, soldier, killed at Zutphen in the Low Countries.

1587 Mary, Queen of Scots, beheaded.
Marlowe's *Tamburlaine* (*Part I*) first staged.

1588 Defeat of the Spanish Armada.
Marlowe's *Tamburlaine* (*Part II*) first staged.

1589 Marlowe's *Jew of Malta* and Kyd's *Spanish Tragedy* (a 'revenge tragedy' and one of the most popular plays of Elizabethan times).

1590 Spenser's *Faerie Queene* (Books I-III) published.

1592 Marlowe's *Doctor Faustus* and *Edward II* first staged. Witchcraft trials in Scotland.
Robert Greene, a rival playwright, refers to Shakespeare as 'an upstart crow' and 'the only Shake-scene in a country'.

Titus Andronicus
Henry VI, Parts I, II and III
Richard III

1593 London theatres closed by the plague.
Christopher Marlowe killed in a Deptford tavern.

Two Gentlemen of Verona
Comedy of Errors
The Taming of the Shrew
Love's Labour's Lost

1594 Shakespeare's company becomes The Lord Chamberlain's Men.

Romeo and Juliet

1595 Raleigh's first expedition to Guiana. Last expedition of Drake and Hawkins (both died).

Richard II
A Midsummer Night's Dream

1596 Spenser's *Faerie Queene* (Books IV-VI) published. James Burbage buys rooms at Blackfriars and begins to convert them into a theatre.

King John
The Merchant of Venice
Shakespeare's son Hamnet dies. Shakespeare's father is granted a coat of arms.

1597 James Burbage dies; his son Richard, a famous actor, turns the Blackfriars Theatre into a private playhouse.

Henry IV (Part I)
Shakespeare buys and redecorates New Place at Stratford.

1598 Death of Philip II of Spain.

Henry IV (Part II)
Much Ado About Nothing

1599 Death of Edmund Spenser. The Globe Theatre completed at Bankside by Richard and Cuthbert Burbage.

Henry V
Julius Caesar
As You Like It

1600 Fortune Theatre built at Cripplegate.
East India Company founded for the extension of English trade and influence in the East.
The Children of the Chapel begin to use the hall at Blackfriars.

Merry Wives of Windsor
Troilus and Cressida

1601

Hamlet
Twelfth Night

1602 Sir Thomas Bodley's library opened at Oxford.

1603 Death of Queen Elizabeth. James I comes to the throne. Shakespeare's company becomes The King's Men. Raleigh tried, condemned and sent to the Tower.

1604 Treaty of peace with Spain.

Measure for Measure
Othello
All's Well that Ends Well

1605 The Gunpowder Plot: an attempt by a group of Catholics to blow up the Houses of Parliament.

1606 Guy Fawkes and other plotters executed.

Macbeth
King Lear

1607 Virginia, in America, colonized.
A great frost in England.

Antony and Cleopatra
Timon of Athens
Coriolanus
Shakespeare's daughter, Susanna, married to Dr. John Hall.

1608 The company of the Children of the Chapel Royal (who had performed at Blackfriars for ten years) is disbanded.
John Milton born.
Notorious pirates executed in London.

Richard Burbage leases the Blackfriars Theatre to six of his fellow actors, including Shakespeare.
Pericles, Prince of Tyre

1609

Shakespeare's *Sonnets* published.

1610 A great drought in England.

Cymbeline

1611 Chapman completes his great translation of the *Iliad*, the story of Troy.
Authorized Version of the Bible published.

A Winter's Tale
The Tempest

1612 Webster's *The White Devil* first staged.

Shakespeare's brother, Gilbert, dies.

1613 Globe Theatre burnt down during a performance of *Henry VIII* (the firing of small cannon set fire to the thatched roof).
Webster's *Duchess of Malfi* first staged.

Henry VIII
Two Noble Kinsmen
Shakespeare buys a house at Blackfriars.

1614 Globe Theatre rebuilt 'in far finer manner than before'.

1616 Ben Jonson publishes his plays in one volume.
Raleigh released from the Tower in order to prepare an expedition to the gold mines of Gùiana.

Shakespeare's daughter, Judith, marries Thomas Quiney.
Death of Shakespeare on his birthday, April 23rd.

1618 Raleigh returns to England and is executed on the charge for which he was imprisoned in 1603.

1623 Publication of the Folio edition of Shakespeare's plays.

Death of Anne Shakespeare (née Hathaway).

MONEY IN SHAKESPEARE'S DAY

It is extremely difficult, if not impossible, to relate the value of money in our time to its value in another age and to compare prices of commodities today and in the past. Many items are simply not comparable on grounds of quality or serviceability.

There was a bewildering variety of coins in use in Elizabethan England. As nearly all English and European coins were gold or silver, they had intrinsic value apart from their official value. This meant that foreign coins circulated freely in England and were officially recognized, for example, the French crown (écu) worth about 30p (72 cents), and the Spanish ducat worth about 33p (79 cents). The following table shows some of the coins mentioned by Shakespeare and their relation to one another.

GOLD	British	American	SILVER	British	American
sovereign (heavy type)	£1.50	$3.60	shilling	10p	24c
sovereign (light type)	66p–£1	$1.58–$2.40	groat	1½p	4c
angel	33p–50p	79c–$1.20			
royal	50p	$1.20			
noble	33p	79c			
crown	25p	60c			

A comparison of the following prices in Shakespeare's time with the prices of the same items today will give some idea of the change in the value of money.

ITEM	PRICE British	PRICE American	ITEM	PRICE British	PRICE American
beef, per lb.	½p	1c	cherries (lb.)	1p	2c
mutton, leg	7½p	18c	7 oranges	1p	2c
rabbit	3½p	9c	1 lemon	1p	2c
chicken	3p	8c	cream (quart)	2½p	6c
potatoes (lb.)	10p	24c	sugar (lb.)	£1	$2.40
carrots (bnch.)	1p	2c	sack (wine) (gal.)	14p	34c
8 artichokes	4p	9c	tobacco (oz.)	25p	60c
1 cucumber	1p	2c	biscuits (lb.)	12½p	30c

19

INTRODUCTION

'The tragedy of a man who could not make up his mind' –
this is how the Olivier film of *Hamlet* describes the theme of
the play. When *you* have read or seen it, however, will you
agree? What has fascinated generations of audiences and
readers, is that it is not so easy to sum up for good and all,
in one short sentence, what the play is about, because its
situations and characters are seen differently by different
people, like those in real life. This is particularly the case
with Hamlet himself, for we each tend to feel closest to those
sides of his changeable personality in which we recognize
ourselves and our friends, while at other times finding him
as remote and mysterious as do the other characters in the
play.

This is what makes *Hamlet* one of the few plays that
appeals as much when you read it as when you see it, though
for quite different reasons. When reading it, for instance,
you are free to make up your own mind about what sort of
person not only Hamlet, but each of the other characters,
seems to you. Is the real Hamlet the accomplished, elegant
prince portrayed by Olivier in his film, chivalrous towards
his mother, melancholy, but never losing his dignity or
acting ignobly? Or should we see him as a frustrated
adolescent, rebelling against a mother and step-father he
cannot respect, and a society whose standards he despises?
To some he is a scholarly day-dreamer who finds it difficult
to translate his ideas into action, while to others he seems a
naturally sociable person, a born leader, who is forced by
circumstances to retire into himself. Exactly how much does
he resent not being king? Is he, or isn't he, in love with
Ophelia? Finally, was Hamlet really mad for some or all of
the time, or did he merely encourage the idea that he was
insane, for some secret purpose? Before we can begin to
answer this last question we have to take another look at the
people around us and try to decide exactly what we mean by
'sane' behaviour. In the play, the contrast between Hamlet's
and Ophelia's 'madness' may help us to arrive at some sort of
conclusion.

Many of the rest of the characters offer the reader a similar choice. Is Claudius just a fairy-tale cruel step-father, a debauched and power-drunk villain, or an efficient, if ruthless, administrator whose attempts to run Denmark smoothly are continually threatened by a neurotic step-son? How far, in fact, is the theme of the play the struggle for power between these two men? Is Gertrude a silly, selfish, perhaps wicked, woman, a slave to her instincts, or really a well-intentioned and affectionate wife and mother, doing her best, as she saw it, by her country and her son? Is Ophelia as innocent as she seems? Why does Hamlet treat her father so contemptuously? Are Rosencrantz and Guildenstern willing accomplices of Claudius, hoping to gain something for themselves, or are they well-meaning young men, caught up against their will in a dangerous conflict they fail to understand?

If you are reading the play, you are also free to decide for yourself exactly what happens at certain points during the action of the play. Does Hamlet overhear the plot to eavesdrop on him? How is the play-within-a-play (Act III, Scene ii) put on, and why doesn't Claudius seem to notice anything strange at first? Why does the queen take the drink meant for Hamlet, in the last scene, and how does Hamlet obtain Laertes' sword? What are the reactions of the courtiers to the events in Act III, Scene ii; Act III, Scene iii and the final scene? In a stage production, the answers to these and the many other questions posed by this play have already been decided for us by the producer, according to *his* idea of the meaning of the play. Finally, Hamlet is a character whom we get to know largely by what he says to himself when alone, and the effect of these soliloquies can be more intimate when we read them than when we hear an actor deliver them to us as members of an audience.

All this is not to suggest, however, that reading the play can be a substitute for seeing it. Not only are there several incidents, such as the final struggle between Hamlet and Laertes, which look quite tame in the form of stage directions, yet are most gripping when watched, but there are many other points in the play where one can only fully appreciate what is going on when one can see as well as hear. The alarming appearances of the ghost, the royal pomp and ceremony surrounding Claudius, the old-fashioned style of the play-within-the-play, the tension when Hamlet stands behind the praying Claudius, drawn sword in hand, the pathos of Ophelia's distribution of flowers, the sexton's fooling – all these provide not just varied and striking dramatic spectacle but help us to identify ourselves with the changing moods of the play. If you have read the play before seeing it, you will have the added interest of seeing which of the many possible Hamlets appears in the production you are watching – it is said that there are as many Hamlets as there are actors who play him! It is a play, in fact, that should be read, seen, then read again and seen again. It will never grow stale.

LIST OF CHARACTERS

CLAUDIUS *King of Denmark*
HAMLET *son to the former and nephew to the present King*
POLONIUS *Lord Chamberlain*
HORATIO *friend to Hamlet*
LAERTES *son to Polonius*

VOLTEMAND
CORNELIUS
ROSENCRANTZ
GUILDENSTERN } *courtiers*
OSRIC
A GENTLEMAN

A PRIEST } *officers*
MARCELLUS
BERNARDO
FRANCISCO *a soldier*
REYNALDO *servant to Polonius*
PLAYERS
TWO CLOWNS *grave-diggers*
FORTINBRAS *Prince of Norway*
A NORWEGIAN CAPTAIN
ENGLISH AMBASSADORS
GERTRUDE *Queen of Denmark and mother of Hamlet*
OPHELIA *daughter to Polonius*
GHOST OF HAMLET'S FATHER
LORDS, LADIES, OFFICERS, SOLDIERS, SAILORS, MESSENGERS
and ATTENDANTS

THE SCENE: *Denmark*

25

NOTES

ACT ONE

SCENE I

At the beginning of the play we find ourselves looking at a solitary figure, a soldier on guard on the battlements of the King of Denmark's castle, in the cold still hours between midnight and dawn. The abrupt exchange of words that breaks the silence makes us aware immediately of an atmosphere of uncertainty and uneasiness. Bernardo, the officer who has come to relieve Francisco at his post, seems on edge; does Francisco notice this, or not? Why has the scholar Horatio been asked by Bernardo's colleague, Marcellus, to come on duty with him at this unearthly hour? As the scene develops, the contrasting attitudes of the sceptical Horatio and the more easily convinced soldiers, when they all share a strange and frightening experience, are shown very clearly.

Originally, this scene would probably have taken place on the gallery above the Elizabethan stage, which often represented the walls of a castle, etc.

1-2. Francisco, as the sentry on duty, should challenge Bernardo. What does the question show about Bernardo's state of mind?
2. The stress is on *me. unfold yourself:* show who you are.
3. Perhaps this phrase is the watchword.
6. 'You are very prompt,' says Francisco, sounding slightly surprised by Bernardo's eagerness to come on duty.

8-9. We are not told whether tiredness and cold are the only things that make Francisco feel depressed.
8. *this relief:* taking over guard duty.

10. We see later why Bernardo asks this.

13. *rivals of my watch:* 'those who are sharing guard duty with me.' Bernardo seems anxious not to be left alone.

ACT ONE

SCENE I—*Elsinore. The guard-platform of the Castle*

FRANCISCO *at his post. Enter to him* BERNARDO

Bernardo
  Who's there?
Francisco
  Nay, answer me. Stand and unfold yourself.
Bernardo
  Long live the King!
Francisco
  Bernardo?
Bernardo
  He.   5
Francisco
  You come most carefully upon your hour.
Bernardo
  'Tis now struck twelve; get thee to bed, Francisco.
Francisco
  For this relief much thanks. 'Tis bitter cold,
  And I am sick at heart.
Bernardo
  Have you had quiet guard?
Francisco   Not a mouse stirring.   10
Bernardo
  Well, good night.
  If you do meet Horatio and Marcellus,
  The rivals of my watch, bid them make haste.

              Enter HORATIO *and* MARCELLUS

Francisco
  I think I hear them. Stand, ho! Who is there?

15. *liegemen to the Dane:* loyal subjects of the King of Denmark.

16. *Give you:* may God give you.

19. Horatio does not make clear what he means by this remark. Perhaps he feels, what with the climb up to the guard platform and the lateness of the hour, that he is not quite 'all there', or perhaps that only part of him can be seen at the moment. The lightness of his manner contrasts with the earnestness and suppressed excitement of the two officers, probably deliberately: he does not want to look as though he, too, is taking this wild-goose-chase seriously.

21. The vagueness of *thing* creates a more eerie effect than the word 'ghost' would have done. Horatio's brisk tone, however, shows that it will be difficult to persuade him to believe in it.

23-9. Horatio has scoffed at their story of seeing a ghost, so Marcellus has begged him to share the watch with them tonight so that, if it appears, he will know they were not just 'seeing things'. What is more, he may be able to talk with it.

23. *fantasy:* imagination.

25. *of:* by.

29. *approve our eyes:* confirm what we have seen.

31-3. Bernardo, as a soldier, instinctively uses military images like *assail* and *fortified* for his attempts to break down the barriers of Horatio's convictions.

Horatio
  Friends to this ground.
Marcellus   And liegemen to the Dane.   15
Francisco
  Give you good night.
Marcellus   O, farewell, honest soldier!
  Who hath reliev'd you?
Francisco   Bernardo hath my place.
  Give you good night.

Exit

Marcellus   Holla, Bernardo!
Bernardo   Say—
  What, is Horatio there?
Horatio   A piece of him.
Bernardo
  Welcome, Horatio; welcome, good Marcellus.   20
Horatio
  What, has this thing appear'd again to-night?
Bernardo
  I have seen nothing.
Marcellus
  Horatio says 'tis but our fantasy,
  And will not let belief take hold of him
  Touching this dreaded sight, twice seen of us;   25
  Therefore I have entreated him along
  With us to watch the minutes of this night,
  That, if again this apparition come,
  He may approve our eyes and speak to it.
Horatio
  Tush, tush, 'twill not appear.
Bernardo   Sit down awhile,   30
  And let us once again assail your ears,
  That are so fortified against our story,
  What we have two nights seen.
Horatio   Well, sit we down,
  And let us hear Bernardo speak of this.

35. *last night of all:* no longer ago than last night.

36-9. 'When that star to the west of the Pole-star had moved to its present position,' i.e. at about the same time last night (one o'clock).
37. *t'illume:* to light up.

42. As a scholar, Horatio would speak Latin, which was believed to be the right language in which to address a ghost, particularly if you needed to exorcize it (send it away by pronouncing the appropriate religious formula).
43. *'a:* he. *Mark it:* Look hard at it.

45. It was also believed that a ghost could not speak until spoken to. *would be:* wants to be.

46-9. *usurp'st:* By using this word Horatio shows that his attitude to the ghost is hostile. It has no business, he seems to be saying, to appear there in the dark, masquerading as the late King of Denmark. Not surprisingly, the ghost is 'offended' at this!
48. *Denmark:* Kings were often referred to simply by the names of their countries (see line 61).
49. *sometimes:* in the past, at one time.

53. The doubting intellectual of a moment ago is now completely shaken. Understandably, Bernardo sounds rather triumphant.

Bernardo
    Last night of all,   35
    When yond same star that's westward from the pole
    Had made his course t' illume that part of heaven
    Where now it burns, Marcellus and myself,
    The bell then beating one—

Enter GHOST

Marcellus
    Peace, break thee off; look where it comes again.   40
Bernardo
    In the same figure, like the King that's dead.
Marcellus
    Thou art a scholar; speak to it, Horatio.
Bernardo
    Looks 'a not like the King? Mark it, Horatio.
Horatio
    Most like. It harrows me with fear and wonder.
Bernardo
    It would be spoke to.
Marcellus   Question it, Horatio.   45
Horatio
    What art thou that usurp'st this time of night
    Together with that fair and warlike form
    In which the majesty of buried Denmark
    Did sometimes march? By heaven I charge thee, speak!
Marcellus
    It is offended.
Bernardo   See, it stalks away.   50
Horatio
    Stay! speak, speak! I charge thee, speak!

Exit GHOST

Marcellus
    'Tis gone, and will not answer.
Bernardo
    How now, Horatio! You tremble and look pale.

55. *on't:* of it.

56. *might:* could.

57-8. *sensible:* perceived by the senses. *avouch:* proof, backing up; so
'. . . without the solid evidence of my own eyes.'

61. *Norway:* King of Norway.

62. *parle:* parley, conference. It seems that this one turned into a fight.

63. *sledded Polacks:* Polish soldiers using sleds (sledges) for transport.

65. *jump:* just, precisely.

66. *martial stalk:* warlike stride.

67-9. Horatio does not know exactly what attitude to adopt to the
appearance of the ghost, but on the whole he feels it signifies that there
will be an unpleasant disturbance of some kind in Denmark.

70-9. Marcellus asks whether either of them can say why there are so
many preparations for war just now: watch is being kept every night,
cannon are being made every day, weapons are being purchased
through foreign trade and shipbuilders are forced to work every day of
the week. What is the point of this day and night labour? *mart:* trade,
purchasing. *toward:* about to come, 'in the offing'.

79-107. In answer to Marcellus' question, Horatio says it is rumoured
that there will be an invasion from Norway. Some years before, the
then King of Norway, Fortinbras, challenged the late King of Denmark
(whose ghost, they think, they have just seen) to a fight, betting, on the
result of the battle, all his lands against a wager of equal value on the
part of his opponent. Hamlet, the Danish king, won the fight, killed
Fortinbras, and, of course, took the land. Now young Fortinbras, the
son of the dead Norwegian king, has scraped together an army and is
making preparations to take back the land by force.

83. *prick'd:* spurred. *emulate:* ambitious.

Is not this something more than fantasy?
What think you on't?   55

Horatio
Before my God, I might not this believe
Without the sensible and true avouch
Of mine own eyes.

Marcellus   Is it not like the King?

Horatio
As thou art to thyself:
Such was the very armour he had on   60
When he the ambitious Norway combated;
So frown'd he once when, in an angry parle,
He smote the sledded Polacks on the ice.
'Tis strange.

Marcellus
Thus twice before, and jump at this dead hour,   65
With martial stalk hath he gone by our watch.

Horatio
In what particular thought to work I know not;
But, in the gross and scope of mine opinion,
This bodes some strange eruption to our state.] *menace?*

Marcellus
Good now, sit down, and tell me, he that knows,   70
Why this same strict and most observant watch
So nightly toils the subject of the land;
And why such daily cast of brazen cannon,
And foreign mart for implements of war;
Why such impress of shipwrights, whose sore task   75
Does not divide the Sunday from the week;
What might be toward, that this sweaty haste
Doth make the night joint-labourer with the day:
Who is't that can inform me?

Horatio   That can I;
At least, the whisper goes so. Our last king,   80
Whose image even but now appear'd to us,
Was, as you know, by Fortinbras of Norway,
Thereto prick'd on by a most emulate pride,

86-7. *a seal'd compact . . . heraldry:* a legal agreement, binding according to both the law and the code of chivalry.

89. *seiz'd of:* possessed of. This is a legal term.

90-1. *a moiety competent Was gaged:* an equally valuable portion was wagered.

91-2. *which . . . Fortinbras:* which would have become Fortinbras's.

93-4. *comart And carriage . . . design'd:* 'mutual bargain and carrying out of the agreement.' Horatio is determined to make it clear that the King of Denmark's actions were absolutely legal. His bias as a loyal Dane is also shown by the slighting way in which he speaks of the Norwegian king and prince.

96. *unimproved mettle:* immature high-spiritedness.

97. *skirts:* outskirts, distant parts.

98. *Shark'd up:* gathered together, without being too fussy, like a shark snatching prey. *a list of lawless resolutes:* a gang of desperadoes.

99. *food and diet:* This can be taken both literally (fighting being their way of obtaining their keep) and as a metaphor, meaning 'something to feed their appetite for adventure.'

100. *stomach:* This picks up both the above ideas, as the word can mean 'courage'.

102. *of us:* from Denmark.

102-3. *by strong hand . . . compulsatory:* by force.

106. *head:* cause.

107. *romage:* bustle.

109. *Well may it sort:* It fits in well. *portentous:* warning, ominous.

110-11. The fact that the apparition wore armour (the ghost of a dead king might be expected to wear his usual royal garments) misleads all three men into thinking that its appearance is something to do with the Norwegian trouble.

112-25. *mote:* speck of dust. Horatio's mind is disturbed and irritated by the ghost. Even so, his scholar's mind now recalls how far stranger things have been seen in the past, such as when Julius Caesar was assassinated (Shakespeare had just written his *Julius Caesar*, so these tales would be fresh in his mind). It was still believed in Elizabethan days – and even Horatio seems prepared to accept the idea – that the close connection between human affairs and the rest of the universe meant that a disturbance such as the death of a king was accompanied by phenomena like storms, earthquakes, eclipses, etc. (Even nowadays, people's instinctive feeling that there must be some sort of connection between the rest of the universe and themselves is revealed by the popularity of horoscopes, which are based on the old idea that the stars have some sort of influence on human affairs).

113. *palmy:* flourishing. The palm was a symbol of success.

115. *sheeted:* wrapped in the shrouds they were buried in.

116. *gibber:* chatter meaninglessly.

117. *stars with trains of fire:* meteors or comets.

118-20. *the moist star . . . eclipse:* the moon (which affects the movement of the sea, the kingdom of the Roman god *Neptune*) was in eclipse, so that it was almost as dark as the end of the world.

Dar'd to the combat; in which our valiant Hamlet—
For so this side of our known world esteem'd him— 85
Did slay this Fortinbras; who, by a seal'd compact,
Well ratified by law and heraldry,
Did forfeit, with his life, all those his lands
Which he stood seiz'd of, to the conqueror;
Against the which a moiety competent 90
Was gaged by our king; which had return'd
To the inheritance of Fortinbras,
Had he been vanquisher; as, by the same comart
And carriage of the article design'd,
His fell to Hamlet. Now, sir, young Fortinbras, 95
Of unimproved mettle hot and full,
Hath in the skirts of Norway, here and there,
Shark'd up a list of lawless resolutes,
For food and diet, to some enterprise
That hath a stomach in't; which is no other, 100
As it doth well appear unto our state,
But to recover of us, by strong hand
And terms compulsatory, those foresaid lands
So by his father lost; and this, I take it,
Is the main motive of our preparations, 105
The source of this our watch, and the chief head
Of this post-haste and romage in the land.

Bernardo

I think it be no other but e'en so.
Well may it sort, that this portentous figure
Comes armed through our watch; so like the King 110
That was and is the question of these wars.

Horatio

A mote it is to trouble the mind's eye.
In the most high and palmy state of Rome,
A little ere the mightiest Julius fell,
The graves stood tenantless, and the sheeted dead 115
Did squeak and gibber in the Roman streets;
As, stars with trains of fire, and dews of blood,
Disasters in the sun; and the moist star

121-3. *precurse, harbingers* and *prologue:* all refer to signs that come before some terrible event.
122. *still:* always.
123. *omen:* the happening of which there have been forewarnings (rather than the warnings themselves in this case).

125. *climatures:* regions.

126-39. When the ghost unexpectedly reappears and makes what seems a pleading gesture, Horatio makes a more determined effort to find out why it has come, now that he is not so taken by surprise.
127. *I'll cross it:* To cross the path of a ghost was thought to be dangerous, as by doing that you came under its evil influence. *blast:* lay a harmful spell on, 'put the evil eye on'. *illusion:* Horatio is still trying to tell himself that the apparition is unreal.

131. *That may ... to me:* 'Which will relieve you of anxiety and make me feel I have done some good.' Horatio is the sort of person whose chief wish is always to do the right and honourable thing.
133. *thou art privy to:* you have secret knowledge of.
134. *happily:* perhaps.

136-7. *Or if ... earth:* 'If you have buried a hoard of wrongfully acquired wealth.' This crime, as were the two other reasons Horatio has just suggested for the ghost's appearance, was thought to be a common cause of restlessness among the souls of the dead: if a treasure was hidden it was useless, instead of being put to some good purpose, like helping the poor.

140. *partisan:* a kind of long spear, with a large head. No weapon, of course, would be able to stop a ghost!

143-56. Marcellus expresses an instinctive reverence for the regal figure of the ghost, but Horatio, characteristically, still refuses to assume it is the dead Hamlet, calling it *a guilty thing.* It was commonly believed, as Horatio here says, that at the crowing of the cock, a warning of the approach of day, spirits had to go back where they came from – probably hell or purgatory.

Upon whose influence Neptune's empire stands
Was sick almost to doomsday with eclipse;   *120*
And even the like precurse of fear'd events,
As harbingers preceding still the fates
And prologue to the omen coming on,
Have heaven and earth together demonstrated
Unto our climatures and countrymen.   *125*

Re-enter GHOST

But, soft, behold! Lo, where it comes again!
I'll cross it, though it blast me. Stay, illusion.

GHOST spreads its arms

If thou hast any sound or use of voice,
Speak to me.
If there be any good thing to be done,   *130*
That may to thee do ease and grace to me,
Speak to me.
If thou art privy to thy country's fate,
Which happily foreknowing may avoid,
O, speak!   *135*
Or if thou hast uphoarded in thy life
Extorted treasure in the womb of earth,
For which, they say, you spirits oft walk in death,

The cock crows

Speak of it. Stay, and speak. Stop it, Marcellus.

Marcellus
Shall I strike at it with my partisan?   *140*

Horatio
Do, if it will not stand.

Bernardo   'Tis here!

Horatio   'Tis here!

Exit GHOST

Marcellus
'Tis gone!
We do it wrong, being so majestical,
To offer it the show of violence;
For it is, as the air, invulnerable,   *145*

37

154. *extravagant and erring:* wandering.
154·5. *hies To his confine:* has to go back to its prison.

156. *made probation:* proved.

158-9. *ever 'gainst . . . celebrated:* whenever Christmas comes round.

160. *This bird of dawning:* the cock.

162. *wholesome:* safe from the influence of spirits. *strike:* exert an evil influence – another reference to the idea that the stars have some sort of connection with human beings.
163. *takes:* bewitches.
164. *hallowed:* holy. *gracious:* benign.

165. Horatio, as usual, is cautious!

166-7. After the strange and terrifying experience that they have just gone through in the darkness, they are reassured to see the ordinary, everyday world return with the dawn, which seems to Horatio like a homely peasant going off to work early, wrapped in his rough cloak. *russet:* a coarse, homespun fabric of an in-between colour, either reddish or greyish. This serene description of the coming of daylight, followed by a brisk statement of what the three men are going to do next, prepares the way for the complete change of mood in the next scene.
168-73. Horatio, superior in status to the other two, is the one to take the lead in saying what their next move is to be.
170. This is the first time we have heard the son of the dead king mentioned, even though he is the main character of the play.
173. *As needful . . . duty:* as our affection and loyalty demand.

And our vain blows malicious mockery.

Bernardo

It was about to speak, when the cock crew.

Horatio

And then it started like a guilty thing
Upon a fearful summons. I have heard
The cock, that is the trumpet to the morn,   *150*
Doth with his lofty and shrill-sounding throat
Awake the god of day; and at his warning,
Whether in sea or fire, in earth or air,
Th' extravagant and erring spirit hies
To his confine; and of the truth herein   *155*
This present object made probation.

Marcellus

It faded on the crowing of the cock.
Some say that ever 'gainst that season comes
Wherein our Saviour's birth is celebrated,
This bird of dawning singeth all night long;   *160*
And then, they say, no spirit dare stir abroad,
The nights are wholesome, then no planets strike,
No fairy takes, nor witch hath power to charm,
So hallowed and so gracious is that time.

Horatio

So have I heard, and do in part believe it.   *165*
But look, the morn, in russet mantle clad,
Walks o'er the dew of yon high eastward hill.
Break we our watch up; and, by my advice,
Let us impart what we have seen to-night
Unto young Hamlet; for, upon my life,   *170*
This spirit, dumb to us, will speak to him.
Do you consent we shall acquaint him with it,
As needful in our loves, fitting our duty?

Marcellus

Let's do't, I pray; and I this morning know
Where we shall find him most convenient.   *175*

Exeunt

The opening of this scene is in striking contrast with the last; now we are inside the castle of Elsinore, on the following morning, in the brightly lit main hall, where the whole court is assembled ceremoniously for an important meeting chaired by the new king, who is a middle-aged man – not the 'young Hamlet' whom we might expect to see on the throne. His rather pompous, self-satisfied manner is very different from the silent dignity of his predecessor's ghost. Probably he is trying to impress everyone with his authority, for it is not long since the last king died, and the country needs to feel it has someone capable in his place. Also, there are one or two awkward matters to be dealt with; the best way to cope with them, he seems to feel, is to behave as though everyone is pleased with the way things have turned out. But there is one young man (who, we soon learn, is Hamlet himself) making things difficult for the king by looking gloomy, and taking no interest in the proceedings.

1-16. The King's first words reveal the surprising fact that it is not the dead king Hamlet's son but his brother who is now on the throne. Claudius goes on to explain that though it was, of course, natural and right for him and Denmark as a whole to mourn their loss, he has been sensible enough not to forget himself entirely in his grief. He has enlivened the funeral ceremonies with a wedding celebration, by marrying his former sister-in-law, Gertrude. (She had shared the throne with her former husband, i.e. was an *imperial jointress*, so this helped Claudius to become king.) He reminds the courtiers that this step was taken with their full approval.

1. *yet:* still. *our:* as in the rest of this speech, Claudius is here using the 'royal plural' when speaking of himself. This was the custom for kings, helping to give an impression of dignity and self-importance.

2. *green:* fresh. *that:* though.

4. *contracted . . . woe:* united in looking mournful.

5. *discretion:* commonsense, self-restraint. *nature:* natural affection, particularly for one's family.

8. *sometime sister:* sister-in-law that was.

10. *Have we:* I have. *defeated:* subdued.

11. *With . . . eye:* 'With one cheerful and one tearful eye.' This rather absurd image shows how difficult it is for Claudius to gloss over the bad taste of his hasty marriage.

13. *In equal scale . . . dole:* balancing sadness with happiness.

17-39. Claudius, having dealt with these rather delicate personal matters, turns briskly to a purely political one, the Fortinbras threat referred to in the previous scene. He suggests that Fortinbras had tried to take advantage of the fact that Denmark had lost its king, and shows that he himself intends to cope with the situation promptly and cleverly by diplomatic means: the Norwegian king, Fortinbras's uncle, is being told to stop his nephew's activities. War will be unnecessary.

17. *that:* what.

18-20. *Holding . . . frame:* underestimating Claudius's ability to cope with the situation, or thinking the country must be disorganized and confused because of his brother's death.

SCENE II—*Elsinore. The Castle*

Flourish. Enter CLAUDIUS *King of Denmark,* GERT-
RUDE *the Queen, and* COUNCILLORS, *including*
POLONIUS, *his son* LAERTES, VOLTEMAND, CORNELIUS
and HAMLET

King

> Though yet of Hamlet our dear brother's death
> The memory be green; and that it us befitted
> To bear our hearts in grief, and our whole kingdom
> To be contracted in one brow of woe;
> Yet so far hath discretion fought with nature   5
> That we with wisest sorrow think on him,
> Together with remembrance of ourselves.
> Therefore our sometime sister, now our queen,
> Th' imperial jointress to this warlike state,
> Have we, as 'twere with a defeated joy,   10
> With an auspicious and a dropping eye,
> With mirth in funeral, and with dirge in marriage,
> In equal scale weighing delight and dole,
> Taken to wife; nor have we herein barr'd
> Your better wisdoms, which have freely gone   15
> With this affair along. For all, our thanks.
> Now follows that you know: young Fortinbras,
> Holding a weak supposal of our worth,
> Or thinking by our late dear brother's death
> Our state to be disjoint and out of frame,   20

21. *Co-leagued . . . advantage:* combined with his illusion of his own superiority.

23. *Importing:* asking for. *those lands:* See Horatio's account of the quarrel, in the previous scene (lines 79-107).

24. *with all bands of law:* entirely legally.

25. *our most valiant brother:* By such phrases as these, Claudius tries to keep in with those who may have preferred his brother.

27. *we have here writ:* Claudius has already had the necessary documents prepared.

29. *impotent and bed-rid:* he is a helpless invalid.

30-3. *to suppress . . . subject:* to stop him going any further, because the army is composed of Norwegian citizens.

33-9. The two ambassadors who are sent on the mission are given strict orders to stick to their detailed instructions (*delated articles*) and not to act on their own initiative. Why?

39. *let your haste . . . duty:* if you are quick I shall be able to see that you are loyal to me.

41. *nothing:* not at all.

42-50. Having shown how firm he can be in the country's interests, the king now turns to the son of an important politician, Polonius, and, ingratiatingly repeating his name several times, asks what he can do for him. What is behind this behaviour?

43. *suit:* request.

44. *speak of reason:* ask anything within reason. *Dane:* king of Denmark (see note on Act I, Scene i, line 48).

45. *lose your voice:* waste your breath.

46. *That . . . asking:* that will not be given almost before it is asked.

47. *native:* closely related.

48. *instrumental:* useful, necessary.

50. *dread:* respected. Laertes repays the king's flattery of his father with a subservient kind of politeness.

51. *favour:* kind permission.

Co-leagued with this dream of his advantage—
He hath not fail'd to pester us with message
Importing the surrender of those lands
Lost by his father, with all bands of law,
To our most valiant brother. So much for him.   25
Now for ourself, and for this time of meeting,
Thus much the business is: we have here writ
To Norway, uncle of young Fortinbras—
Who, impotent and bed-rid, scarcely hears
Of this his nephew's purpose—to suppress   30
His further gait herein, in that the levies,
The lists, and full proportions, are all made
Out of his subject; and we here dispatch
You, good Cornelius, and you, Voltemand,
For bearers of this greeting to old Norway;   35
Giving to you no further personal power
To business with the King more than the scope
Of these delated articles allow.
Farewell; and let your haste commend your duty.

Cornelius and Voltemand

In that and all things will we show our duty.   40

King

We doubt it nothing, heartily farewell.

      Exeunt VOLTEMAND *and* CORNELIUS

And now, Laertes, what's the news with you?
You told us of some suit; what is't, Laertes?
You cannot speak of reason to the Dane
And lose your voice. What wouldst thou beg, Laertes,   45
That shall not be my offer, not thy asking?
The head is not more native to the heart,
The hand more instrumental to the mouth,
Than is the throne of Denmark to thy father.
What wouldst thou have, Laertes?

Laertes   My dread lord,   50
Your leave and favour to return to France;
From whence though willingly I came to Denmark
To show my duty in your coronation,

56. *bow them to:* submissively request. *pardon:* permission to go.

57. Claudius again flatters Polonius by seeking his advice.

58. *'A hath:* he has.
59. *laboursome petition:* repeated requests.
60. *Upon . . . consent:* I firmly agreed to what he wanted.
62. *Take thy fair hour:* use this good opportunity well.
63. *And thy best graces . . . will:* And may your good qualities enable you to use your leisure well.
64. Claudius has left till last the most tricky item on his agenda, the matter of what to do with young Hamlet, his nephew (in Shakespeare's time *cousin* meant simply 'relation') and, now, step-son, who might well have been on the throne himself at this moment.
65-7. Hamlet's response to Claudius's gracious manner is sarcastic: as the king has just reminded him, they are closer than mere relatives (*kin*), but yet without any natural affection for each other (*kind*), and he does not like being called 'son' (*sun*) by his uncle. *too much in the sun* also means 'exposed to the weather', i.e. turned out of house and home – in this case, his throne – or 'having too much attention from the king' (the sun was commonly associated with kingship). His opening remarks, therefore, show Hamlet's resentment of the situation, his dislike of Claudius, and his refusal to play his uncle's game and pretend that all is well between them.
66. *How is it . . . hang on you?* The king asks why Hamlet is still gloomy.
68-73. Hamlet's mother begs him to stop mourning for his father, as everyone, she says, has to die sometime. How will this remark, coming from her, strike Hamlet?
68. *nighted colour:* Hamlet is wearing black mourning, in contrast, it seems, to the rest of the court, including his mother, who are wearing their normal dress or, possibly, even the gay garments suited to the wedding which has recently been celebrated.
70. *vailed lids:* downcast eyes.
73. *nature:* this world.
74. *Ay, madam, it is common:* In what tone does Hamlet say this – polite agreement, sulky indifference, bitter reproach?
75. The queen asks why her son behaves as though he were the only person who has ever been bereaved.
76-86. Hamlet is stung into a retort of some length (up to now all his remarks have been very brief). Neither his black garments nor his mournful behaviour really represent his grief, for they are merely outward signs of mourning, easy to adopt, whereas what he feels inwardly is beyond expression.
78. *customary suits of solemn black:* conventional mourning garments.
79. *windy . . . breath:* sighs.
80. *fruitful river:* floods of tears.

Yet now, I must confess, that duty done,
My thoughts and wishes bend again toward France,   55
And bow them to your gracious leave and pardon.

King

Have you your father's leave? What says Polonius?

Polonius

'A hath, my lord, wrung from me my slow leave
By laboursome petition; and at last
Upon his will I seal'd my hard consent.   60
I do beseech you, give him leave to go.

King

Take thy fair hour, Laertes; time be thine,
And thy best graces spend it at thy will!
But now, my cousin Hamlet, and my son—

Hamlet [*Aside*]

A little more than kin, and less than kind.   65

King

How is it that the clouds still hang on you?

Hamlet

Not so, my lord; I am too much in the sun.

Queen

Good Hamlet, cast thy nighted colour off,
And let thine eye look like a friend on Denmark.
Do not for ever with thy vailed lids   70
Seek for thy noble father in the dust.
Thou know'st 'tis common—all that lives must die,
Passing through nature to eternity.

Hamlet

Ay, madam, it is common.

Queen   If it be,
Why seems it so particular with thee?   75

Hamlet

Seems, madam! Nay, it is; I know not seems.
'Tis not alone my inky cloak, good mother,
Nor customary suits of solemn black,
Nor windy suspiration of forc'd breath,
No, nor the fruitful river in the eye,   80

81. *haviour of the visage:* facial expression.

82. *forms, moods, shapes:* outward signs.

83. *seem:* Hamlet is hurt particularly by his mother's use of this word – if she had said 'is' it would not have sounded so unsympathetic.
84. *play:* act.

85-6. The rhyming couplet at the end of this speech sounds final – as though Hamlet has said what he wishes to say and now relapses into his former silence.

86. *the trappings and the suits of woe:* dark clothes that are merely the symbols of grief.

87-117. Claudius takes up Gertrude's point: death is something one has to learn to accept – to fail to do so is not only weak and foolish but irreligious, for it shows a lack of faith in the afterlife and in Providence. Hamlet must now think of Claudius as his father and, to show that he means this, the king now publicly announces that his step-son should inherit the throne from him.

90. *That father lost, lost his:* the father (Hamlet's grandfather) whom Hamlet's father had lost had, in turn, lost his father.

90-2. *and the survivor . . . sorrow:* It was the duty of the son who survived his father to observe the customary period of mourning. *obsequious:* relating to obsequies or funeral ceremonies.

93. *condolement:* mourning.

95. *incorrect to heaven:* disobedient to God.

96. *unfortified:* not strengthened by religious faith.

97. *An understanding . . . unschool'd:* an immature attitude.

98-101. What is the use, asks Claudius, of insisting on taking something to heart which is inevitable and as ordinary as any everyday experience?

101. *Fie!* is an exclamation of disgust. *fault:* insult.

102. *A fault against-the dead:* It is no compliment to the dead to grieve when they die, for it is to be hoped that they have gone to heaven. *nature:* the natural order of things, or family feelings.

103-6. *whose common theme . . . be so:* commonsense (*reason*) has often had to cope with a father's death and, from the beginning of time right up to now, has always declared it to be inevitable. *the first corse:* Claudius's reference to this is rather unfortunate, as, according to the Bible, the first man who died was Abel, killed by his brother Cain!

107. *unprevailing:* of no avail, useless. *us:* me. Claudius is again using the royal plural.

108. *the world:* all the listening courtiers.

109. *most immediate:* next in line.

112-17. Having, he hopes, created a good impression by this announcement, which, of course, costs him nothing, Claudius finishes by saying that he wishes Hamlet to stay at the Danish court, though the prince had asked to go back to university (*school*) at Wittenberg. Why does the king grant Laertes's request, but not Hamlet's, although the latter wanted to continue his studies while the former probably just wanted to amuse himself?

114. *retrograde to:* contrary to.

115. *bend you to:* give way and.

Nor the dejected haviour of the visage,
Together with all forms, moods, shapes of grief,
That can denote me truly. These, indeed, seem;
For they are actions that a man might play;
But I have that within which passes show— 85
These but the trappings and the suits of woe.

King

'Tis sweet and commendable in your nature, Hamlet,
To give these mourning duties to your father;
But you must know your father lost a father;
That father lost, lost his; and the survivor bound, 90
In filial obligation, for some term
To do obsequious sorrow. But to persever
In obstinate condolement is a course
Of impious stubbornness; 'tis unmanly grief;
It shows a will most incorrect to heaven, 95
A heart unfortified, a mind impatient,
An understanding simple and unschool'd;
For what we know must be, and is as common
As any the most vulgar things to sense,
Why should we in our peevish opposition 100
Take it to heart? Fie! 'tis a fault to heaven,
A fault against the dead, a fault to nature,
To reason most absurd; whose common theme
Is death of fathers, and who still hath cried,
From the first corse till he that died to-day, 105
'This must be so'. We pray you throw to earth
This unprevailing woe, and think of us
As of a father; for let the world take note
You are the most immediate to our throne;
And with no less nobility of love 110
Than that which dearest father bears his son
Do I impart toward you. For your intent
In going back to school in Wittenberg,
It is most retrograde to our desire;
And we beseech you bend you to remain 115
Here, in the cheer and comfort of our eye,

47

118. *lose her prayers:* beg in vain.

120. Hamlet, who has not deigned to reply to Claudius, pointedly addresses his consent to his mother only; even then his politeness is rather distant; he calls her simply 'madam', not 'mother'.

121-8. Claudius hastily passes over Hamlet's rudeness, and puts an end to the discussion before there is further awkwardness.

122. *Be as ourself in Denmark:* Take upon yourself all the royal privileges that I have.

123. *gentle and unforc'd accord:* polite and spontaneous agreement.

124. *to:* at. *in grace whereof:* in celebration of which.

125-8. Claudius says that every toast he drinks that day (the king, we see from the rest of the play, is fond of feasting) will be accompanied by the firing of a big cannon.

127. *rouse:* carousal, drinking bout. *bruit again:* echo.

128. *Re-speaking earthly thunder:* imitating the thunder of the guns.

129-59. As soon as he is left alone, Hamlet, who has seemed so poised up to now, bursts into a passionate cry that he wishes he were dead. It is not, as we might expect, resentment of Claudius's condescending treatment, when he himself had probably expected to become king when his father died, that most upsets him – nor is it simply grief at his father's death. These things are insignificant beside the disgust he feels at his mother's betrayal of his father's memory in marrying, so soon after his death, someone as inferior to him as Claudius. His disillusionment colours his feelings about the whole of the world: everything and everybody is futile and rotten.

129. *too too:* The repetition movingly conveys Hamlet's weary longing to be rid of his body: if only he could melt, like the icicle his chilly manner up to now has resembled.

130. *resolve:* dissolve, melt.

131-2. Hamlet wishes that God had not forbidden suicide.

134. *uses:* ways, customs. Perhaps Hamlet is prompted to say this partly because the ceremonious formality surrounding the king in the first part of this scene seems to him empty and false.

135. *Fie on't:* An expression of great disgust and disapproval.

135-7. To Hamlet, the world, particularly Denmark, is degenerate and corrupt, like a neglected garden full of coarse weeds. *merely:* only, exclusively.

138. Now we learn what a very short time ago it was that his father died.

139-40. Compared with Claudius, Hamlet's father was like a Sun-God (*Hyperion*). A *satyr*, in Greek mythology, was an ugly, lecherous creature, half man, half goat.

141. *might:* would. *beteem:* allow.

143. *Must I remember?* Hamlet's thoughts are agonizing, yet he cannot stop himself brooding. Compare this with *Let me not think on't* (line 146). *hang on him:* cling to him.

144-5. *As if . . . fed on:* As if the more she had of him, the more she wanted. *within a month:* Less than a month after her first husband died, Gertrude accepted Claudius.

146. *Frailty, thy name is woman:* women are fickleness incarnate.

147. *or ere:* before.

48

Our chiefest courtier, cousin, and our son.

Queen

Let not thy mother lose her prayers, Hamlet:
I pray thee stay with us; go not to Wittenberg.

Hamlet

I shall in all my best obey you, madam. 120

King

Why, 'tis a loving and a fair reply.
Be as ourself in Denmark. Madam, come;
This gentle and unforc'd accord of Hamlet
Sits smiling to my heart; in grace whereof,
No jocund health that Denmark drinks to-day 125
But the great cannon to the clouds shall tell,
And the King's rouse the heaven shall bruit again,
Re-speaking earthly thunder. Come away.

Flourish. Exeunt all but HAMLET

Hamlet

O, that this too too solid flesh would melt,
Thaw, and resolve itself into a dew! 130
Or that the Everlasting had not fix'd
His canon 'gainst self-slaughter! O God! God!
How weary, stale, flat, and unprofitable,
Seem to me all the uses of this world!
Fie on't! Ah, fie! 'tis an unweeded garden, 135
That grows to seed; things rank and gross in nature
Possess it merely. That it should come to this!
But two months dead! Nay, not so much, not two.
So excellent a king that was to this
Hyperion to a satyr; so loving to my mother, 140
That he might not beteem the winds of heaven
Visit her face too roughly. Heaven and earth!
Must I remember? Why, she would hang on him
As if increase of appetite had grown
By what it fed on; and yet, within a month— 145
Let me not think on't. Frailty, thy name is woman!—
A little month, or ere those shoes were old

149. *Niobe:* a mythical Greek woman who wept so much at the death of her children that she was turned into a fountain.

150. *a beast . . . reason:* an animal which has no understanding to guide it.

153. *Hercules:* the legendary strong man who was famous for having rid the world of a number of nuisances. Even in his misery, Hamlet still keeps a sense of humour: he feels inadequate to take on the Herculean task of putting the world right. Incidentally, Hamlet is no physical weakling, as we see later in the play.

154. The tears were *unrighteous* because they were insincere.

155. *flushing:* redness. *galled:* sore.

156. *post:* rush.

157. *dexterity:* agility. *incestuous:* Marriage between brother- and sister-in-law was regarded by the Church in Shakespeare's time as a form of incest. This explains some of Hamlet's disgust at his mother's behaviour and of his wish to die, for he feels involved in her shame. He is obsessed, too, with the idea that Gertrude just couldn't wait to get into Claudius's bed.

159. Ironically, Hamlet expresses a feeling of total isolation and lack of any outlet for his emotion just as Horatio, his friend, arrives with news that will give him the opportunity to do something about the situation.

160-1. At first Hamlet's greeting is off-hand, until he shakes off his gloom and recognizes his university friend.

163. Hamlet insists that Horatio should regard himself as his friend, not his 'servant'.

164. It is rather surprising that Hamlet did not know Horatio was at court – unless Horatio arrived late the previous day and was taken to see the ghost immediately.

165-7. Notice the way that Hamlet's greeting to the three men differs according to their ranks. *even:* evening.

169. *a truant disposition:* I am playing truant. Horatio tries to turn off the question with a joke.

170-3. 'You can't get me to believe that,' says Hamlet

With which she followed my poor father's body,
Like Niobe, all tears—why she, even she—
O God! a beast that wants discourse of reason   150
Would have mourn'd longer—married with my uncle,
My father's brother; but no more like my father
Than I to Hercules. Within a month,
Ere yet the salt of most unrighteous tears
Had left the flushing in her galled eyes,   155
She married. O, most wicked speed, to post
With such dexterity to incestuous sheets!
It is not, nor it cannot come to good.
But break, my heart, for I must hold my tongue.

Enter HORATIO, MARCELLUS, *and* BERNARDO

Horatio
Hail to your lordship!
Hamlet   I am glad to see you well.   160
Horatio—or I do forget myself.
Horatio
The same, my lord, and your poor servant ever.
Hamlet
Sir, my good friend. I'll change that name with you.
And what make you from Wittenberg, Horatio?
Marcellus?   165
Marcellus
My good lord!
Hamlet
I am very glad to see you. [*To Bernardo*] Good even, sir.—
But what, in faith, make you from Wittenberg?
Horatio
A truant disposition, good my lord.
Hamlet
I would not hear your enemy say so;   170
Nor shall you do my ear that violence,
To make it truster of your own report
Against yourself. I know you are no truant.
But what is your affair in Elsinore?

175. A slightly bitter reference to Claudius's fondness for feasting.

177. *prithee:* pray thee (I beg you).

179. *hard upon:* very soon after.

180-4. After a sarcastic comment that the two ceremonies were timed so closely for the sake of economy, the food cooked for the first being served cold for the second, Hamlet confesses something of his unhappiness. *dearest:* greatest. *Or ever:* before. *methinks:* it seems to me.

185. *Where, my lord?* Why does Horatio ask this?

186. *I saw him once:* Perhaps Horatio was just about to tell Hamlet of the ghost, then hesitates, and finishes the sentence lamely.

187. *'A:* he.

189-90. Horatio at last springs the news on Hamlet, so suddenly that the prince does not at first know what he is talking about.

192. *Season your admiration:* control your wonder.
193. *attent:* attentive. *deliver:* describe.

We'll teach you to drink deep ere you depart. *175*

Horatio
My lord, I came to see your father's funeral.

Hamlet
I prithee do not mock me, fellow-student;
I think it was to see my mother's wedding.

Horatio
Indeed, my lord, it followed hard upon.

Hamlet
Thrift, thrift, Horatio! The funeral bak'd-meats *180*
Did coldly furnish forth the marriage tables.
Would I had met my dearest foe in heaven
Or ever I had seen that day, Horatio!
My father—methinks I see my father.

Horatio
Where, my lord?

Hamlet   In my mind's eye, Horatio. *185*

Horatio
I saw him once; 'a was a goodly king.

Hamlet
'A was a man, take him for all in all,
I shall not look upon his like again.

Horatio
My lord, I think I saw him yesternight.

Hamlet
Saw who? *190*

Horatio
My lord, the King your father.

Hamlet   The King my father!

Horatio
Season your admiration for a while
With an attent ear, till I may deliver,
Upon the witness of these gentlemen,
This marvel to you.

Hamlet   For God's love, let me hear. *195*

Horatio
Two nights together had these gentlemen,

199. *A figure like your father:* Horatio has not yet committed himself to saying that it is a genuine ghost.

200. *Armed . . . cap-a-pe:* armed fully, from head to foot.

203. *oppress'd:* overwhelmed with amazement.

204. *truncheon:* As commander of the Danish forces the king would have carried a baton as a symbol of his office.

204-5. *distill'd . . . fear:* sweating with fright.

207. *dreadful:* fearful.

212. *These hands are not more like:* the apparition was as similar to the king as one of my hands is to the other.

216. *it:* its.

216-17. *did address . . . speak:* began to move as though it wanted to speak.

218. *even:* just.

224. *Indeed, indeed:* Hamlet has a habit of repeating words.

Marcellus and Bernardo, on their watch,
In the dead waste and middle of the night,
Been thus encounter'd. A figure like your father,
Armed at point exactly, cap-a-pe,   *200*
Appears before them, and with solemn march
Goes slow and stately by them; thrice he walk'd
By their oppress'd and fear-surprised eyes,
Within his truncheon's length; whilst they, distill'd
Almost to jelly with the act of fear,   *205*
Stand dumb and speak not to him. This to me
In dreadful secrecy impart they did;
And I with them the third night kept the watch;
Where, as they had delivered, both in time,
Form of the thing, each word made true and good, *210*
The apparition comes. I knew your father;
These hands are not more like.

Hamlet   But where was this?

Marcellus
  My lord, upon the platform where we watch.

Hamlet
  Did you not speak to it?

Horatio   My lord, I did;
But answer made it none; yet once methought *215*
It lifted up it head and did address
Itself to motion, like as it would speak;
But even then the morning cock crew loud,
And at the sound it shrunk in haste away
And vanish'd from our sight.

Hamlet   'Tis very strange. *220*

Horatio
  As I do live, my honour'd lord, 'tis true;
And we did think it writ down in our duty
To let you know of it.

Hamlet
  Indeed, indeed, sirs, but this troubles me.
  Hold you the watch to-night?

All   We do, my lord. *225*

226. Hamlet, like Horatio, is not the sort of person to take a story on trust, and he begins to cross-question them, but fails to catch them out.

229. *beaver:* visor of a helmet.

234. *would:* wish.

236. *Very like, very like:* Hamlet repeats the phrase absent-mindedly while he works out his next questions.

237-8. The disagreement of the witnesses on this minor point would convince Hamlet, rather than otherwise: if they had made up the tale they would be careful to agree with each other. *tell:* count.

239. *grizzl'd:* grey.

241. *a sable silver'd:* black, with a few grey hairs. Convinced, Hamlet decides to try to see it.

Hamlet

Arm'd, say you?

All Arm'd, my lord.

Hamlet

From top to toe?

All My lord, from head to foot.

Hamlet

Then saw you not his face?

Horatio

O yes, my lord; he wore his beaver up.

Hamlet

What, look'd he frowningly? 230

Horatio

A countenance more in sorrow than in anger.

Hamlet

Pale or red?

Horatio

Nay, very pale.

Hamlet And fix'd his eyes upon you?

Horatio

Most constantly.

Hamlet I would I had been there.

Horatio

It would have much amaz'd you. 235

Hamlet

Very like, very like. Stay'd it long?

Horatio

While one with moderate haste might tell a hundred.

Both

Longer, longer.

Horatio

Not when I saw't.

Hamlet His beard was grizzl'd—no?

Horatio

It was, as I have seen it in his life, 240
A sable silver'd.

Hamlet I will watch to-night;

242. *Perchance:* perhaps. *warr'nt:* guarantee (warrant).

243-5. Hamlet says that if the apparition looks like his father he will speak to it even if silence might be wiser, as it might be a devil from hell.

247. *Let it . . . still:* go on keeping quiet about it.

248. *hap:* happen.

249. *Give . . . tongue:* take it in, but don't talk about it.

250. *requite your loves:* repay your loyalty.

251. *'twixt:* between.

253. Hamlet corrects their use of the word *duty*. They should speak of friendship, he says, just as he feels friendship for them.

254. *in arms:* Hamlet feels that his father's warlike appearance is a bad omen.

255. *doubt:* suspect.

255-7. Hamlet can hardly wait for night to come. Unlike Horatio and the others, he instinctively feels that the apparition's reason for coming is not to warn the country of military danger, but to disclose some evil deeds done in the past, that will rise up like dead bodies out of the ground.

SCENE III

Like Hamlet, we have to wait in suspense until night. Meanwhile, we see more of the Polonius family: Laertes, having obtained permission to return to France, is saying goodbye to his sister, and warning her against Hamlet, who has been paying her attentions.

1. *My necessaries are embark'd:* my luggage is on board.

2-3. *as the winds . . . assistant:* whenever the wind is favourable and messengers are available.

Perchance 'twill walk again.
Horatio   I warr'nt it will.
Hamlet
If it assume my noble father's person,
I'll speak to it, though hell itself should gape
And bid me hold my peace. I pray you all,   *245*
If you have hitherto conceal'd this sight,
Let it be tenable in your silence still;
And whatsomever else shall hap to-night,
Give it an understanding, but no tongue;
I will requite your loves. So, fare you well—   *250*
Upon the platform, 'twixt eleven and twelve,
I'll visit you.
All   Our duty to your honour.
Hamlet
Your loves, as mine to you; farewell.

Exeunt all but HAMLET

My father's spirit in arms! All is not well.
I doubt some foul play. Would the night were come! *255*
Till then sit still, my soul. Foul deeds will rise,
Though all the earth o'erwhelm them, to men's eyes.

Exit

SCENE III—*Elsinore. The house of Polonius*

Enter LAERTES *and* OPHELIA *his sister*

Laertes
My necessaries are embark'd. Farewell.
And, sister, as the winds give benefit
And convoy is assistant, do not sleep,
But let me hear from you.
Ophelia   Do you doubt that?

5-10. Laertes warns Ophelia to consider Hamlet's interest in her merely a flirtation.

6. *a fashion and a toy in blood:* a passing fancy and a trivial passion.

7. Laertes says that Hamlet's interest in Ophelia is a result of his youth – just as spring produces flowers.

8. *Forward:* early.

9. *suppliance of a minute:* something to wile away a short time.

10. Ophelia hesitantly queries her brother's denial that Hamlet is seriously in love with her.

11-14. Laertes says that people grow in mind as well as body, developing their ideas and tastes as they grow older. *nature crescent:* growing being. *this temple:* the body, which houses the soul. *waxes:* grows.

15-16. *no soil . . . will:* now his motives may be entirely pure. *cautel:* trick.

16-24. Laertes points out that Hamlet, being the prince, cannot choose whoever he fancies for his wife.

18. *birth:* rank.

19. *unvalued:* unimportant.

20. *Carve:* choose.

21. *The sanity . . . state:* the well-being of Denmark.

22-4. *circumscrib'd . . . head:* restricted to what the state, of which he is the head, will approve and agree to.

25-8. Laertes says that Ophelia would be wise not to believe any of Hamlet's promises which he is not able to carry out with the full consent of the country.

29-32. *Then weigh . . . importunity:* consider how your reputation will suffer if you believe his declarations too easily, or fall in love with him or give in to his uncontrolled pestering and let him rob you of your precious chastity.

34-5. Ophelia must not let her feelings take her too far. Laertes compares the situation to a battle between her and her emotions: she must keep out of range of physical desire.

36-42. 'Young girls can't be too careful,' says Laertes.

36. *chariest:* most cautious. *prodigal:* reckless.

38. *Virtue . . . strokes:* even if one is the embodiment of virtue people will gossip.

Laertes
  For Hamlet, and the trifling of his favour,   5
  Hold it a fashion and a toy in blood,
  A violet in the youth of primy nature,
  Forward not permanent, sweet not lasting,
  The perfume and suppliance of a minute;
  No more.

Ophelia   No more but so?

Laertes   Think it no more;   10
  For nature crescent does not grow alone
  In thews and bulk, but as this temple waxes,
  The inward service of the mind and soul
  Grows wide withal. Perhaps he loves you now,
  And now no soil nor cautel doth besmirch   15
  The virtue of his will; but you must fear,
  His greatness weigh'd, his will is not his own;
  For he himself is subject to his birth:
  He may not, as unvalued persons do,
  Carve for himself; for on his choice depends   20
  The sanity and health of this whole state;
  And therefore must his choice be circumscrib'd
  Unto the voice and yielding of that body
  Whereof he is the head. Then if he says he loves you,
  It fits your wisdom so far to believe it   25
  As he in his particular act and place
  May give his saying deed; which is no further
  Than the main voice of Denmark goes withal.
  Then weigh what loss your honour may sustain,
  If with too credent ear you list his songs,   30
  Or lose your heart, or your chaste treasure open
  To his unmaster'd importunity.
  Fear it, Ophelia, fear it, my dear sister;
  And keep you in the rear of your affection,
  Out of the shot and danger of desire.   35
  The chariest maid is prodigal enough
  If she unmask her beauty to the moon.
  Virtue itself scapes not calumnious strokes;

39-42. Comparing his sister to a spring flower in bud, Laertes points out that these are particularly susceptible to disease.

44. *Youth to itself rebels:* you are your own worst enemy.

45-51. When her brother has come to the end of his rather pompous sermon, Ophelia, while agreeing to be careful, teases him by suggesting that he had better practise what he preaches.

47. *ungracious:* unholy.

49. *puff'd and reckless libertine:* self-satisfied, wild playboy.

50. *the primrose path of dalliance:* the easy way of pleasure (contrasted with the *thorny way to heaven,* line 48).

51. *recks not his own rede:* takes no notice of his own advice. *O, fear me not:* Laertes tells her not to worry about his conduct.

53-4. *A double blessing . . . leave:* Laertes says that he is doubly well-off in being able to have his father's blessing twice over, for now they have a second opportunity of saying goodbye.

55-81. Though Polonius begins by telling him to hurry, like his son he enjoys the opportunity of delivering a sermon. He tells Laertes how he should behave now that he is going out into the world away from home. Like Laertes, he seems more concerned about what sort of impression his family creates in the eyes of the world, than with the moral rights and wrongs of behaviour.

55. *Yet:* still.

57. *stay'd for:* waited for.

58. *precepts:* pieces of advice.

59. *Look thou character:* be sure you write.

59-60. Polonius tells Laertes to keep his thoughts to himself, and never to do anything that is unsuited to the occasion.

61. *Be thou familiar . . . vulgar:* be sociable, but don't make yourself cheap.

62. *adoption tried:* loyalty proved.

63. *Grapple . . . steel:* hold tight to them.

64-5. *But . . . courage:* Don't greet every fine new acquaintance as a bosom friend immediately. (The phrase describes a hand that has been shaken so often that the palm has become insensitive.) *new-hatch'd, unfledg'd:* The image is of a baby bird, without feathers.

65-7. Laertes is to avoid getting into a quarrel but, if he finds himself involved in one, he must make his enemy regret it.

68. *Give . . . voice:* Listen to what everyone has to say, but don't agree too readily with anyone.

69. *censure:* opinion.

70-2. Polonius tells his son not to spare any expense on clothes, but they must look expensive without being elaborate and showy, for people show what they are like by what they wear.

The canker galls the infants of the spring
Too oft before their buttons be disclos'd;   40
And in the morn and liquid dew of youth
Contagious blastments are most imminent.
Be wary, then; best safety lies in fear:
Youth to itself rebels, though none else near.

Ophelia

I shall the effect of this good lesson keep   45
As watchman to my heart. But, good my brother,
Do not, as some ungracious pastors do,
Show me the steep and thorny way to heaven,
Whiles, like a puff'd and reckless libertine,
Himself the primrose path of dalliance treads   50
And recks not his own rede.

Laertes   O, fear me not!

Enter POLONIUS

I stay too long. But here my father comes.
A double blessing is a double grace;
Occasion smiles upon a second leave.

Polonius

Yet here, Laertes! Aboard, aboard, for shame!   55
The wind sits in the shoulder of your sail,
And you are stay'd for. There—my blessing with thee!
And these few precepts in thy memory
Look thou character. Give thy thoughts no tongue,
Nor any unproportion'd thought his act.   60
Be thou familiar, but by no means vulgar.
Those friends thou hast, and their adoption tried,
Grapple them to thy soul with hoops of steel;
But do not dull thy palm with entertainment
Of each new-hatch'd, unfledg'd courage. Beware   65
Of entrance to a quarrel; but, being in,
Bear't that th' opposed may beware of thee.
Give every man thy ear, but few thy voice;
Take each man's censure, but reserve thy judgment.
Costly thy habit as thy purse can buy,   70

73-4. The aristocracy of France are very particular about what they wear and spend a lot of money on their garments.

75-7. Both borrowing and lending are to be avoided, for if you lend money you may never see it, or the friend you lent it to, again, and if you borrow money you do not learn to economize. Polonius's mistrust of human nature is obvious here.

78-80. *to thine own self be true. . . man:* Polonius's advice is summed up by his statement that if Laertes does not let himself down he will be doing his duty by everyone. How safe a guide is this to how one should behave? Later in the play Laertes has a chance to put these principles into practice.

81. *season:* preserve.

83. *The time invites you:* it is time to go. *tend:* wait.

88. Polonius, who makes a habit of listening to other people's conversations, quickly pounces on Laertes's remark, and finds he has another opportunity to deliver some advice. Suspicious about Hamlet's intentions, he, too, warns Ophelia against him.

90. *Marry:* indeed (literally, 'by Mary') – a common exclamation in Shakespeare's time. *well bethought!* a good idea!

93. *Have . . . bounteous:* have been too generous in your readiness to see him.

94. *put on me:* suggested to me. Polonius did not notice it for himself.

95. *in way of caution:* by way of a warning.

96-7. Polonius tells Ophelia that his daughter ought to have more pride in herself and her reputation.

But not express'd in fancy; rich, not gaudy;
For the apparel oft proclaims the man;
And they in France of the best rank and station
Are of a most select and generous choice in that.
Neither a borrower nor a lender be;   75
For loan oft loses both itself and friend,
And borrowing dulls the edge of husbandry.
This above all—to thine own self be true,
And it must follow, as the night the day,
Thou canst not then be false to any man.   80
Farewell; my blessing season this in thee!

Laertes
Most humbly do I take my leave, my lord.

Polonius
The time invites you; go, your servants tend.

Laertes
Farewell, Ophelia; and remember well
What I have said to you.

Ophelia   'Tis in my memory lock'd,   85
And you yourself shall keep the key of it.

Laertes
Farewell.

Exit

Polonius
What is't, Ophelia, he hath said to you?

Ophelia
So please you, something touching the Lord Hamlet.

Polonius
Marry, well bethought!   90
'Tis told me he hath very oft of late
Given private time to you; and you yourself
Have of your audience been most free and bounteous.
If it be so—as so 'tis put on me,
And that in way of caution—I must tell you   95
You do not understand yourself so clearly
As it behoves my daughter and your honour.

99. *made many tenders:* offered many tokens.

101. *green:* immature, like an unripe fruit. Laertes, too, compared her to a young plant.
102. *Unsifted . . . circumstance:* inexperienced in these dangerous matters.

104. Ophelia's inability to think for herself is not surprising, as both her father and brother seem in the habit of treating her like a silly young girl who must accept the advice of men-of-the-world like themselves. Her father's tone of brisk contempt has shaken her faith in Hamlet's sincerity.
106-9. Punning on the word *tenders*, Polonius says that Ophelia has accepted mere token money, instead of real currency, from Hamlet, and she must offer herself for sale (*tender*, line 107) at a higher price, otherwise she will show (*tender*, line 109) her father to be a fool, for not having stopped her. The last phrase could also mean that Polonius was afraid that Ophelia might have an illegitimate child, as *fool* was a common word for 'baby'.
108-9. *not to crack . . . thus:* Polonius compares his complicated punning to overworking a horse.
110-11. Indignantly, Ophelia defends herself and Hamlet, but she is talked down by her father. *importun'd with:* repeatedly assured me of.
112. Polonius sarcastically twists her use of *fashion* to mean 'passing fancy'. *go to:* get along with you.
113. *given countenance to:* confirmed.
115. Woodcocks were thought to be stupid birds, as they are so easily trapped in snares (*springes*). The bird, here, is of course Ophelia, and Hamlet's promises are the snares.
115-23. In a tone of worldly wisdom, Polonius says that it is all too easy to make extravagant promises when physical desire is aroused. The flames of passion have no real warmth: they are gone almost as soon as they appear and seem about to come to something. Therefore, Ophelia must not mistake Hamlet's infatuation for the fire of real love, but must keep away from him.
122-3. Show that he will have to offer more than a mere request to see you before you start negotiating with him. The diplomatic terms – *entreatments* and *parle* – show that he thinks of the situation as one to be treated like a conflict between two opposing parties trying to reach a settlement, not as a love affair.
123-6. Like Laertes, Polonius emphasizes Hamlet's youth, in trying to convince Ophelia that his love will not last.
125. *with a larger tether may he walk:* he can act more freely than you can.
126. *In few:* in short.

What is between you? Give me up the truth.

Ophelia

He hath, my lord, of late made many tenders
Of his affection to me. 100

Polonius

Affection! Pooh! You speak like a green girl,
Unsifted in such perilous circumstance.
Do you believe his tenders, as you call them?

Ophelia

I do not know, my lord, what I should think.

Polonius

Marry, I will teach you: think yourself a baby 105
That you have ta'en these tenders for true pay
Which are not sterling. Tender yourself more dearly;
Or—not to crack the wind of the poor phrase,
Running it thus—you'll tender me a fool.

Ophelia

My lord, he hath importun'd me with love 110
In honourable fashion.

Polonius

Ay, fashion you may call it; go to, go to.

Ophelia

And hath given countenance to his speech, my lord,
With almost all the holy vows of heaven.

Polonius

Ay, springes to catch woodcocks! I do know, 115
When the blood burns, how prodigal the soul
Lends the tongue vows. These blazes, daughter,
Giving more light than heat—extinct in both,
Even in their promise, as it is a-making—
You must not take for fire. From this time 120
Be something scanter of your maiden presence;
Set your entreatments at a higher rate
Than a command to parle. For Lord Hamlet,
Believe so much in him, that he is young,
And with a larger tether may he walk 125
Than may be given you. In few, Ophelia,

127. *brokers:* go-betweens.

128. *Not of that dye . . . show:* not what they appear from their clothes (*investments:* used in its financial sense, picking up the rest of the business imagery – *brokers, bonds,* etc. – implying that Polonius sees his daughter as property to be bought and sold in marriage).

129-31. *But . . . beguile:* Hamlet's promises are only a way of making his immoral advances seem attractive and acceptable. He makes them sound like genuine contracts (Polonius means 'promises of marriage') in order to seduce you. *suits:* this picks up the garment imagery of line 128.

131. *This is for all:* to sum up.

133-4. Ophelia must not misuse any more of her leisure time by talking to Hamlet.

135. *Look to't:* see to it. *Come your ways:* come along.

136. Ophelia, completely crushed by her father's overbearing manner, agrees to give Hamlet up. If he trusted in her loyalty, he will be disappointed. She, like his mother, will have let him down.

SCENE IV

Midnight has come at last. While waiting in tense expectancy for the ghost to appear, Hamlet and the others attempt to make casual conversation about the weather and the customs of the Danish court.

1. *shrewdly:* sharply. Hamlet is perhaps shivering with excitement as well as cold.

2. *eager:* keen.

3. *lacks of:* is not quite.

5. *season:* time.

6. *held his wont:* made it his habit.

7. Horatio asks why trumpets are being blown and guns fired in the middle of the night. *pieces:* cannon.

8-9. *The King . . . wassail:* Hamlet explains that Claudius is sitting up late drinking and revelling.

9. *the swagg'ring upspring reels:* There are various possible explanations of this phrase, the two most likely being (i) that it refers to a drunken reveller dancing a wild German dance, the *up-spring,* and (ii) that it means 'new-fangled revelry' (*reels:* revels). Whichever Hamlet intended, it is clear from his use of such words as *swaggering* that he does not approve of his uncle's fondness for noisy drinking parties.

10. *Rhenish:* wine from the German Rhineland, which Claudius pours down his throat (*drains*) in large quantities.

Do not believe his vows; for they are brokers,
Not of that dye which their investments show,
But mere implorators of unholy suits,
Breathing like sanctified and pious bonds,   130
The better to beguile. This is for all—
I would not, in plain terms, from this time forth
Have you so slander any moment leisure
As to give words or talk with the Lord Hamlet.
Look to't, I charge you. Come your ways.   135

Ophelia

I shall obey, my lord.

Exeunt

SCENE IV—*Elsinore. The guard-platform of the Castle*

Enter HAMLET, HORATIO *and* MARCELLUS

Hamlet

The air bites shrewdly; it is very cold.

Horatio

It is a nipping and an eager air.

Hamlet

What hour now?

Horatio   I think it lacks of twelve.

Marcellus

No, it is struck.

Horatio

Indeed? I heard it not. It then draws near the season   5
Wherein the spirit held his wont to walk.

A flourish of trumpets, and two pieces go off

What does this mean, my lord?

Hamlet

The King doth wake to-night and takes his rouse,
Keeps wassail, and the swagg'ring up-spring reels,
And, as he drains his draughts of Rhenish down,   10

11. *bray:* He sarcastically compares the music the king has ordered to accompany his drinking of a toast (see Act I, Scene ii, lines 125-8) to the cry of a donkey.

12. *The triumph of his pledge:* to celebrate the toast he drinks.

13. *Ay, marry, is't:* Yes, indeed it is.

14-16. *though I am native here . . . observance:* Hamlet says that, though he is Danish too, he thinks it is a custom that Denmark would be more respected for breaking with than keeping.

17-18. The adjective *heavy-headed* indicates what effect the revelry has on those who indulge in it, while other countries both to the east and the west of Denmark criticize and condemn it.

19. *clepe:* call.

19-20. *with swinish phrase . . . addition:* label us pigs (*addition:* a style of address, such as 'Sir').

20-2. *it takes . . . attribute:* The idea that Danes are drunkards takes away the best part of the credit they should have for their achievements, even though these may be outstanding.

23-38. What he has just said of Denmark causes Hamlet to reflect that the same is also true of individuals: one small fault will often ruin an otherwise great and gifted man. (This is what causes the downfall of most heroes of tragedy. Has Hamlet shown any signs of believing his own character to contain a flaw?)

24. *vicious mole of nature:* malignant natural blemish.

25-6. *As in their birth . . . origin:* Such as in the circumstances of their birth, which they cannot help, as no-one can choose how to be born.

27. *o'ergrowth . . . complexion:* overdevelopment of some trait of the personality.

28. *Oft breaking down . . . reason:* Bursting the barriers of reason. Hamlet describes the mind as being surrounded by barricades which are broken down by madness.

29. *o'er-leavens:* blows up, distorts (like yeast fermenting in bread).

30. *the form of plausive manners:* pleasant behaviour.

32. *Being . . . star:* whether inborn or the result of bad luck (another reference to the idea that the stars affect human destiny.

33. *virtues else:* other good qualities.

34. *as man may undergo:* as one man may accumulate.

35. *general censure:* the opinion of the majority. *take corruption From:* be spoiled by.

36-8. The exact meaning of *eale* and *of a doubt* is uncertain, but the general idea is that a little of something base in a fine substance (such as wine or gold) will ruin the whole of it.

38. Just when the tension of the opening of the scene has been relaxed by Hamlet's long, thoughtful speech, the ghost startles him, and the audience, by suddenly appearing.

39. *ministers of grace:* servants of God, angels. Hamlet's first instinct is to protect his friends and himself by prayer, in case Horatio is right in suspecting that the apparition is a devil. Then the prince's courage and curiosity overcome his fears, and he invites the ghost to speak, taking the risk of calling it his father.

40. *spirit of health:* good spirit. *goblin damn'd:* fiend from hell.

41. *blasts:* used in two senses – 'gusts of hot air', and 'evil influences'.

The kettle-drum and trumpet thus bray out
The triumph of his pledge.

Horatio   Is it a custom?

Hamlet
Ay, marry, is't;
But to my mind, though I am native here
And to the manner born, it is a custom   15
More honour'd in the breach than the observance.
This heavy-headed revel east and west
Makes us traduc'd and tax'd of other nations;
They clepe us drunkards, and with swinish phrase
Soil our addition; and, indeed, it takes   20
From our achievements, though perform'd at height,
The pith and marrow of our attribute.
So, oft it chances in particular men
That, for some vicious mole of nature in them,
As in their birth, wherein they are not guilty,   25
Since nature cannot choose his origin;
By the o'ergrowth of some complexion,
Oft breaking down the pales and forts of reason;
Or by some habit that too much o'er-leavens
The form of plausive manners—that these men,   30
Carrying, I say, the stamp of one defect,
Being nature's livery or fortune's star,
His virtues else, be they as pure as grace,
As infinite as man may undergo,
Shall in the general censure take corruption   35
From that particular fault. The dram of eale
Doth all the noble substance of a doubt
To his own scandal.

Enter GHOST

Horatio   Look, my lord, it comes.

Hamlet
Angels and ministers of grace defend us!
Be thou a spirit of health or goblin damn'd,   40
Bring with thee airs from heaven or blasts from hell,

43. *questionable:* also used in two senses – 'asking to be questioned' and 'unidentifiable'.

45. Hamlet pauses, after going so far as to address the ghost by the name of the dead king, but to his intense disappointment it remains silent.

47. *canoniz'd bones . . . death:* consecrated and buried bones.

48. *cerements:* winding sheets, shrouds.

49. *enurn'd:* entombed.

50-1. *Hath op'd . . . again:* 'Has opened its heavy stone jaws to vomit you up again.' Hamlet visualizes with a mixture of awe and repulsion his father's corpse resurrecting itself (see also Act I, Scene ii, lines 256–7 for a similar picture).

52. *corse:* corpse. *complete steel:* full armour.

53. *Revisits . . . moon:* comes back in the moonlight (to this earth).

54-6. *and we fools of nature . . . souls:* making us foolish mortals (or 'children of nature') disturb ourselves with fears of supernatural things which we do not understand.

57. *wherefore?* what for?

59. *As if . . . desire:* As if it wanted to say something.

60. *with what courteous action:* in what a dignified way.

61. *removed ground:* remote place.

63. That Hamlet is no coward is shown by the way he decides without hesitation to follow the ghost, in spite of his friends' warnings; in fact, the more they try to dissuade him, the more obstinate he becomes. The prince does not like to be crossed.

65. Hamlet says his life is not worth anything to him (in Act I, Scene ii, lines 129-32 he said he wished he could die).

66-7. In spite of his doubts about life and himself, Hamlet has none about the immortality of the soul.

69-78. Horatio suggests that the apparition may be an evil one which is trying to drive Hamlet mad, and perhaps cause him to kill himself. He points out that, if the ghost leads Hamlet to the top of a cliff, he may succumb to the quite common human impulse to jump when looking down from a height. Horatio's reference to madness and suicide suggests that in spite of the steadiness of his own nature he has an instinctive awareness that Hamlet is disturbed and unhappy.

69. *flood:* sea.

Be thy intents wicked or charitable,
Thou com'st in such a questionable shape
That I will speak to thee. I'll call thee Hamlet,
King, father, royal Dane. O, answer me!   45
Let me not burst in ignorance, but tell
Why thy canoniz'd bones, hearsed in death,
Have burst their cerements; why the sepulchre
Wherein we saw thee quietly enurn'd
Hath op'd his ponderous and marble jaws   50
To cast thee up again. What may this mean
That thou, dead corse, again in complete steel
Revisits thus the glimpses of the moon,
Making night hideous, and we fools of nature
So horridly to shake our disposition   55
With thoughts beyond the reaches of our souls?
Say, why is this? wherefore? What should we do?

GHOST *beckons* HAMLET

Horatio
  It beckons you to go away with it,
  As if it some impartment did desire
  To you alone.
Marcellus   Look with what courteous action   60
  It waves you to a more removed ground.
  But do not go with it.
Horatio   No, by no means.
Hamlet
  It will not speak; then I will follow it.
Horatio
  Do not, my lord.
Hamlet   Why, what should be the fear?
  I do not set my life at a pin's fee;   65
  And for my soul, what can it do to that,
  Being a thing immortal as itself?
  It waves me forth again; I'll follow it.
Horatio
  What if it tempt you toward the flood, my lord,

73

71. *beetles o'er his base:* overhangs.

73. *deprive your sovereignty of reason:* overthrow your reason.

75. *toys of desperation:* silly, desperate ideas.

76. *Without more motive:* The place, alone, is sufficient to put the idea of suicide into the mind.

78. *waves:* beckons.

79-86. *Go on; I'll follow thee:* This is spoken, of course, to the ghost.

80-6. Horatio and Marcellus have taken the liberty of grabbing him, to prevent him following the ghost, but, after an angry struggle, Hamlet succeeds in shaking them off – which shows he is no weakling, since Marcellus, for one, is a soldier.

81. *Be rul'd:* Do what we say.

82. *petty arture:* little artery. We would say 'nerve' in this connection.

83. *hardy:* strong. *The Nemean lion:* an immensely fierce beast which could not be wounded by any arrow; one of the creatures that Hercules killed (see note on Act I, Scene ii, line 153). *nerve:* sinew.

85. *lets:* hinders. With a grim sense of humour, Hamlet threatens to create another ghost by killing anyone who holds him back.

87. Horatio says anxiously that Hamlet is going out of his mind.

89. *Have after:* 'Let's follow. *To what issue . . . come?* What will come of this?

90. The ugly word *rotten* recalls Hamlet's description of the corruption of the world in Act I, Scene ii, and his statement *Foul deeds will rise* (Act I, Scene ii, line 256).

91. Horatio is an optimist, with a simple faith in the power of good, but Marcellus says 'Come on, don't leave it to heaven.'

Or to the dreadful summit of the cliff 70
That beetles o'er his base into the sea,
And there assume some other horrible form,
Which might deprive your sovereignty of reason
And draw you into madness? Think of it:
The very place puts toys of desperation, 75
Without more motive, into every brain
That looks so many fathoms to the sea
And hears it roar beneath.

Hamlet   It waves me still.
Go on; I'll follow thee.

Marcellus
You shall not go, my lord.

Hamlet   Hold off your hands. 80

Horatio
Be rul'd; you shall not go.

Hamlet   My fate cries out,
And makes each petty arture in this body
As hardy as the Nemean lion's nerve.

GHOST *beckons*

Still am I call'd. Unhand me, gentlemen.
By heaven, I'll make a ghost of him that lets me. 85
I say, away! Go on; I'll follow thee.

Exeunt GHOST *and* HAMLET

Horatio
He waxes desperate with imagination.

Marcellus
Let's follow; 'tis not fit thus to obey him.

Horatio
Have after. To what issue will this come?

Marcellus
Something is rotten in the state of Denmark. 90

Horatio
Heaven will direct it.

Marcellus   Nay, let's follow him.

Exeunt

SCENE V

This scene follows immediately after the last. The ghost has led Hamlet to a remote place on the walls of the castle.

2. At last the ghost breaks its long silence, solemnly telling Hamlet to listen to it carefully.

2-4. With the coming of dawn, the ghost will have to return to the fires of purgatory (see Act I, Scene i, lines 149-56 for this belief). Any trace Hamlet may still have of suspicion and fear melts away in pity.

6. *bound:* obliged, in duty bound.

7. With the word *revenge* the ghost finally reveals what is on its mind; Horatio and the others were a long way from the mark in their assumption that Denmark's political crisis had brought it there. In Act I, Scene iv, line 90, however, Marcellus came near the truth.

8. In what tone does Hamlet say this? Is he simply querying what it is he has to avenge, or is he shocked and startled? Is it altogether a surprise to him (see line 40, below)?

10. *Doom'd for a certain term:* condemned for a fixed period.

11-13. The fact that his father, whom Hamlet and others admired as a good man, has to suffer punishment in purgatory until all his sins are burnt away, must horrify Hamlet, but at least the flames are not those of hell.

14. *prison-house:* purgatory.

16. *harrow up:* distress. We talk of a 'harrowing' story.

17. *start from their spheres:* jump from their sockets. It was believed for centuries that the planets and stars moved round the earth fixed in transparent spheres.

18-20. Hamlet's hair would stand out on end, like quills on an angry porcupine.

21. *eternal blazon:* revelation of the supernatural world.

76

SCENE V—*Elsinore. The battlements of the Castle*

Enter GHOST *and* HAMLET

Hamlet
Whither wilt thou lead me? Speak. I'll go no further.
Ghost
Mark me.
Hamlet   I will.
Ghost   My hour is almost come,
When I to sulph'rous and tormenting flames
Must render up myself.
Hamlet   Alas, poor ghost!
Ghost
Pity me not, but lend thy serious hearing   5
To what I shall unfold.
Hamlet   Speak; I am bound to hear.
Ghost
So art thou to revenge, when thou shalt hear.
Hamlet
What?
Ghost
I am thy father's spirit,
Doom'd for a certain term to walk the night,   10
And for the day confin'd to fast in fires,
Till the foul crimes done in my days of nature
Are burnt and purg'd away. But that I am forbid
To tell the secrets of my prison-house,
I could à tale unfold whose lightest word   15
Would harrow up thy soul, freeze thy young blood,
Make thy two eyes, like stars, start from their spheres,
Thy knotted and combined locks to part,
And each particular hair to stand an end,
Like quills upon the fretful porpentine.   20
But this eternal blazon must not be

22. *List, list, O, list!* The repetition conveys powerfully the ghost's earnest wish for Hamlet to take in what it is saying.

24. Hamlet is deeply moved. We know already how grieved he was at his father's death.

25. *unnatural:* To Elizabethan ears, this would, in itself, suggest that it was a member of King Hamlet's family who killed him, so ignoring the claims of 'natural affection', with which, like 'kind' (see note on Act I, Scene ii, line 65), it is usually associated in Shakespeare.

29. *Haste me to know't:* hurry up and tell me.
29-31. In the excitement of the moment, Hamlet talks of flying with the speed of thought to take revenge, yet it takes him a long time to get round to it, as the rest of the play shows.
31. *apt:* ready and willing.
32. *duller:* more lifeless. *fat:* thick, or damp and sweaty, or both. The ghost is probably not thinking of any particular plant.
33. *Lethe wharf:* the bank of the river Lethe, in the Greek underworld. Whoever drank its waters forgot all his past experiences. The ghost means that Hamlet would have to be extraordinarily insensitive and lazy to fail to do something about his father's murder.
35. *given out:* stated officially. *orchard:* This word just means garden in Shakespeare.
36-8. *the whole ear . . . abus'd:* the whole of Denmark is grossly deceived by being given a false account of the cause of the king's death.
38. *know:* let me tell you.
39-40. *The serpent . . . crown:* it was Claudius who killed him.

40. *O my prophetic soul!* "I thought so!" How long, do you think, has Hamlet suspected his uncle of this crime?

42. The ghost refers with horror to the fact that, from the Church's point of view, the marriage between Gertrude and Claudius was incestuous (see note on Act I, Scene ii, line 157). *adulterate:* adulterous. This is the first suggestion that Gertrude was having an affair with Claudius even before her first husband died, unless the ghost is using the word very loosely.
43. *witchcraft of his wits:* The ghost obviously does not want to believe that Claudius stole his wife from him by fair means.
44. *wit:* cunning.
47. *falling off:* deterioration, 'come-down'.
48-50. *whose love . . . marriage:* whose love was holy, and lived up to our marriage vows.
50-1. *decline Upon:* lower herself to.

To ears of flesh and blood. List, list, O, list!
If thou didst ever thy dear father love—

Hamlet
O God!

Ghost
Revenge his foul and most unnatural murder.   25

Hamlet
Murder!

Ghost
Murder most foul, as in the best it is;
But this most foul, strange, and unnatural.

Hamlet
Haste me to know't, that I, with wings as swift
As meditation or the thoughts of love,   30
May sweep to my revenge.

Ghost   I find thee apt;
And duller shouldst thou be than the fat weed
That roots itself in ease on Lethe wharf,
Wouldst thou not stir in this. Now, Hamlet, hear:
'Tis given out that, sleeping in my orchard,   35
A serpent stung me; so the whole ear of Denmark
Is by a forged process of my death
Rankly abus'd; but know, thou noble youth,
The serpent that did sting thy father's life
Now wears his crown.

Hamlet   O my prophetic soul!   40
My uncle!

Ghost
Ay, that incestuous, that adulterate beast,
With witchcraft of his wits, with traitorous gifts—
O wicked wit and gifts that have the power
So to seduce!—won to his shameful lust   45
The will of my most seeming virtuous queen.
O Hamlet, what a falling off was there,
From me, whose love was of that dignity
That it went hand in hand even with the vow
I made to her in marriage; and to decline   50

51-2. *a wretch . . . mine:* The ghost's self-righteousness here is understandable if one considers how much cause he has to despise Claudius.
53-7. The ghost goes on to say that, whereas a really virtuous person cannot be persuaded to do wrong however angelic the would-be seducer seems, lustful feelings will cause people like Gertrude to become 'fed up' with a virtuous partner and try to satisfy themselves with disgusting indulgence.

58. *But soft:* The ghost pulls itself up short, for not much time is left.

60. *of:* in.

61. *Upon my secure hour:* while I was relaxing, free from care.

62. Claudius came prepared with a little bottle of poisonous juice from a deadly plant (such as henbane or hemlock).

63. *porches:* entrances, openings. It was believed in Shakespeare's day that people could be poisoned in the way described.

64. *leperous distilment:* The concentrated juice caused an effect like leprosy on the body.

65. *Holds such an enmity:* Causes such a violent reaction.

66. *quicksilver:* This liquid metal (mercury) is also poisonous.

67. *gates and alleys:* ducts and veins.

68. *posset:* curdle, coagulate.

69. *eager droppings:* drops of acid. Sour wine or vinegar, for example, have this effect in curdling milk.

70. *thin:* free-flowing. *wholesome:* healthy.

71. *instant tetter:* instantaneous rash. *bark'd about:* formed a scaly eruption like bark.

72. *lazar-like:* like leprosy.

75. *dispatch'd:* deprived.

76-7. Hamlet's father was killed while his sins were full-blown, i.e. before he had time to be prepared for death with the proper religious rites, confessing his sins, receiving absolution for them, and being given the last sacraments.

78. *account:* judgement by God.

80. This heart-felt cry expresses the ghost's horror both at its own predicament and at Claudius's callousness in causing his own brother to suffer in this way.

81. *nature:* family affection, the 'natural' feeling of a son for a father.

83. *luxury:* lechery.

84-8. The ghost cautions Hamlet to avoid two things, however he goes about obtaining his revenge: he must beware of endangering his sanity, and he must not think up ways of hurting his mother – she will be sufficiently punished by God and her own conscience. Is the ghost implying that Gertrude collaborated in the murder of her first husband, or just that she feels guilty about having remarried so soon? We cannot know this yet.

Upon a wretch whose natural gifts were poor
To those of mine!
But virtue, as it never will be moved,
Though lewdness court it in a shape of heaven,
So lust, though to a radiant angel link'd,   55
Will sate itself in a celestial bed
And prey on garbage.
But soft! methinks I scent the morning air.
Brief let me be. Sleeping within my orchard,
My custom always of the afternoon,   60
Upon my secure hour thy uncle stole,
With juice of cursed hebona in a vial,
And in the porches of my ears did pour
The leperous distilment; whose effect
Holds such an enmity with blood of man   65
That swift as quicksilver it courses through
The natural gates and alleys of the body;
And with a sudden vigour it doth posset
And curd, like eager droppings into milk,
The thin and wholesome blood. So did it mine;   70
And a most instant tetter bark'd about,
Most lazar-like, with vile and loathsome crust,
All my smooth body.
Thus was I, sleeping, by a brother's hand
Of life, of crown, of queen, at once dispatch'd;   75
Cut off even in the blossoms of my sin,
Unhousel'd, disappointed, unanel'd;
No reck'ning made, but sent to my account
With all my imperfections on my head.
O, horrible! O, horrible! most horrible!   80
If thou hast nature in thee, bear it not;
Let not the royal bed of Denmark be
A couch for luxury and damned incest.
But, howsomever thou pursuest this act,
Taint not thy mind, nor let thy soul contrive   85
Against thy mother aught; leave her to heaven,
And to those thorns that in her bosom lodge

89. *matin:* morning.

90. The glow-worm begins to let its faint light die away.

92-112. As the ghost fades into the pale light of dawn, Hamlet is left alone, shaking with reaction from his emotional encounter (lines 94-5), but strangely excited, too. His anger against Claudius is mixed with a kind of glee, for his instinctive hatred of him is now fully justified, and he has an aim in life – revenge – to replace his miserable frustration (Act I, Scene ii, line 159). He vows to forgo all other interests. (What about Ophelia?)

93. *And shall I couple hell?* Hamlet asks whether he should mention hell as well as heaven and earth, in his exclamations. He considers briefly the possibility that the ghost may be a demon, but the rest of his speech shows that he has accepted it as genuine, at least, for the time being. *O, fie!* Hamlet either rejects his moment of doubt, or exclaims in disgust at his uncle's wickedness.

94. *grow not instant old:* 'don't become like those of an old man in a moment.' Hamlet is trembling.

96-7. *whiles memory . . . globe:* 'as long as this head of mine contains any memories at all.' Hamlet's use of the word *distracted* may suggest that he feels the balance of his mind has been disturbed.

98. Hamlet compares his memory to a tablet, often made of ivory, which an Elizabethan gentleman would carry, using it as a kind of notebook to jot down ideas (which could later be rubbed off, as with a child's slate). Hamlet is going to erase from his mind everything but what the ghost has told him to do.

99. *fond:* foolish. *records:* notes, memos.

100. *saws:* sayings. *forms:* sketches. *pressures:* impressions.

101. *That youth . . . there:* The ideas with which Hamlet has filled his mind till now suddenly seem juvenile to him.

105. In spite of the ghost's warning, Hamlet's anger is directed against his mother almost as fiercely as against his uncle.

106-10. Now he takes out his actual tables (see note on line 98, above) and writes down a comment on Claudius's hypocrisy in concealing his wickedness under a flattering manner. Is this a completely normal way to behave?

110. *word:* watchward, motto, vow.

112. Hamlet perhaps swears this oath on the cross-shaped hilt of the sword which he uses later in the scene (lines 147-80).

112-15. The anxious calls of his friends rouse Hamlet from his reverie: after a last solemn *so be it*, he braces himself to face their inevitable questions, adopting, as he often does when excited, a frivolous manner.

113. *secure:* protect.

To prick and sting her. Fare thee well at once.
The glowworm shows the matin to be near,
And gins to pale his uneffectual fire.   90
Adieu, adieu, adieu! Remember me.

Exit

Hamlet
O all you host of heaven! O earth! What else?
And shall I couple hell? O, fie! Hold, hold, my heart;
And you, my sinews, grow not instant old,
But bear me stiffly up. Remember thee!   95
Ay, thou poor ghost, whiles memory holds a seat
In this distracted globe. Remember thee!
Yea, from the table of my memory
I'll wipe away all trivial fond records,
All saws of books, all forms, all pressures past,   100
That youth and observation copied there,
And thy commandment all alone shall live
Within the book and volume of my brain,
Unmix'd with baser matter. Yes, by heaven!
O most pernicious woman!   105
O villain, villain, smiling, damned villain!
My tables—meet it is I set it down
That one may smile, and smile, and be a villain;

Writing

At least I am sure it may be so in Denmark.
So, uncle, there you are. Now to my word: 110
It is 'Adieu, adieu! Remember me'.
I have sworn't.
Horatio [*Within*]   My lord, my lord!

Enter HORATIO *and* MARCELLUS

Marcellus
Lord Hamlet!
Horatio   Heavens secure him!

116. Hamlet playfully echoes Marcellus's shout, imitating a falconer calling his hawk back to his hand.

118. *O, wonderful!* As the other two come panting up to him, Hamlet teases them with a mock-serious hint of being about to reveal a fascinating secret to them.

121-2. Hamlet is perhaps about to tell them something of what happened, but he breaks off as though unsure whether he can trust them. For a second time, however, they promise to keep his secret, this time with a binding oath.

123-4. Again Hamlet seems about to confide in them, but he ends his sentence lamely with an obvious truth (how might the sentence have finished?). *never a:* no. *arrant knave:* out-and-out scoundrel.

125-6. Horatio drily points out that he has told them nothing.

126-32. Hamlet abruptly tries to dismiss the others.
127. *circumstance:* beating about the bush.

129. Hamlet tells them to go and do whatever they have to do, or fancy doing.

132. Do you think he says this jestingly or seriously?

133. Instead of pretending to see nothing odd about the prince's behaviour, and obeying him, Horatio courteously but firmly refuses to be fobbed off with nonsense.

Hamlet
  So be it!

Marcellus
  Illo, ho, ho, my lord!   *115*

Hamlet
  Hillo, ho, ho, boy! Come, bird, come.

Marcellus
  How is't, my noble lord?

Horatio   What news, my lord?

Hamlet
  O, wonderful!

Horatio
  Good my lord, tell it.

Hamlet   No; you will reveal it.

Horatio
  Not I, my lord, by heaven!

Marcellus   Nor I, my lord.   *120*

Hamlet
  How say you, then; would heart of man once think it?
  But you'll be secret?

Both   Ay, by heaven, my lord!

Hamlet
  There's never a villain dwelling in all Denmark
  But he's an arrant knave.

Horatio
  There needs no ghost, my lord, come from the grave *125*
  To tell us this.

Hamlet   Why, right; you are in the right;
  And so, without more circumstance at all,
  I hold it fit that we shake hands and part;
  You, as your business and desire shall point you—
  For every man hath business and desire,   *130*
  Such as it is; and for my own poor part,
  Look you, I will go pray.

Horatio
  These are but wild and whirling words, my lord.

134-40. Suddenly made aware by Horatio's implied reproach that he is behaving uncivilly, and perhaps impressed by Horatio's sturdy loyalty, Hamlet seems again about to relate the ghost's message, and yet again cuts himself short; possibly he was about to tell Horatio, and suddenly realized that Marcellus, who was not a close friend, was listening.

136. *Saint Patrick* was the patron saint of purgatory so, by using this unusual oath, Hamlet may have been hinting to Horatio that the ghost really was genuine, as ghosts should not be able to wander from heaven or hell.

137. *Touching:* about, concerning.

138. *honest ghost:* genuine ghost, not a devil masquerading.

140. *O'ermaster't as you may:* conquer it as well as you can.

143. Horatio's loyalty and desire to help Hamlet are shown by the way he promises without knowing the request.

144. Why is Hamlet so insistent that even the news that a ghost has been seen should not get around?

145, 146. *In faith:* more or less equivalent to 'on my honour'.

147. The hilt of Hamlet's sword, being cross-shaped, would serve, like a Bible, to make an oath binding. Also, of course, for Hamlet the sword symbolizes the revenge he means to take.

149-81. The mysterious voice of the ghost, rising up from beneath their feet as though from hell, or the ground where the ex-king's body was buried, no doubt impresses Horatio and Marcellus deeply. Hamlet's behaviour, however, is strange: the awe and pity with which he addressed the ghost earlier have been replaced by a facetious tone. His conduct seems excited, perhaps even unhinged. Maybe he is trying to frighten the others into silence by pretending he is in league with the spirit world (*truepenny* was a name associated with the familiar spirit of a magician. Moving from place to place, as Hamlet makes them all do, was also a feature of magical rites).

150. These words are addressed to the ghost. *truepenny:* good fellow.

151-2. Hamlet speaks to Horatio and Marcellus. *cellarage:* space below the stage.

152. *Propose the oath:* say what oath is to be sworn.

Hamlet

   I am sorry they offend you, heartily;

   Yes, faith, heartily.

Horatio   There's no offence, my lord.   135

Hamlet

   Yes, by Saint Patrick, but there is, Horatio,

   And much offence too. Touching this vision here—

   It is an honest ghost, that let me tell you.

   For your desire to know what is between us,

   O'ermaster't as you may. And now, good friends,   140

   As you are friends, scholars, and soldiers,

   Give me one poor request.

Horatio

   What is't, my lord? We will.

Hamlet

   Never make known what you have seen to-night.

Both

   My lord, we will not.

Hamlet   Nay, but swear't.

Horatio   In faith,   145

   My lord, not I.

Marcellus   Nor I, my lord, in faith.

Hamlet

   Upon my sword.

Marcellus   We have sworn, my lord, already.

Hamlet

   Indeed, upon my sword, indeed.

Ghost [*Cries under the stage*]

   Swear.

Hamlet

   Ha, ha, boy! say'st thou so? Art thou there truepenny?   150

   Come on. You hear this fellow in the cellarage:

   Consent to swear.

Horatio   Propose the oath, my lord.

Hamlet

   Never to speak of this that you have seen,

   Swear by my sword.

156. *Hic et ubique:* Latin for here and everywhere. *shift our ground:* move somewhere else.

162. Hamlet disrespectfully compares the ghost's way of speaking from beneath their feet, however often they move, to a mole burrowing through the ground.

163. *pioneer:* digger, miner. *remove:* move.

164. Even Horatio is thoroughly out of his depth.

165. Promptly picking up Horatio's *strange*, Hamlet tells him to welcome a new experience in the way he would give hospitality to a stranger.

166-7. Hamlet gently teases his friend for having relied too much on rational explanations of such things as ghosts; *your* is probably used in an indefinite sense, however, as it is often in Shakespeare (compare Act V, Scene i, line 163-4). Hamlet too was a scholar.

169. The word 'swear' is understood at the beginning of this line, for Hamlet is giving the oath in detail. *so help you mercy:* as you hope for God's mercy.

170-9. Hamlet makes the others promise that however oddly he may behave from now on, they must not go around looking, knowing, and saying that, if they chose, they could explain the reason for his behaviour. He hints (line 171-2) that he may, in fact, decide to act in a crazy way. What do you think are his reasons for saying this?

174. *encumber'd thus:* folded.

175. *doubtful:* ambiguous, with a double meaning.

176. *an if:* if.

177. *list:* wanted. *There be:* there are people who could speak.

178. *giving out:* hinting. *note:* indicate.

180. *most:* greatest. Hamlet makes the oath binding by connecting it with religion.

182. With another sudden change of mood, Hamlet tells the ghost compassionately that it can be at peace at last, and then he amicably but briskly says goodbye to his friends.

183. *With all my love . . . you:* My very best wishes to you.

Ghost [*Beneath*]

  Swear.   155

Hamlet

  Hic et ubique? Then we'll shift our ground.

  Come hither, gentlemen,

  And lay your hands again upon my sword.

  Swear by my sword

  Never to speak of this that you have heard.   160

Ghost [*Beneath*]

  Swear, by his sword.

Hamlet

  Well said, old mole! Canst work i' th' earth so fast?

  A worthy pioneer! Once more remove, good friends.

Horatio

  O day and night, but this is wondrous strange!

Hamlet

  And therefore as a stranger give it welcome.   165

  There are more things in heaven and earth, Horatio,

  Than are dreamt of in your philosophy.

  But come.

  Here, as before, never, so help you mercy,

  How strange or odd some'er I bear myself—   170

  As I perchance hereafter shall think meet

  To put an antic disposition on—

  That you, at such times, seeing me, never shall,

  With arms encumber'd thus, or this head-shake,

  Or by pronouncing of some doubtful phrase,   175

  As 'Well, well, we know' or 'We could, an if we would'

  Or 'If we list to speak' or 'There be, an if they might'

  Or such ambiguous giving out, to note

  That you know aught of me—this do swear,

  So grace and mercy at your most need help you.   180

Ghost [*Beneath*]

  Swear.

Hamlet

  Rest, rest, perturbed spirit! So, gentlemen,

  With all my love I do commend me to you;

184. *so poor a man as Hamlet.* Either he is speaking modestly of himself, or he is commenting dryly on the fact that he has been cheated of the crown.

185. *friending:* friendship.

186. *shall not lack:* shall be done.

187. *And still . . . pray:* Please keep this a permanent secret.

188-9. Do you think Hamlet says this to the others or just to himself? *The time is out of joint:* Things are in a state of confusion. *O cursed spite . . . right:* The enthusiasm for revenge which the conversation with the ghost aroused has died down to a reluctant sense of duty; the reaction from his excitement is setting in. Is anything in particular upsetting Hamlet about the task he has to do?

190. *Nay, come:* right, then.

And what so poor a man as Hamlet is
May do t'express his love and friending to you, *185*
God willing, shall not lack. Let us go in together;
And still your fingers on your lips, I pray.
The time is out of joint. O cursed spite,
That ever I was born to set it right!
Nay, come, let's go together. *190*

Exeunt

ACT TWO

SCENE I

Some time must elapse between the last scene and this one, for here Polonius is sending a servant with money and letters to Laertes, who was only just leaving for France on the day when Hamlet met the ghost, but who has been long enough in Paris by now to have acquired some sort of independent reputation. In fact, Reynaldo's chief job is to spy on Laertes, and report back on his behaviour to Polonius. This is something of a surprise after the impression we were given in Act I, Scene iii of an affectionate father-son relationship. Has Laertes given his father cause to suspect him of wild behaviour, or is Polonius's action chiefly prompted by his own love of intrigue and being 'in the know'? No wonder Hamlet is so cautious and suspicious if this is the sort of thing that generally goes on in the Danish court.

1. *notes:* letters.

3. *You shall do marvellous wisely:* it would be an excellent idea.

4. *inquire:* inquiries.

5. The fact that Reynaldo guessed that some spying on Laertes would be a good idea reveals a lot about the characters of both Laertes and Polonius.

7-68. Polonius gives Reynaldo detailed instructions about how to tackle the investigation. One gets the impression that, if he could, he would rather have enjoyed doing it himself!

7. *Enquire me:* find out for me. *Danskers:* Danes.

8-9. *how, and who ... expense:* 'why they are there, who they are, what their income is, where they live, who their friends are and how much they spend.' Reynaldo will be busy!

10. *encompassment ... question:* roundabout method of inquiry.

11-12. In this way Reynaldo will come to the heart of the matter more successfully than if he asked direct questions about Laertes.

13. *Take you ... of him:* say you know him vaguely.

15. *in part:* slightly. *mark this:* take this in.

17. By repeating these words Polonius gives the impression that he has prepared this speech word for word beforehand. It is almost as though he is reading it from notes. *not well:* Reynaldo must not give the impression of being a personal friend.

19. *Addicted:* given to. *put on him:* accuse him of.

20. *forgeries:* invented faults. *rank:* gross.

22-4. *such wanton ... liberty:* the sort of irresponsible little faults that are usually found in a young man who is free to do what he wants.

ACT TWO

SCENE I—*Elsinore. The house of Polonius*

Enter POLONIUS *and* REYNALDO

Polonius
Give him this money and these notes, Reynaldo.
Reynaldo
I will, my lord.
Polonius
You shall do marvellous wisely, good Reynaldo,
Before you visit him, to make inquire
Of his behaviour.
Reynaldo   My lord, I did intend it.   5
Polonius
Marry, well said; very well said. Look you, sir,
Enquire me first what Danskers are in Paris;
And how, and who, what means, and where they keep,
What company, at what expense; and finding
By this encompassment and drift of question   10
That they do know my son, come you more nearer
Than your particular demands will touch it.
Take you, as 'twere, some distant knowledge of him;
As thus: 'I know his father and his friends,
And in part him'. Do you mark this, Reynaldo?   15
Reynaldo
Ay, very well, my lord.
Polonius
'And in part him'—but you may say 'not well;
But if't be he I mean, he's very wild;
Addicted so and so'; and there put on him
What forgeries you please; marry, none so rank   20
As may dishonour him; take heed of that;
But, sir, such wanton, wild, and usual slips

93

24. *gaming:* gambling.

26. *Drabbing:* associating with prostitutes.

27. *that:* drabbing.

28. *as you . . . charge:* provided you phrase the accusation delicately.
29. *put another scandal on him:* accuse him of anything else.
30. *is open to incontinency:* goes beyond reasonable limits.
31. *breathe:* speak of. *quaintly:* discreetly.
32. *taints of liberty:* little faults which result from too much freedom.
33. *the flash . . . mind:* the self-expression of a young spark.
34. *savageness:* wildness. *unreclaimed blood:* untamed spirit.

35. *Of general assault:* that attacks many young men.

36. *Wherefore:* why.

37. *would:* want to. Reynaldo seems to feel that Polonius is asking him to go too far. *here's my drift:* this is what I'm getting at.
38. *fetch of warrant:* justifiable trick.
39-45. Polonius says that when Reynaldo has made these insinuations about Laertes, as though they were common gossip, his listener will follow up the subject, if he has any evidence of Laertes indulging in the vices named by Reynaldo.

45. *closes . . . consequence:* replies in the following manner.
46. *or so:* or something like that.
47-8. *According . . . country:* in whatever way is usual to the speaker and the country he comes from.
49. *does 'a this:* he does this.
49-51. Polonius has become so wrapped up in finding just the right phrase for the next stage in his imaginary conversation that he has lost the thread completely. His fumbling attempt to pick it up again shows up his pomposity and lack of real dignity or sense. *By the mass:* a mild oath. *leave:* stop.

As are companions noted and most known
To youth and liberty.

Reynaldo   As gaming, my lord.

Polonius

Ay, or drinking, fencing, swearing, quarrelling,   25
Drabbing—you may go so far.

Reynaldo

My lord, that would dishonour him.

Polonius

Faith, no; as you may season it in the charge.
You must not put another scandal on him,
That he is open to incontinency;   30
That's not my meaning. But breathe his faults so quaintly
That they may seem the taints of liberty;
The flash and outbreak of a fiery mind,
A savageness in unreclaimed blood,
Of general assault.

Reynaldo   But, my good lord—   35

Polonius

Wherefore should you do this?

Reynaldo   Ay, my lord,
I would know that.

Polonius   Marry, sir, here's my drift,
And I believe it is a fetch of warrant:
You laying these slight sullies on my son,
As 'twere a thing a little soil'd wi' th' working,   40
Mark you,
Your party in converse, him you would sound,
Having ever seen in the prenominate crimes
The youth you breathe of guilty, be assur'd
He closes with you in this consequence—   45
'Good sir' or so, or 'friend' or 'gentleman'
According to the phrase or the addition
Of man and country.

Reynaldo   Very good, my lord.

Polonius

And then, sir, does 'a this—'a does—What was I about

52-3. Reynaldo dryly supplies Polonius's cue – he seems used to this sort of situation!

55. *He:* Reynaldo's imaginary listener.

57. *such:* so-and-so.
58. *a':* he. *o'ertook in's rouse:* overcome by drink.
59. *falling out at tennis:* quarrelling over a game of tennis. Tennis was regarded as a frivolous sport in Shakespeare's time.

61. *Videlicet:* that is to say.

63. *Your bait . . . truth:* You obtain the truth by fishing for it with a bit of a lie. We would say, 'a sprat to catch a mackerel.' *carp:* also means criticism; Polonius is punning.
64-6. Polonius informs Reynaldo that men of understanding and influence, such as he fancies himself, make a habit of obtaining information in roundabout ways.
65. *windlasses:* winding, indirect approaches (a hunting term). *assays of bias:* oblique methods; following up his other references to sport Polonius here refers to the game of bowls, where the ball used, being weighted on one side, follows a curving path. This effect is called the *bias.*
67. *by my former lecture and advice:* as I have just described.
68. *Shall you my son:* Reynaldo will discover what Laertes has been up to. *have me:* follow me.
69. *God buy ye:* goodbye (literally, 'God be with you').
70. *Good my lord!* Reynaldo's way of saying goodbye to his master is, of course, more formal than Polonius's way of speaking to him.
71. *inclination:* disposition. *in yourself:* for yourself.

73. *ply his music:* go his own way. *Well:* yes.

to say? By the mass, I was about to say something;   50
where did I leave?

Reynaldo

At 'closes in the consequence', at 'friend or so' and
'gentleman'.

Polonius

At 'closes in the consequence'—ay, marry,
He closes thus: 'I know the gentleman;   55
I saw him yesterday, or t'other day,
Or then, or then; with such, or such; and, as you say,
There was 'a gaming; there o'ertook in's rouse;
There falling out at tennis'; or perchance
'I saw him enter such a house of sale'   60
Videlicet, a brothel, or so forth.
See you now
Your bait of falsehood take this carp of truth;
And thus do we of wisdom and of reach,
With windlasses and with assays of bias,   65
By indirections find directions out;
So, by my former lecture and advice,
Shall you my son. You have me, have you not?

Reynaldo

My lord, I have.

Polonius   God buy ye; fare ye well.

Reynaldo

Good my lord!   70

Polonius

Observe his inclination in yourself.

Reynaldo

I shall, my lord.

Polonius

And let him ply his music.

Reynaldo   Well, my lord.

Polonius

Farewell!

Exit REYNALDO

75. Ophelia's distraught manner, so different from that of the meek girl we met in Act I, Scene iii, indicates immediately to her father that something is wrong, but though she has run to him for comfort his attitude is impatient, until he learns that the cause of her distress may be to his advantage.

76. *affrighted:* frightened.

78-101. Ophelia describes how Hamlet has just burst into her room, looking dishevelled and wildly unhappy, and without speaking, grabbed her wrist, examined her at arm's length for some time, and then left, as though disappointed.

78. *closet:* private room.

79. *doublet all unbrac'd:* tunic unfastened (Hamlet was normally elegantly dressed (see Act III, Scene i, line 154), so Ophelia was alarmed by the change in his appearance).

80. *No hat upon his head:* The Elizabethans often wore hats indoors. *fouled:* dirty.

81. *down-gyved:* fallen crumpled.

83. *piteous in purport:* expressing such grief.

84-5. *As if . . . horrors:* What may Hamlet have been about to tell Ophelia?

86. Polonius immediately jumps to the flattering conclusion that the prince, genuinely in love with Ophelia after all, has gone mad with grief because she has kept him at a distance recently, on her father's orders. (Untidy dress was thought to be a symptom of being in love).

87. Ophelia's reaction to Hamlet's apparent madness, in contrast to her father's, is one of compassion, rather than triumph at her 'conquest.'

91. *falls to such perusal of:* examines.

92. *As 'a would:* as if he wanted to. Why did Hamlet study her face so intently? Perhaps he was just taking a last, long look before saying goodbye to their love affair (is there any reason why he should have to give Ophelia up?) or perhaps he was asking himself whether she could be trusted with his secret: that he must avenge his father's death (is she the kind of girl who can keep things to herself?)

94. Hamlet nodded slowly and sadly. He seemed to have had a gloomy idea confirmed. Ophelia does not say she spoke to him; what expression had probably been on her face?

98-101. As Hamlet walked out, he kept his head turned back, to look at Ophelia until she was out of sight. *adoors:* of the door. *bended:* turned.

Enter OPHELIA

How now, Ophelia! What's the matter?   75

Ophelia

O my lord, my lord, I have been so affrighted!

Polonius

With what, i' th' name of God?

Ophelia

My lord, as I was sewing in my closet,
Lord Hamlet, with his doublet all unbrac'd,
No hat upon his head, his stockings fouled,   80
Ungarter'd and down-gyved to his ankle;
Pale as his shirt, his knees knocking each other,
And with a look so piteous in purport
As if he had been loosed out of hell
To speak of horrors—he comes before me.   85

Polonius

Mad for thy love?

Ophelia   My lord, I do not know,
But truly I do fear it.

Polonius   What said he?

Ophelia

He took me by the wrist, and held me hard;
Then goes he to the length of all his arm,
And, with his other hand thus o'er his brow,   90
He falls to such perusal of my face
As 'a would draw it. Long stay'd he so.
At last, a little shaking of mine arm,
And thrice his head thus waving up and down,
He rais'd a sigh so piteous and profound   95
As it did seem to shatter all his bulk
And end his being. That done, he lets me go,
And, with his head over his shoulder turn'd,
He seem'd to find his way without his eyes;
For out adoors he went without their helps   100
And to the last bended their light on me.

103. *This is . . . love:* this is the frenzied behaviour typical of someone in love.

104-7. Love destroys itself with its own violence, and no other human emotion causes people to behave in a wilder way.

107. *I am sorry:* Polonius finishes this sentence in lines 112-13.

109. *as you did command:* in Act I, Scene iii.

110. *repel:* send back.

110-11. *denied His access to me:* refused to let him see me.

112-13. Polonius says he regrets that he did not observe Hamlet more carefully and take him more seriously.

113. *did but trifle:* was just playing with Ophelia's affections.

114. *wreck thee:* get you into trouble. *beshrew my jealousy:* curse my suspicions.

115-18. *it is as proper . . . discretion:* Polonius says that it is as natural for someone of his age (he pompously uses the 'royal plural') to be over-cautious as it is for the young to be rash.

119. *close:* secret.

119-20. *might move . . . love:* More trouble might be caused by hiding the reason for Hamlet's madness than by Claudius's anger when he is told of it. Why is Polonius so ready to rush off to the king with his news, in spite of the fact that Claudius might resent his step-son becoming involved with someone of Ophelia's standing? Polonius has obviously weighed up the pros and cons, and his excited manner suggests that he hopes to get something out of the situation. He is, of course, quite unaware that Hamlet has better reasons for going mad (or pretending to be mad – see Act I, Scene v, lines 171-2) than frustration over Ophelia; but Polonius is the sort of person who sees things chiefly as they concern him!

SCENE II

This scene is set in the lobby of the castle, a kind of entrance hall where casual encounters between members of the court might take place, where visitors could be greeted and where Hamlet, we learn, makes a habit of walking up and down, reading. This is a scene packed with varied encounters which show what a fierce battle of wits Hamlet will have to fight if he is to win his way through the intrigue and hypocrisy of the Danish court. He adopts so many poses, from that of a melancholy lunatic to that of the affable, urbane Prince of Denmark, that we begin to wonder whether any or all of them are the real Hamlet. Claudius opens the scene by ceremoniously greeting two schoolfriends of Hamlet's, whom he has summoned to spy on Hamlet. As they are two nobodies, who have to make their way in the world somehow, they are only too glad to curry favour with a powerful king.

2-4. *Moreover . . . hasty sending:* Claudius says that he sent for them in such a hurry because, besides wanting to see them very much (this unconvincing flattery goes down well with the two young men), he needs their help.

Polonius

Come, go with me. I will go seek the King.
This is the very ecstasy of love,
Whose violent property fordoes itself,
And leads the will to desperate undertakings   *105*
As oft as any passion under heaven
That does afflict our natures. I am sorry—
What, have you given him any hard words of late?

Ophelia

No, my good lord; but, as you did command,
I did repel his letters, and denied   *110*
His access to me.

Polonius   That hath made him mad.
I am sorry that with better heed and judgment
I had not quoted him. I fear'd he did but trifle,
And meant to wreck thee; but beshrew my jealousy!
By heaven, it is as proper to our age   *115*
To cast beyond ourselves in our opinions
As it is common for the younger sort
To lack discretion. Come, go we to the King.
This must be known; which, being kept close, might move
More grief to hide than hate to utter love.   *120*
Come.

Exeunt

SCENE II—*Elsinore. The Castle*

Flourish. Enter KING, QUEEN, ROSENCRANTZ, GUILDEN-
STERN *and* ATTENDANTS

King

Welcome, dear Rosencrantz and Guildenstern!
Moreover that we much did long to see you,
The need we have to use you did provoke
Our hasty sending. Something have you heard

101

5. *Hamlet's transformation:* the change that has come over Hamlet.

6-7. *Sith . . . that it was:* since neither in his appearance nor his personality is he the same person as before. We realize from this statement that Hamlet must have been acting oddly for some time, and that Claudius does not believe his behaviour is simply caused by grief at his father's death (as in Act I, Scene ii).

8. *More than:* other than, besides.

8-9. *put him . . . himself:* altered him.

10. *deem of:* judge.

10-18. Claudius begs them, since they have been brought up with Hamlet from childhood and are of his own age and disposition, to be so kind as to stay at the court for a while, to encourage Hamlet to amuse himself and to find out, when a suitable opportunity occurs, whether he has some secret trouble that, if discovered, could be put right. (If the ghost told the truth, Claudius may be afraid that Hamlet knows too much; but he disguises his anxiety to know what is going on in Hamlet's mind by pretending to be an anxious parent.)

19-26. The queen's manner seems more sincere than her husband's; she pins her faith on Hamlet's affection for his friends, and appeals to their good nature.

21. *To whom . . . adheres:* of whom he is fonder.

22. *gentry:* courtesy. *good will:* kindness.

23. *expend:* spend.

24. *For the supply . . .,hope:* to keep our hope alive, and reward it with success.

25-6. The queen hints that they will be rewarded very generously.

26-9. Rosencrantz points out that there is no need for the king and queen to beg them to help: they could force them to.

29-32. Perhaps feeling that his partner has struck the wrong note, Guildenstern hastily assures the king and queen that they are very ready to obey. They do not seem to have a moment's hesitation about spying on their friend.

33-4. The repetition of their names makes the two sound rather ridiculous – they are so nondescript that they can hardly be told apart. *gentle:* noble.

36. *too much changed son:* The queen's anxiety sounds genuine. *some of you:* spoken to the attendants.

Of Hamlet's transformation; so I call it,   5
Sith nor th' exterior nor the inward man
Resembles that it was. What it should be,
More than his father's death, that thus hath put him
So much from th' understanding of himself,
I cannot deem of. I entreat you both   10
That, being of so young days brought up with him,
And sith so neighboured to his youth and haviour,
That you vouchsafe your rest here in our court
Some little time; so by your companies
To draw him on to pleasures, and to gather,   15
So much as from occasion you may glean,
Whether aught to us unknown afflicts him thus
That, open'd, lies within our remedy.

Queen

Good gentlemen, he hath much talk'd of you;
And sure I am two men there is not living   20
To whom he more adheres. If it will please you
To show us so much gentry and good will
As to expend your time with us awhile
For the supply and profit of our hope,
Your visitation shall receive such thanks   25
As fits a king's remembrance.

Rosencrantz   Both your Majesties
Might, by the sovereign power you have of us,
Put your dread pleasures more into command
Than to entreaty.

Guildenstern   But we both obey,
And here give up ourselves, in the full bent,   30
To lay our service freely at your feet,
To be commanded.

King

Thanks, Rosencrantz and gentle Guildenstern.

Queen

Thanks, Guildenstern and gentle Rosencrantz.
And I beseech you instantly to visit   35
My too much changed son. Go, some of you,

38. *practices:* actions. The word also means 'intrigues', so it is an apt description of what they are about to do.

39. *Aye amen:* again this sounds heartfelt.

40-1. Polonius bustles in importantly, announcing the return of the ambassadors who were sent to Norway in Act I, Scene ii, to deal with the threat of Fortinbras's invasion. *joyfully:* This indicates that they were successful, so, whatever Claudius's private morals may be, he is shown to be a clever diplomat and an efficient king.

42. *Thou still . . . news:* you always bring good news.

43-9. Claudius's casually polite reply delights Polonius, especially as the word *father* is a stroke of luck for him: it could lead naturally to discussion of Ophelia. What is more, the king seems in a good mood.

44-5. Polonius, like Rosencrantz and Guildenstern, takes every opportunity to assure the king of his loyalty: he puts it on the same level as his religion.

47-8. *Hunts . . . us'd to do:* is not as keen on the scent of intrigue as it used to be. Polonius prides himself on his ability to ferret out secrets.

49. *very:* real. Polonius probably employs a discreet whisper when mentioning Hamlet's madness, for Gertrude has not heard (lines 54-5).

50. A really impulsive remark escapes from the normally suave king's lips, but Polonius enjoys whetting the king's appetite for his tit-bit of news by keeping him in suspense. Also, Claudius will be in a still better mood when he has heard of the ambassadors' complete success.

52. *the fruit:* the dessert, the next course. *that great feast:* the ambassadors' news.

53. *do grace to:* honour.

55. *head and source:* cause. *distemper:* mental disturbance.

56. *doubt:* fear. *main:* chief cause.

57. *our o'erhasty marriage:* Gertrude already feels some misgiving, perhaps even the pangs of conscience of which the ghost spoke, about the indiscreet speed at which she remarried.

And bring these gentlemen where Hamlet is.

Guildenstern

Heavens make our presence and our practices
Pleasant and helpful to him!

Queen   Aye amen!

Exeunt ROSENCRANTZ, GUILDENSTERN *and*
some ATTENDANTS
Enter POLONIUS

Polonius

Th' ambassadors from Norway, my good lord,   40
Are joyfully return'd.

King

Thou still hast been the father of good news.

Polonius

Have I, my lord? I assure you, my good liege,
I hold my duty, as I hold my soul,
Both to my God and to my gracious King;   45
And I do think—or else this brain of mine
Hunts not the trail of policy so sure
As it hath us'd to do—that I have found
The very cause of Hamlet's lunacy.

King

O, speak of that; that do I long to hear.   50

Polonius

Give first admittance to th' ambassadors;
My news shall be the fruit to that great feast.

King

Thyself do grace to them, and bring them in.

Exit POLONIUS

He tells me, my dear Gertrude, he hath found
The head and source of all your son's distemper.   55

Queen

I doubt it is no other but the main,
His father's death and our o'erhasty marriage.

58. *sift him:* find out what he thinks. Claudius could mean either Polonius or Hamlet here. Which do you think more likely?

59. *what from our brother Norway:* 'what does the king of Norway say?' Kings habitually addressed each other as *brother*.

60. *Most fair . . . desires:* he sends very courteous replies to your salutations and requests.

61-80. Voltimand says that after their first audience with him, the Norwegian king sent a message forbidding his nephew Fortinbras to enlist more soldiers; he had been under the impression that they were intended to fight the Poles. But when he found that they really were meant to invade Denmark, and that Fortinbras had been taking advantage of his uncle's invalid state, he arrested and rebuked him, and obtained a promise that he would never try to fight against Claudius again. When Fortinbras vowed this, the king of Norway was so pleased that he gave him a generous allowance and permission to employ his newly gathered army against Poland. Now he asks Claudius to give his nephew a safe conduct through Denmark for this purpose.

67. *falsely borne in hand:* abused.

69. *in fine:* in the end.

79-80. *On such regards . . . down:* on the conditions about safety and free passage that are given in the document.

80. *It likes us well:* I approve.

81. *at our more considered time:* when I have more time for thought.

83. *well-took:* well carried out.

84. *at night we'll feast together:* Claudius seizes the opportunity for another banquet.

King
    Well, we shall sift him.

[*Re-enter* POLONIUS, *with* VOLTEMAND *and* CORNELIUS]

                    Welcome, my good friends!
    Say, Voltemand, what from our brother Norway?
Voltemand
    Most fair return of greetings and desires.   60
    Upon our first, he sent out to suppress
    His nephew's levies; which to him appear'd
    To be a preparation 'gainst the Polack;
    But, better look'd into, he truly found
    It was against your Highness. Whereat griev'd,   65
    That so his sickness, age, and impotence,
    Was falsely borne in hand, sends out arrests
    On Fortinbras; which he, in brief, obeys;
    Receives rebuke from Norway; and, in fine,
    Makes vow before his uncle never more   70
    To give th' assay of arms against your Majesty.
    Whereon old Norway, overcome with joy,
    Gives him threescore thousand crowns in annual fee,
    And his commission to employ those soldiers,
    So levied as before, against the Polack;   75
    With an entreaty, herein further shown,

                    Gives a paper

    That it might please you to give quiet pass
    Through your dominions for this enterprise,
    On such regards of safety and allowance
    As therein are set down.
King   It likes us well;   80
    And at our more considered time we'll read,
    Answer, and think upon this business.
    Meantime we thank you for your well-took labour.
    Go to your rest; at night we'll feast together.
    Most welcome home!
                    Exeunt AMBASSADORS *and* ATTENDANTS

85-105. Dismissing politics impatiently, Polonius embarks on a long unnecessary preamble to what he has to say about Hamlet – perhaps he is nervous about what sort of reception it will get. Even the gentle queen is driven to interrupt. Yet Polonius begins by saying he will speak briefly and to the point!

86. *liege:* lord. *expostulate:* hold forth about.

87. *What majesty should be:* how royalty should behave (i.e. Hamlet). *what duty is:* how a subject should act (i.e. Polonius).

89. *Were nothing:* would be useless.

90. *wit:* In Shakespeare's day this meant the ability to make clever, neat remarks, rather than amusing ones. Polonius obviously thinks this is a quality which he himself possesses!

91. *tediousness:* longwindedness. *limbs and outward flourishes:* superficial decoration (*limbs* contrasts with *soul*, line 90).

93. *Mad call I it:* Perhaps Polonius has seen a look of displeasure cross his sovereigns' faces at his blunt announcement, for he hurriedly excuses the word – but this involves him in more verbal complications.

95. *More matter with less art:* come to the point instead of trying to say things cleverly.

97-8. Having sworn he is speaking simply, Polonius still cannot resist this unnecessary word-play. *'tis true 'tis pity:* indeed it is a pity. *And pity 'tis 'tis true:* and it is a pity it is true. *figure:* figure of speech.

100-3. *and now remains . . . cause:* Now what they have to do is to discover what has produced this result, that is, Hamlet's illness, for, by the law of cause and effect, it must have a reason. Polonius puns again, with *effect and defect*.

104. *Thus it remains . . . thus:* that is how it is, and I'll now proceed.

105. *Perpend:* a pompous way of saying 'consider'.

106. *have while she is mine:* Polonius coyly hints at the idea of Ophelia getting married.

107. *mark:* look.

108. *this:* a letter from Hamlet to Ophelia. *gather and surmise:* see what you can make of this.

109-24. The letter is certainly a strange one. It is just possible that Hamlet wrote it to support the idea that he was mad, guessing that Ophelia would take it straight to her father; but something in the intensity of its tone makes one feel that it was a very private communication, meant for her alone, that is now exposed to the curious and critical gaze of Polonius and the king and queen.

109-10. Apart from the word *beautified* (and this could just mean 'beautiful' in those days) to which Polonius takes exception, probably thinking that it hints that Ophelia makes up her face too much, the elaborate opening is like that of the average Elizabethan love-letter.

111-12. *But you shall hear:* The king or the queen must have shown signs of impatience. Hamlet was probably expressing a hope that Ophelia would carry the verses he wrote around with her. In early days, women often used the bodice of their dresses as a kind of pocket, to carry letters and even money. *etc.:* Polonius mutters over the next part of the letter.

115. *stay:* wait. Polonius enjoys keeping his listeners in suspense over the authorship of the letter.

Polonius   This business is well ended.   *85*
  My liege, and madam, to expostulate
  What majesty should be, what duty is,
  Why day is day, night night, and time is time,
  Were nothing, but to waste night, day, and time.
  Therefore, since brevity is the soul of wit,   *90*
  And tediousness the limbs and outward flourishes,
  I will be brief. Your noble son is mad.
  Mad call I it; for, to define true madness,
  What is't but to be nothing else but mad?
  But let that go.
Queen   More matter with less art.   *95*
Polonius
  Madam, I swear I use no art at all.
  That he's mad, 'tis true: 'tis true 'tis pity;
  And pity 'tis 'tis true. A foolish figure!
  But farewell it, for I will use no art.
  Mad let us grant him, then; and now remains   *100*
  That we find out the cause of this effect;
  Or rather say the cause of this defect,
  For this effect defective comes by cause.
  Thus it remains, and the remainder thus.
  Perpend.   *105*
  I have a daughter—have while she is mine—
  Who in her duty and obedience, mark,
  Hath given me this. Now gather, and surmise.

Reads

  'To the celestial, and my soul's idol, the most
beautified Ophelia.' That's an ill phrase, a vile *110*
phrase; 'beautified' is a vile phrase. But you shall
hear. Thus: [*Reads*] 'In her excellent white bosom,
these, &c.'
Queen
  Came this from Hamlet to her?
Polonius
  Good madam, stay awhile; I will be faithful.   *115*

116-19. This simple, neat little poem is in startling contrast to the elaborate opening and the abrupt, down-to-earth style of the next sentence. Hamlet uses *doubt* in two senses – 'disbelieve' (lines 116, 117, 119) and 'suspect' (line 118). It was still generally believed in Shakespeare's time that the sun went round the earth and that the stars were made of fire.

120. *ill at these numbers:* no good at writing poetry.

120-1. *I have not art to reckon my groans:* Hamlet says he hasn't the skill to sum up his feelings in rhyme. The declaration of love that follows sounds all the more sincere for its simplicity.

123-4. *whilst this machine is to him:* 'while my body belongs to me, while I live.' This phrase strikes an odd note in the otherwise conventional ending. Other Elizabethan writers had seen the likeness between the human body and a machine (both being a combination of working parts) but Hamlet's use of the term here sounds somewhat cynical, as though he felt his body to be an encumbrance and he is preoccupied with the idea of getting rid of it (compare Act I, Scene ii, lines 129-30).

125-8. Ophelia, as well as giving her father the letter, has given him all the details about Hamlet's advances to her. *fell out:* happened.

128-30. Claudius quickly sees that Hamlet is not likely to have gone mad for love unless Ophelia had repulsed him. This puts Polonius in an awkward position – the king will either think that he encouraged his daughter to try to rise above her station and marry the prince, or he has to admit that he distrusted Hamlet's intentions.

131-50. Polonius asks the king to imagine what he would have thought of Polonius if he had done nothing. He explains at length why he forbade Ophelia to see Hamlet, saying it was unsuitable to encourage such a match because Hamlet is her superior in rank – he does not mention that he thought Hamlet might behave dishonourably!

132. *hot:* passionate.

133-4. Polonius in fact had noticed nothing until he was warned by others.

136-8. Polonius describes how he might have just noted the situation in his mind (a *table-book* was a memorandum pad) and said and done nothing, shutting his mind to it.

139. *round:* straight.

140. *my young mistress:* that little madam. *bespeak:* address.

141. *out of thy star:* moving in different circles from you.

142. *prescripts:* orders.

143. *lock . . . resort:* lock herself up so that he couldn't be with her.

145. *Which done:* when this had been said. *took the fruits of my advice:* benefited by my advice.

146. *he repelled:* when he was rejected. *a short tale to make:* to put it briefly.

110

Reads

'Doubt thou the stars are fire;
    Doubt that the sun doth move;
    Doubt truth to be a liar;
    But never doubt I love.

O dear Ophelia, I am ill at these numbers. I have   120
not art to reckon my groans; but that I love thee best,
O most best, believe it. Adieu.
                Thine evermore, most dear lady, whilst
                  this machine is to him, HAMLET.'

This, in obedience, hath my daughter shown me;   125
And more above, hath his solicitings,
As they fell out by time, by means, and place,
All given to mine ear.

King   But how hath she
Receiv'd his love?

Polonius   What do you think of me?

King
As of a man faithful and honourable.   130

Polonius
I would fain prove so. But what might you think,
When I had seen this hot love on the wing,
As I perceiv'd it, I must tell you that,
Before my daughter told me—what might you,
Or my dear Majesty your queen here, think,   135
If I had play'd the desk or table-book;
Or given my heart a winking, mute and dumb;
Or look'd upon this love with idle sight—
What might you think? No, I went round to work,
And my young mistress thus I did bespeak: 140
'Lord Hamlet is a prince out of thy star;
This must not be'. And then I prescripts gave her,
That she should lock herself from his resort,
Admit no messengers, receive no tokens.
Which done, she took the fruits of my advice;   145
And he repelled, a short tale to make,

147-50. Polonius goes on to describe the symptoms of what we would call a nervous breakdown: Hamlet first became depressed, then went off his food, became sleepless and unbalanced and light-headed, finally lapsing into his present state of wild insanity. Perhaps this really did happen, or maybe Polonius is describing what he imagines would have been the logical stages by which Hamlet became 'mad'.

151. Reserving his own judgement, Claudius inquires whether Gertrude is convinced by Polonius's theory.

152. *very like:* very likely.

153-5. Seeing the king still hesitating, Polonius enquires whether he has ever been known to be wrong about something.

156. *Take this from this:* Polonius points to his head and shoulders, meaning that Claudius can put him to death if he is wrong.

157-9. Polonius claims he is infallible, able to find the truth even if it were hidden in the centre of the earth – a rather unwise boast, as in a moment Hamlet finds it easy to make a fool of him.

159. *try it:* test the theory.

162-7. Polonius has a plan ready: Ophelia is to be used as a decoy. In conversation with her Hamlet should reveal if he is mad for love; Polonius and Claudius will eavesdrop on them.

162. *loose:* turn her loose, make her available to him. This was the phrase used for releasing a cow in the same field as a bull; an idea picked up by *keep a farm and carters.* Polonius's tenderness about Ophelia's honour seems to have disappeared.

163. *arras:* a tapestry curtain covering a wall.

165. *thereon:* because of that.

166-7. Polonius says that if he is wrong he will have to give up politics and go in for farming.

168. As the other two are deep in conversation, it is the queen who first notices Hamlet, who shames their plotting to spy on this 'raving madman' by walking in quietly reading. The queen's comment seems to reproach the two men for their unimaginative attitude to her sick and unhappy, but harmless, son. Perhaps Hamlet was in time to overhear the plot to eavesdrop on him. If he did, his odd manner when he finds Ophelia waiting for him in this very spot (in Act III, Scene i) is understandable. *sadly:* seriously, soberly. *wretch:* a more affectionate term in Shakespeare's day than it is now.

169-70. Polonius hurriedly asks the king and queen to go, and takes his leave of them, so that he can pursue his investigations into the extent of Hamlet's insanity immediately. *board:* tackle, accost.

Fell into a sadness, then into a fast,
Thence to a watch, thence into a weakness,
Thence to a lightness, and, by this declension,
Into the madness wherein now he raves   *150*
And all we mourn for.

King   Do you think 'tis this?

Queen

It may be, very like.

Polonius

Hath there been such a time—I would fain know that—
That I have positively said ''Tis so',
When it prov'd otherwise?

King   Not that I know.   *155*

Polonius

Take this from this, if this be otherwise.
If circumstances lead me, I will find
Where truth is hid, though it were hid indeed
Within the centre.

King   How may we try it further?

Polonius

You know sometimes he walks four hours together, *160*
Here in the lobby.

Queen   So he does, indeed.

Polonius

At such a time I'll loose my daughter to him.
Be you and I behind an arras then;
Mark the encounter: if he love her not,
And be not from his reason fall'n thereon,   *165*
Let me be no assistant for a state,
But keep a farm and carters.

King   We will try it.

Enter HAMLET, *reading on a book*

Queen

But look where sadly the poor wretch comes reading.

Polonius

Away, I do beseech you, both away:

113

172. *God-a-mercy:* thank God.

173. Refusing to be put off by Hamlet's distant manner, Polonius coyly inquires whether Hamlet is well enough to recognize him.

174. Seeing that this busybody will not let him continue with his book, Hamlet decides to play up to him, and show him up at the same time. *Excellent:* perfectly. *fishmonger:* By calling Polonius this, Hamlet is not just implying that he is too mad to be able to distinguish this eminent politician from a shopkeeper: this word, in Elizabethan times, was a slang term for someone who hired out prostitutes (who were called 'fish' or 'fishmongers' daughters'). This suggests that Hamlet did indeed overhear Polonius's plan to use his daughter as a bait; or at least, he realizes Polonius regards his daughter as a marketable commodity (see note on Act I, Scene iii, lines 127-31). Hamlet is disgusted by Polonius's hypocrisy.

175. Polonius is too stupid to realize he is being teased.

178-9. The glimpses we have been given into the amount of intrigue that goes on at the Danish court justifies Hamlet's bitter comment about human nature.

181. *sun . . . dog:* It was believed in Shakespeare's time that the sun's heat alone was responsible for the breeding of maggots in rotten meat. **182.** *good kissing carrion:* flesh (the dog's) suitable for kissing, and therefore breeding. The mention of kissing leads naturally on to Ophelia. Hamlet says that, as life is so easily conceived, Polonius had better keep Ophelia out of sight if he doesn't want her to become pregnant. *the sun:* Hamlet may be referring to himself, the prince, in particular (see note on Act I, Scene ii, line 67), who could so easily seduce someone of lower standing like Ophelia. All this shows clearly how well Hamlet knows what suspicions have been in Polonius's mind. *look to't:* watch out.

186-9. Polonius triumphantly seizes on the only thing that makes sense to him, the mention of his daughter, and concludes Hamlet's love really has driven him quite mad. *How say you by that?* 'what do you say to that?' Polonius converses with himself. *much extremity:* a great deal. It is hard to imagine Polonius as a distraught lover!

114

I'll board him presently. O, give me leave.   *170*

Exeunt KING *and* QUEEN

How does my good Lord Hamlet?
Hamlet
Well, God-a-mercy.
Polonius
Do you know me, my lord?
Hamlet
Excellent well; you are a fishmonger.
Polonius
Not I, my lord.   *175*
Hamlet
Then I would you were so honest a man.
Polonius
Honest, my lord!
Hamlet
Ay, sir; to be honest, as this world goes, is to be one
man pick'd out of ten thousand.
Polonius
That's very true, my lord.   *180*
Hamlet
For if the sun breed maggots in a dead dog, being a
good kissing carrion—Have you a daughter?
Polonius
I have, my lord.
Hamlet
Let her not walk i' th' sun. Conception is a blessing.
But as your daughter may conceive—friend, look to't.   *185*
Polonius
How say you by that? [*Aside*] Still harping on my
daughter. Yet he knew me not at first; 'a said I was a
fishmonger. 'A is far gone, far gone. And truly in my
youth I suffer'd much extremity for love. Very near
this. I'll speak to him again.—What do you read, my   *190*
lord?

192. *Words, words, words:* How does Hamlet say this – sadly, absent-mindedly, impatiently?

193. *matter:* subject-matter.

194. Hamlet deliberately misunderstands him, but Polonius still fails to realize he is being teased.

196-204. *the satirical rogue:* the real or imaginary author of the book. Hamlet may well be inventing this description of a senile old man as an exaggerated portrait of Polonius, for he shows it is aimed at him in lines 202-4.

198. *purging . . . gum:* discharging a gummy fluid, like resin.

199. *wit:* sense, intelligence.

200. *hams:* thighs.

201-2. *I hold it not honesty . . . down:* Returning to the idea of *honesty*, which he here uses in the sense of 'right and proper behaviour', Hamlet says it is not tactful to describe old men so unflatteringly for, after all, Polonius is old.

202-4. *you yourself . . . backward:* Polonius would have to go a long way back through his life to be young again like Hamlet. Perhaps the idea of a *crab* is suggested by Polonius edging round to try and get a look at Hamlet's book.

205-6. Polonius begins to suspect dimly that Hamlet may not be all that mad after all, but decides on a soothing approach: fresh air was supposed to be bad for the sick, so he suggests that Hamlet leaves the lobby.

207. Quickly seeing the other meaning of this phrase also, Hamlet again, and in line 216, expresses a longing for death.

208. *pregnant:* full of meaning.

209-11. *a happiness . . . delivered of:* sometimes madmen can express themselves more neatly than reasonable, sane people.

212. *suddenly:* immediately. *contrive the means of:* arrange.

215-17. Hamlet has abandoned any attempt to be polite to this silly old man, and is openly sarcastic, saying that it is a pleasure to be rid of him; then he lapses back into melancholy. *withal:* with.

116

Hamlet
  Words, words, words.
Polonius
  What is the matter, my lord?
Hamlet
  Between who?
Polonius
  I mean, the matter that you read, my lord.   *195*
Hamlet
  Slanders, sir; for the satirical rogue says here that old
  men have grey beards; that their faces are wrinkled;
  their eyes purging thick amber and plum-tree gum;
  and that they have a plentiful lack of wit, together
  with most weak hams—all which, sir, though I most *200*
  powerfully and potently believe, yet I hold it not
  honesty to have it thus set down; for you yourself,
  sir, shall grow old as I am, if, like a crab, you could
  go backward.
Polonius [Aside]
  Though this be madness, yet there is method in't.— *205*
  Will you walk out of the air, my lord?
Hamlet
  Into my grave?
Polonius
  Indeed, that's out of the air. *[Aside]* How pregnant
  sometimes his replies are! a happiness that often
  madness hits on, which reason and sanity could not *210*
  so prosperously be delivered of. I will leave him, and
  suddenly contrive the means of meeting between him
  and my daughter.—My lord, I will take my leave of
  you.
Hamlet
  You cannot, sir, take from me anything that I will *215*
  more willingly part withal—except my life, except my
  life, except my life.

Enter ROSENCRANTZ *and* GUILDENSTERN

219. *these tedious old fools:* Hamlet despises not only Polonius but all people like him.

220. Polonius seems to know why Rosencrantz and Guildenstern are there.

224-6. At first, as when he greeted Horatio in Act I, Scene ii, Hamlet, suspecting nothing, throws off his gloom in his delight at seeing his friends (who also have come from abroad). At first the conversation takes the form of the sort of witty small-talk that is popular with gay young men.

227. *As the indifferent . . . earth:* so-so.

228. *Happy . . . over-happy:* fortunate in not being too well off.

229. *the very button:* the button at the very top.

230. Picking up the personification of fortune as a woman, Hamlet suggests that they are not as badly off as they might be.

232-3. *Then . . . favours:* then you are moderately well off. *favours:* charms.

234. *privates:* intimate acquaintances; but no doubt Guildenstern also intends it to have the improper meaning which Hamlet picks up in the next line: this is the sort of joke which Rosencrantz and Guildenstern appreciate.

235-6. *she is a strumpet:* Hamlet jokes rather wryly that Fortune behaves like a whore.

237. They have come unprepared with a reason for their presence, and this weak remark (perhaps prompted by their fear of Hamlet's discovering that their motive for being present is not honest!) leads Hamlet to inquire more pointedly why they are there.

Polonius

Fare you well, my lord.

Hamlet

These tedious old fools!

Polonius

You go to seek the Lord Hamlet; there he is.   220

Rosencrantz [*To Polonius*]

God save you, sir!

Exit POLONIUS

Guildenstern

My honour'd lord!

Rosencrantz

My most dear lord!

Hamlet

My excellent good friends! How dost thou, Guildenstern? Ah, Rosencrantz! Good lads, how do you   225
both?

Rosencrantz

As the indifferent children of the earth.

Guildenstern

Happy in that we are not over-happy;
On fortune's cap we are not the very button.

Hamlet

Nor the soles of her shoe?   230

Rosencrantz

Neither, my lord.

Hamlet

Then you live about her waist, or in the middle of her
favours?

Guildenstern

Faith, her privates we.

Hamlet

In the secret parts of Fortune? O, most true; she is a   235
strumpet. What news?

Rosencrantz

None, my lord, but that the world's grown honest.

238. *Then is doomsday near:* that's not likely.

240. Still speaking lightly, Hamlet makes another jocular reference to Fortune.

242-8. Like Polonius, Rosencrantz and Guildenstern are rather slow on the uptake, but when they finally realize that the heir to the throne says he feels frustrated in Denmark, their conventional disapproval shows Hamlet that it is no good trying to confide his feelings to them.

245-6. *confines, wards:* cells.

249-50. *there is nothing . . . so:* If the other two had been more on the spot they might have realized that this detached philosophical remark is hardly that of a confused madman.

252-3. Hamlet's remarks give Rosencrantz an idea: perhaps Hamlet is discontented because he is not on the throne. *'tis:* Denmark is.
254-6. Hamlet's passionate reply shows that the idea that mere ambition could have caused his unhappiness is absurd but his 'friends' press on with this line of enquiry, as being the most obvious explanation to them (for they themselves are ambitious).
254. *bounded:* confined.
256. *bad dreams:* Does Hamlet mean that he really has nightmares (what might they be about?) or is he hinting that he has mad fantasies? He might simply mean that he has depressing thoughts.
257-9. Guildenstern perseveringly brings the conversation back to the point, though pretending to talk jestingly. *the very substance . . . dream:* what the ambitious man achieves is only a pale reflection of what he hoped for.
260-4. Hamlet outdoes them at their own game, and with a swift piece of logic proves that greatness is worth nothing. He argues that, as being a king is the dream of a beggar, and a dream is a shadow (line 260) then a king must be the shadow of a beggar. The beggar, therefore, is the solid object (body) that throws this shadow. Though Hamlet is just teasing the others here, with his subtle reasoning, the unreality and pointlessness of kingship and fame is an idea that occupies him a great deal later on.

Hamlet
Then is doomsday near. But your news is not true.
Let me question more in particular. What have you,
my good friends, deserved at the hands of Fortune, *240*
that she sends you to prison hither?

Guildenstern
Prison, my lord!

Hamlet
Denmark's a prison.

Rosencrantz
Then is the world one.

Hamlet
A goodly one; in which there are many confines, *245*
wards, and dungeons, Denmark being one o' th'
worst.

Rosencrantz
We think not so, my lord.

Hamlet
Why, then, 'tis none to you; for there is nothing
either good or bad, but thinking makes it so. To me *250*
it is a prison.

Rosencrantz
Why, then your ambition makes it one; 'tis too
narrow for your mind.

Hamlet
O God, I could be bounded in a nutshell and count
myself a king of infinite space, were it not that I have *255*
bad dreams.

Guildenstern
Which dreams indeed are ambition; for the very
substance of the ambitious is merely the shadow of a
dream.

Hamlet
A dream itself is but a shadow. *260*

Rosencrantz
Truly, and I hold ambition of so airy and light a
quality that it is but a shadow's shadow.

264. *outstretch'd:* puffed up, conceited, or stretched out as a monument on a tomb. *Shall we to th' court:* either 'Shall we join the rest of the court' (to put an end to the conversation) or 'This sort of witty talk is fashionable among courtiers.'

265. *by my fay, I cannot reason:* 'by my faith,' says Hamlet, 'I can't follow an argument any more.' He has just proved he can make circles round the other two!

266. Rosencrantz and Guildenstern say they will go with him.

267-9. Hamlet chooses to take their words as meaning that they will offer their services to him. *No such matter:* certainly not. *sort:* class. *the rest of my servants:* While pretending to pay them a compliment, Hamlet indicates that he thinks of them as attendants rather than friends, now.

269. *most dreadfully attended:* Hamlet leaves Rosencrantz and Guildenstern, and us, to wonder whether he meant (a) that he has not as many attendants as he should have, as a prince (this would encourage their ambition theory), or (b) that he is constantly followed around – by them, for example, or (c) that he is haunted by terrible dreams. *in the beaten way of friendship:* speaking as friend to friend.

270. *what make you:* what are you doing.

271. *occasion:* motive. For all their talk about the folly of ambition, Rosencrantz and Guildenstern decide to keep in with the king rather than tell the truth to their old friend, but something in their manner tells Hamlet that they are lying.

272. *Beggar that I am:* Hamlet implies that as he can only dream about being a king at the moment he is just a beggar (see lines 263-4 above). He plays up to their idea that he resents not being on the throne, for he now sees that this forms a useful disguise for what is really on his mind.

273-4. *dear:* He is probably sarcastic by now. *too dear a half-penny:* not worth much. He is not very grateful to them.

275. *inclining:* inclination. *free visitation:* voluntary visit. *deal justly with:* be honest with. Hamlet makes a last appeal to their loyalty.

277. Guildenstern's hesitation gives the game away.

278. *to th'purpose:* the truth.

279-81. *there is a kind . . . colour:* you look guilty, and your sense of shame prevents you concealing it.

283. *To what end?* why? Rosencrantz plays for time.

284. *That you must teach me:* you will have to tell me that. *conjure:* appeal to.

284-9. Hamlet begs them, for friendship's sake, because they are of the same generation, because they have always been fond of each other, and because of anything else that a more eloquent speaker than he might name, to be open with him.

Hamlet

    Then are our beggars bodies, and our monarchs and
    outstretch'd heroes the beggars' shadows. Shall we to
    th' court? for, by my fay, I cannot reason.   *265*

Both

    We'll wait upon you.

Hamlet

    No such matter. I will not sort you with the rest of
    my servants; for, to speak to you like an honest man,
    I am most dreadfully attended. But, in the beaten
    way of friendship, what make you at Elsinore?   *270*

Rosencrantz

    To visit you, my lord; no other occasion.

Hamlet

    Beggar that I am, I am even poor in thanks; but I
    thank you; and sure, dear friends, my thanks are too
    dear a half-penny. Were you not sent for? Is it your
    own inclining? Is it a free visitation? Come, come, *275*
    deal justly with me. Come, come; nay, speak.

Guildenstern

    What should we say, my lord?

Hamlet

    Why any thing. But to th' purpose: you were sent
    for; and there is a kind of confession in your looks,
    which your modesties have not craft enough to *280*
    colour; I know the good King and Queen have sent
    for you.

Rosencrantz

    To what end, my lord?

Hamlet

    That you must teach me. But let me conjure you by
    the rights of our fellowship, by the consonancy of our *285*
    youth, by the obligation of our ever-preserved love,
    and by what more dear a better proposer can charge
    you withal, be even and direct with me, whether you
    were sent for or no?

290-3. At this appeal, and probably because the game is up anyway, they admit that they were asked to come.

291. *I have an eye of you:* I see what you are up to.

292. *hold not off:* don't refuse.

294-5. *so shall . . . discovery:* 'I shall forestall your explanation.' Hamlet adds contemptuously that in that case their duty to the king and queen will not be infringed. The eloquent speech that follows, however, tells them nothing about the cause of his 'madness' except that he is depressed, which they knew already.

296-7. *but wherefore I know not:* We know that the meeting with the ghost might explain some of Hamlet's odd behaviour, but obviously he will not trust these two with this secret.

297-8. *forgone . . . exercises:* become lethargic, and given up taking exercise.

298-9. *it goes . . . disposition:* I feel so depressed. *goodly frame:* splendid structure.

300. *sterile promontory:* desolate headland (in an ocean of misery).

301-3. *canopy . . . fire:* Hamlet describes the sky as others might see it – a beautiful painted ceiling, decorated with golden stars.

304. *foul . . . vapours:* nasty conglomeration of clouds.

304-9. *What a piece of work . . . animals:* Hamlet parodies the enthusiastic view of human beings that many Elizabethans held. Maybe man is a splendid object, he suggests, but, like Denmark, what appears attractive to others has lost its appeal for him.

306. *infinite in faculties:* unlimited in his abilities. *express:* perfect.

308. *apprehension:* understanding.

309. *paragon:* most perfect specimen.

310. *quintessence of dust:* highly refined earth. Perhaps Hamlet is once again preoccupied with the idea that death ends all man's glory, and he will return 'dust to dust'.

311. *your smiling:* Hamlet finds that the others' reaction to this glimpse of what is going on in his heart seems to be an embarrassed smirk.

313-19. Rosencrantz, remembering, perhaps, that the queen has asked them to find Hamlet some amusements, changes the subject to something he feels may take the prince out of himself.

317. *lenten entertainment:* gloomy reception. *players:* company of actors.

318. *coted:* overtook.

319. It is interesting that the actors came to seek Hamlet's patronage, rather than the king's.

Rosencrantz [*Aside to* GUILDENSTERN]
  What say you? 290

Hamlet [*Aside*]
  Nay, then, I have an eye of you.—If you love me,
  hold not off.

Guildenstern
  My lord, we were sent for.

Hamlet
  I will tell you why; so shall my anticipation prevent
  your discovery, and your secrecy to the King and 295
  Queen moult no feather. I have of late—but wherefore I know not—lost all my mirth, forgone all
  custom of exercises; and indeed it goes so heavily
  with my disposition that this goodly frame, the earth,
  seems to me a sterile promontory; this most excellent 300
  canopy the air, look you, this brave o'er-hanging
  firmament, this majestical roof fretted with golden
  fire—why, it appeareth no other thing to me than a
  foul and pestilent congregation of vapours. What a
  piece of work is a man! How noble in reason! how 305
  infinite in faculties! in form and moving, how express
  and admirable! in action, how like an angel! in
  apprehension, how like a god! the beauty of the
  world! the paragon of animals! And yet, to me, what
  is this quintessence of dust? Man delights not me— 310
  no, nor woman neither, though by your smiling you
  seem to say so.

Rosencrantz
  My lord, there was no such stuff in my thoughts.

Hamlet
  Why did ye laugh, then, when I said 'Man delights
  not me'? 315

Rosencrantz
  To think, my lord, if you delight not in man, what
  lenten entertainment the players shall receive from
  you. We coted them on the way; and hither are they
  coming to offer you service.

320-7. For a while, Hamlet is indeed distracted from his brooding and gaily describes what a good audience he will be for them. Shakespeare takes the opportunity to express a few opinions about drama in his day.

321. *on:* from.

322. *foil and target:* sword and shield.

322-3. *the lover . . . gratis:* the actor playing an unhappy lover will not sigh in vain.

323. *humorous man:* the actor playing an eccentric character part.

324-5. *whose lungs . . . sere:* whose laughter is easily triggered off.

325-6. *the lady . . . halt for't:* the woman in the play (this would always be acted by a boy in Elizabethan times) will be allowed to speak as she wishes, even if it means that the rhythm of the verse will suffer.

328. *Even those:* the very ones. *wont:* used to.

329. *the tragedians of the city:* Perhaps Shakespeare is thinking of a London company of his own time.

330. *How . . . travel?* Why are they on tour? Hamlet adds that both their reputation and their finances would have benefited if they had stayed where they were.

332-3. *their inhibition . . . innovation:* Rosencrantz probably means that they cut down on their city performances because of the latest fashion – a company of child actors which, he goes on to say, is so popular that the established companies have had to go into the provinces to make a living.

334. *Do . . . estimation:* are they so well thought of?

338. *their endeavour . . . pace:* they maintain their usual standard.

339-41. *an eyrie . . . clapp'd for't:* a nestful of children whose squeaky voices, like those of baby birds, shout down everyone else, and are outrageously applauded.

342-4. *berattle . . . thither:* The private company of boy actors has satirized the public, or 'common' theatres, as they call them, so much that many gallants hesitate to visit them for fear of being attacked themselves by the playwrights' pens (*goose quills*).

345-6. *Who maintains . . . escoted?* Who backs and pays them?

346. *pursue the quality:* follow the profession.

346-7. *no longer than they can sing:* until their voices break.

347-51. *Will they not say . . . succession:* Hamlet asks whether they won't feel later on, if they become professional actors (as they may have to, if they have no better source of income) that their playwrights harmed their careers by making them belittle their future calling.

Hamlet

He that plays the king shall be welcome—his Majesty 320
shall have tribute on me; the adventurous knight
shall use his foil and target; the lover shall not sigh
gratis; the humorous man shall end his part in peace;
the clown shall make those laugh whose lungs are
tickle a' th' sere; and the lady shall say her mind 325
freely, or the blank verse shall halt for't. What
players are they?

Rosencrantz

Even those you were wont to take such delight in—
the tragedians of the city.

Hamlet

How chances it they travel? Their residence, both in 330
reputation and profit, was better both ways.

Rosencrantz

I think their inhibition comes by the means of the
late innovation.

Hamlet

Do they hold the same estimation they did when I
was in the city? Are they so followed? 335

Rosencrantz

No, indeed, are they not.

Hamlet

How comes it? Do they grow rusty?

Rosencrantz

Nay, their endeavour keeps in the wonted pace; but
there is, sir, an eyrie of children, little eyases, that cry
out on the top of question, and are most tyrannically 340
clapp'd for't. These are now the fashion, and so
berattle the common stages—so they call them—that
many wearing rapiers are afraid of goose quills and
dare scarce come thither.

Hamlet

What, are they children? Who maintains 'em? How 345
are they escoted? Will they pursue the quality no
longer than they can sing? Will they not say after-

353. *the nation:* the public. *tarre . . . controversy:* keep the argument going. (Shakespeare himself is doing this!)

354-6. *no money . . . question:* no new play brought in any money unless it dealt with the controversy.

359. *carry it away:* win the day.

360. *Hercules and his load:* the sign of the Globe Theatre, where Shakespeare's company performed. For *Hercules*, see note on Act I, Scene ii, line 153; *his load* was the world, which he carried on his shoulders. Rosencrantz means that the boys are stealing the popularity of the other companies.

362-7. Hamlet's bitterness returns, for this confirms his low opinion of human nature: people are fickle, too, to his father's memory, in hero-worshipping Claudius and buying miniatures of him, while formerly they regarded him with disgust.

366. *'Sblood:* literally means 'God's blood.'

366-7. *something . . . find it out:* 'something strange about this if only one could investigate it properly.' Another comment on the limitations of logic (*philosophy*) – see Act I, Scene v, line 167.

369-78. Again Hamlet's mood changes as a flourish of trumpets off-stage announces the players' arrival. Adopting a pointedly affable manner, he welcomes his ex-friends (rather late) to the castle, shaking their hands ceremoniously and saying that he doesn't want to give the impression that the players are more welcome than they are (but the deliberateness with which he does this makes it clear that it is just a superficial act of courtesy). Then he amuses himself by throwing in a disconcertingly 'mad' remark, just as they may have concluded that he is, after all, sane.

370-1. *th'appurtenance . . . ceremony:* some sort of ceremony should accompany a welcome.

371-2. *comply . . . garb:* greet you in this way. *extent:* extending a welcome.

373. *must show fairly outwards:* will be a pleasant one.

374. *entertainment:* welcome.

wards, if they should grow themselves to common
players—as it is most like, if their means are no
better—their writers do them wrong to make them *350*
exclaim against their own succession?

Rosencrantz

Faith, there has been much to-do on both sides; and
the nation holds it no sin to tarre them to controversy. There was for a while no money bid for
argument, unless the poet and the player went to *355*
cuffs in the question.

Hamlet

Is't possible?

Guildenstern

O, there has been much throwing about of brains.

Hamlet

Do the boys carry it away?

Rosencrantz

Ay, that they do, my lord—Hercules and his load *360*
too.

Hamlet

It is not very strange; for my uncle is King of
Denmark, and those that would make mows at him
while my father lived give twenty, forty, fifty, a
hundred ducats apiece for his picture in little. *365*
'Sblood, there is something in this more than natural,
if philosophy could find it out.

A flourish

Guildenstern

There are the players.

Hamlet

Gentlemen, you are welcome to Elsinore. Your
hands, come then; th' appurtenance of welcome is *370*
fashion and ceremony. Let me comply with you in
this garb; lest my extent to the players, which, I tell
you, must show fairly outwards, should more appear
like entertainment than yours. You are welcome.

375. *my uncle-father and aunt-mother:* This shows Hamlet's distaste for the confusion of his family relationships.

377-8. Hamlet hints mysteriously that he is only mad when the wind is in a certain direction. It was formerly believed that the direction of the wind affected one's moods (the weather the wind brings probably does!): a southerly wind, unlike a northerly one, was good for melancholy people, so at these times, Hamlet has his wits about him. *I know a hawk from a handsaw:* This is like saying 'I know chalk from cheese.' Probably the phrase refers to two birds (*a handsaw:* a kind of heron) or possibly to two kinds of tool (*hawk:* a hooked cutting tool).

380-94. Seeing Polonius bustling up with the already stale news of the players' arrival, Hamlet decides to bait him further, encouraging Rosencrantz and Guildenstern, one on each side of him, to exchange rude remarks with him about the old man, in a loud whisper. Is this behaviour of Hamlet's consistent with the courtesy he shows such people as Horatio and the players?
381. *that great baby:* Polonius. In what way is he like one?
382. *swaddling clouts:* the linen in which a new-born baby used to be wrapped.
383-4. *Happily . . . twice a child:* Perhaps he is in his second childhood.

386-7. *You say right . . . indeed:* Raising his voice, Hamlet continues an imaginary conversation with Rosencrantz and Guildenstern, in an exaggeratedly casual tone. *a:* on.

389. Hamlet mockingly echoes Polonius's words and Polonius pretends to take no notice. *Roscius:* a famous Roman actor. Hamlet shows that he already knows Polonius's news.

392. *Buzz, buzz!* I've heard that before.

393. The rhythm of this line is like the opening of a ballad. The words *on his ass* pick up what Polonius has just said, implying that Polonius's honour is that of a donkey, non-existent.
395-401. Why does Polonius praise the actors so much, though it is obvious that Hamlet knows much more about drama, and this company of players, than he does? (Though Polonius makes this list sound ridiculous, it actually describes fairly accurately the variety of plays that Shakespeare himself wrote!)
396. *pastoral:* a story set in idealized country surroundings.

But my uncle-father and aunt-mother are deceived. *375*

Guildenstern

In what, my dear lord?

Hamlet

I am but mad north-north-west; when the wind is
southerly I know a hawk from a handsaw.

Re-enter POLONIUS

Polonius

Well be with you, gentlemen!

Hamlet

Hark you, Guildenstern, and you too—at each ear a *380*
hearer: that great baby you see there is not yet out
of his swaddling clouts.

Rosencrantz

Happily he is the second time come to them; for they
say an old man is twice a child.

Hamlet

I will prophesy he comes to tell me of the players; *385*
mark it. You say right, sir: a Monday morning; 'twas
then indeed.

Polonius

My lord, I have news to tell you.

Hamlet

My lord, I have news to tell you. When Roscius was
an actor in Rome—   *390*

Polonius

The actors are come hither, my lord.

Hamlet

Buzz, buzz!

Polonius

Upon my honour—

Hamlet

Then came each actor on his ass—

Polonius

The best actors in the world, either for tragedy, *395*
comedy, history, pastoral, pastoral-comical, histori-

398-9. *scene . . . unlimited:* plays which consist strictly of one long scene, with no change of set or time, and, on the other hand, plays where the poet is not bound by traditional limitations and rules like these.

399. *Seneca* and *Plautus:* both Roman playwrights, the first of melodramatic tragedies, and the second of comedies.

400. *For the law . . . liberty:* both for traditional and free drama.

402. Polonius's pompous way of passing judgement reminds Hamlet of another judge: the Biblical *Jephthah* (Judges 11, 38) with whom Polonius had something else in common, a daughter. Hamlet begins to sing a popular ballad about him.

408. Polonius still clings to his theory about Hamlet's 'madness'.

409. *'i th' right:* right.

412. Hamlet implies that Polonius does not necessarily love his daughter.

413-18. Hamlet pretends that Polonius meant to ask what the next line of the song was. In fact, Jephthah sacrificed his daughter, just as Polonius is prepared to use Ophelia as a bait to discover what has made Hamlet mad. (This again suggests that Hamlet overheard the plan; but it might just mean that Hamlet feels that Polonius does not care about Ophelia's happiness.)

414. *As by lot, God wot:* then by chance, God knows.

416. *as most like it was:* as it was likely to.

417. *the first row of the pious chanson:* the first line of the religious song.

418. *abridgement:* interruption. Hamlet refers to the players, whom he now greets warmly and with easy courtesy, dropping the mocking tone in which he had been talking to Polonius.

419-20. *I am glad to see thee well:* Hamlet speaks to one of the individual players.

421. *valanc'd:* fringed (bearded).

132

cal-pastoral, tragical-historical, tragical-comical-his-
torical-pastoral, scene individable, or poem unlimited. Seneca cannot be too heavy nor Plautus too
light. For the law of writ and the liberty, these are   400
the only men.

Hamlet

O Jephthah, judge of Israel, what a treasure hadst
thou!

Polonius

What a treasure had he, my lord?

Hamlet

Why—   405

        'One fair daughter, and no more,
        The which he loved passing well'.

Polonius [*Aside*]

Still on my daughter.

Hamlet

Am I not i' th' right, old Jephthah?

Polonius

If you call me Jephthah, my lord, I have a daughter   410
that I love passing well.

Hamlet

Nay, that follows not.

Polonius

What follows then, my lord?

Hamlet   Why—

        'As by lot, God wot'

and then, you know,   415

        'It came to pass, as most like it was'.

The first row of the pious chanson will show you
more; for look where my abridgement comes.

Enter the PLAYERS

You are welcome, masters; welcome, all.—I am
glad to see thee well.—Welcome, good friends.—O,   420
my old friend! Why thy face is valanc'd since I saw
thee last; com'st thou to beard me in Denmark?—

133

423-7. *my young lady . . . ring:* Hamlet addresses one of the boy actors (see note on line 326 above), teasingly saying he is taller by the height of a high-heeled shoe than he was at their last meeting, and hoping that his voice has not broken yet. Hamlet puns with the words *ring*, referring (*a*) to its pure sound and (*b*) to the fact that if a gold coin had a crack that penetrated into the circle surrounding the sovereign's head it was unfit for use (*uncurrent*).

427-8. *We'll e'en to't . . . see:* We'll try something off the cuff, like dashing sportsmen.

429-30. *taste of your quality:* sample of your skill. *passionate:* full of feeling.

434-5. *pleas'd not the million . . . general:* was not popular with the general public, just as a delicacy like caviare is an acquired taste.

435-7. *as I received it . . . of mine:* as Hamlet, and more experienced critics than he, thought.

437-8. *well digested . . . cunning:* well composed and with a restrained but clever style.

439. *one:* someone.

439-40. *sallets . . . savoury:* no salacious touches to add spice to the subject-matter.

440-1. *no matter . . . affectation:* nothing affected about the language.

442-3. *honest method . . . fine:* straightforward style, good as well as pleasant, and dignified rather than elaborate.

448-62. Having described in this way what he considers to be the best kind of dramatic style, it is odd that when the speech comes it is in very high-flown language indeed. Of course, Shakespeare needed to distinguish the style of the speech from that of *Hamlet* itself, but even so it is so old-fashionedly melodramatic that one wonders whether Hamlet did not have his tongue in his cheek (though it is true that the delivery of the speech affects him strongly).

Aeneas: The Trojan who escaped when his city was burnt by the Greeks and told the story of the fall of Troy to *Dido*, the queen of Carthage, when he was staying with her. *Priam:* the old king of Troy, who was killed by the Greek Pyrrhus. Hamlet has asked for the part of the play which dealt with this killing, and with the grief of Priam's wife, Hecuba, at his death. Is he perhaps thinking of his own father's death, or is he imagining himself as Pyrrhus, ferociously killing Claudius?

448. *tn' Hyrcanian beast:* a tiger.

450. *sable:* the heraldic name for black.

452. *the ominous horse:* the wooden horse in which the Greeks hid to deceive the Trojans.

455. *total gules:* red all over, with blood (gules was the heraldic name for red). *trick'd:* painted.

457. *impasted:* congealed by the heat of the flames of the burning streets.

What, my young lady and mistress! By'r lady, your
ladyship is nearer to heaven than when I saw you last
by the altitude of a chopine. Pray God, your voice, *425*
like a piece of uncurrent gold, be not crack'd within
the ring.—Masters, you are all welcome. We'll e'en
to't like French falconers, fly at anything we see.
We'll have a speech straight. Come, give us a taste of
your quality; come, a passionate speech. *430*

First Player

What speech, my good lord?

Hamlet

I heard thee speak me a speech once, but it was never
acted; or, if it was, not above once; for the play, I
remember, pleas'd not the million; 'twas caviary to
the general. But it was—as I received it, and others *435*
whose judgments in such matters cried in the top of
mine—an excellent play, well digested in the scenes,
set down with as much modesty as cunning. I remember one said there were no sallets in the lines to
make the matter savoury, nor no matter in the phrase *440*
that might indict the author of affection; but call'd it
an honest method, as wholesome as sweet, and by
very much more   handsome than fine. One speech
in it I chiefly lov'd: 'twas Æneas' tale to Dido; and
thereabout of it especially where he speaks of *445*
Priam's slaughter. If it live in your memory, begin at
this line—let me see, let me see:

    'The rugged Pyrrhus, like th' Hyrcanian beast,'
'Tis not so; it begins with Pyrrhus.
'The rugged Pyrrhus, he whose sable arms, *450*
Black as his purpose, did the night resemble
When he lay couched in the ominous horse
Hath now this dread and black complexion smear'd
With heraldry more dismal; head to foot
Now is he total gules, horridly trick'd *455*
With blood of fathers, mothers, daughters, sons,
Bak'd and impasted with the parching streets,

460. *o'er-sized with coagulate gore:* glued all over with clotted blood.

461. *carbuncles:* red gem-stones.

463. *So proceed you:* carry on.

464-5. *accent:* expression. *discretion:* interpretation. Polonius might also have added an ingratiating comment on Hamlet's remarkable memory.

467. Priam's blows fell short because he was too old to fight.

469. *Repugnant to command:* useless.

471. *whiff:* breeze. *fell:* fatal.
472. *unnerved:* limp. *Ilium:* Troy.

474. *Stoops to his base:* crashes to the ground.

475. *Takes prisoner Pyrrhus' ear:* catches his attention.

476. *declining:* falling. *milky:* white.

478. *as a painted tyrant:* still as a villain in a picture.

479. *like a neutral . . . matter:* like someone who has forgotten what he means to do.

481. *against:* just before.

482. *rack:* formation of clouds.

483. *orb below:* earth.

484. *anon:* there and then.

486. *sets him new a-work:* sets him off again.

487-8. In Roman mythology *Cyclops* was one of a group of one-eyed giants who assisted Vulcan to make armour for Mars, the war god. *for proof eterne:* to last for ever.

492. *synod:* assembly.
493. *fellies:* sections of the rim of a wheel. The goddess Fortune was supposed to have a wheel which determined people's luck by the way it turned.

That lend a tyrannous and damned light
To their lord's murder. Roasted in wrath and fire,
And thus o'er-sized with coagulate gore,   460
With eyes like carbuncles, the hellish Pyrrhus
Old grandsire Priam seeks.'
So proceed you.

Polonius
Fore God, my lord, well spoken, with good accent
and good discretion.   465

First Player   'Anon he finds him
Striking too short at Greeks; his antique sword,
Rebellious to his arm, lies where it falls,
Repugnant to command. Unequal match'd,
Pyrrhus at Priam drives, in rage strikes wide;   470
But with the whiff and wind of his fell sword
Th' unnerved father falls. Then senseless Ilium,
Seeming to feel this blow, with flaming top
Stoops to his base, and with a hideous crash
Takes prisoner Pyrrhus' ear. For, lo! his sword,   475
Which was declining on the milky head
Of reverend Priam, seem'd i' th' air to stick.
So, as a painted tyrant, Pyrrhus stood
And, like a neutral to his will and matter,
Did nothing.   480
But as we often see, against some storm,
A silence in the heavens, the rack stand still,
The bold winds speechless, and the orb below
As hush as death, anon the dreadful thunder
Doth rend the region; so, after Pyrrhus' pause,   485
A roused vengeance sets him new a-work;
And never did the Cyclops' hammers fall
On Mars's armour, forg'd for proof eterne,
With less remorse than Pyrrhus' bleeding sword
Now falls on Priam.   490
Out, out, thou strumpet, Fortune! All you gods,
In general synod, take away her power;
Break all the spokes and fellies from her wheel,

137

494. *nave:* hub of a wheel.

496. Polonius's interruption, prompted either by boredom or perhaps uneasiness at all this talk of violence in front of a 'madman', is squashed by Hamlet with a mocking remark about his appearance and his low-brow taste.

497. *It shall to the barber's:* it will be cut. *Prithee:* please.

498. *jig:* comic dance. *tale of bawdry:* bawdy story. The idea of the pompous Polonius relishing such things is amusing.

500. *mobled:* muffled.

501. Hamlet perhaps is struck by the difference between Hecuba's grief and his mother's – or perhaps it is just that the word (not a common one) was unfamiliar to him.

502. Polonius eagerly seizes a chance to try and show that after all he can appreciate good literature!

503. *threat'ning:* likely to put out the fire with her tears.

504. *bisson rheum:* blinding tears. *clout:* rag.

506. *o'er-teemed:* probably means 'exhausted with child-bearing.'

508-9. *Who . . . pronounc'd:* whoever had seen this would have railed against Fortune's tyranny bitterly.

510-16. *But if the gods . . . the gods:* If the gods saw her when she watched her husband being chopped to pieces her cries would have made them weep, if anything to do with human beings can affect them.

517-18. Polonius comments on how carried away by his own speech the actor has become.

519. *'Tis well:* right, that's enough.

520. *Good my lord:* this is the first polite remark Hamlet has made to Polonius for a long time. *well bestowed:* settled in good accommodation.

521. *Do you hear:* Perhaps Polonius looked as though he thought a servant should be asked to do this. *well used:* well treated.

522. *the abstract and brief chronicles of the time:* those who sum up and record what is going on.

And bowl the round nave down the hill of heaven,
As low as to the fiends.'   *495*

Polonius

This is too long.

Hamlet

It shall to the barber's, with your beard. Prithee say
on. He's for a jig, or a tale of bawdry, or he sleeps.
Say on; come to Hecuba.

First Player

'But who, ah, who had seen the mobled queen—'   *500*

Hamlet

'The mobled queen'?

Polonius

That's good; 'mobled queen' is good.

First Player

'Run barefoot up and down, threat'ning the flames
With bisson rheum; a clout upon that head
Where late the diadem stood, and for a robe,   *505*
About her lank and all o'er-teemed loins,
A blanket, in the alarm of fear caught up—
Who this had seen, with tongue in venom steep'd,
'Gainst Fortune's state would treason have pronounc'd.
But if the gods themselves did see her then,   *510*
When she saw Pyrrhus make malicious sport
In mincing with his sword her husband's limbs,
The instant burst of clamour that she made—
Unless things mortal move them not at all—
Would have made milch the burning eyes of heaven, *515*
And passion in the gods.'

Polonius

Look whe'er he has not turn'd his colour, and has
tears in 's eyes. Prithee no more.

Hamlet

'Tis well; I'll have thee speak out the rest of this
soon.—Good my lord, will you see the players well *520*
bestowed? Do you hear: let them be well used; for
they are the abstract and brief chronicles of the time;

523-4. *after your death . . . live:* a 'bad press' while you are alive is worse than having unpleasant things said about you after you die.

525. *use:* treat. *according to their desert:* as they deserve.

526. *God's bodykins:* (sometimes written 'Odd's bodikins') is a mild oath, literally 'God's little body'. Hamlet is provoked by Polonius's stuffy attitude to make another of his disillusioned remarks about human nature, but this time it is tempered with compassion: as everyone is imperfect and deserves a rogue's punishment there is all the more necessity for kindness and generosity.

527. *scape:* escape.

528. *honour and dignity:* importance and rank.

529-30. *Take them in:* Since a polite request has failed, Hamlet issues a curt order.

532. Hamlet pointedly addresses the actors as *friends*, showing how unsuitable Polonius's snobbery is; then he has a private word with the chief player.

536. *ha't:* have it.

537. *study:* learn.

538. *set down:* write.

540-3. Why does Hamlet forbid the players to make fun of Polonius when he himself has been doing it? Noticing Rosencrantz and Guildenstern do not go with the others, Hamlet firmly dismisses them.

545-604. *God buy:* goodbye. With relief at being alone at last, Hamlet is able to drop the many disguises he has adopted during this scene, and give vent to the suppressed anger and self-mistrust that have been building up inside him. The player's emotion on describing the imaginary death of Priam (see line 517) reminded him that he has real cause for grief and indignation, yet he has been idling his time away instead of obtaining revenge. Perhaps he is a coward, he thinks. Would he put up with any of the usual insults to his honour? Yes, perhaps he would. At this, Hamlet catches himself being melodramatic, and feels even more disgusted with himself. Finally, he manages to pull himself together and discuss the plan he has in mind.

546. Hamlet feels that if anyone should be whipped as a rogue (see line 527, and note), it is he.

after your death you were better have a bad epitaph
than their ill report while you live.

Polonius

My lord, I will use them according to their desert. 525

Hamlet

God's bodykins, man, much better. Use every man
after his desert, and who shall scape whipping? Use
them after your own honour and dignity: the less
they deserve, the more merit is in your bounty. Take
them in. 530

Polonius

Come, sirs.

Hamlet

Follow him, friends, We'll hear a play to-morrow.
Dost thou hear me, old friend; can you play 'The
Murder of Gonzago'?

First Player

Ay, my lord. 535

Hamlet

We'll ha't to-morrow night. You could, for a need,
study a speech of some dozen or sixteen lines which
I would set down and insert in't, could you not?

First Player

Ay, my lord.

Hamlet

Very well. Follow that lord; and look you mock him 540
not. [*Exeunt* POLONIUS *and* PLAYERS] My good
friends, I'll leave you till night. You are welcome to
Elsinore.

Rosencrantz

Good my lord!

Exeunt ROSENCRANTZ *and* GUILDENSTERN

Hamlet

Ay, so God buy to you! Now I am alone. 545
O, what a rogue and peasant slave am I!
Is it not monstrous that this player here,

548. *But ... passion:* just because of an imaginary emotion.

549. *force ... conceit:* make himself believe in a figment of his own imagination.

550. *from her working ... wann'd:* his face turned pale.

551. *distraction in's aspect:* frenzy in his expression.

552-3. *his whole function ... conceit:* his whole behaviour matching the idea in his mind.

557. *cue:* cause.

559. *cleave the general ear:* deafen the audience. *horrid:* terrifying.

560. *appal the free:* horrify even those who are innocent.

561. *Confound:* bewilder.

563. The shortness of this line emphasizes the way Hamlet dwells angrily on the contrast between the player and himself.

564. *muddy-mettl'd:* feeble-spirited. *peak:* mope.

565. *John-a-dreams:* a day-dreaming fool. *unpregnant of:* inactive in. *cause:* duty.

567-8. *Upon whose property ... made:* who was wickedly deprived of his crown and his life.

569. *Who calls me villain:* can anyone insult me and get away with it? *pate:* head.

571-2. *gives me the lie ... lungs:* calls me an out-and-out liar.

574. *'Swounds:* God's wounds (a strong oath). *I should take it:* We would add the words 'lying down'.

574-6. *it cannot be ... bitter:* Hamlet says he must be as meek as a dove, and lack the necessary spirit to resent an injury. *gall,* which pigeons' livers were thought not to be able to secrete, was believed to be the source of anger.

577-8. *'a fatted ... offal:* have fed Claudius's guts to all the nearby carrion birds.

579. *kindless:* heartless, lacking any feeling for his family.

580. Another pause, while Hamlet repents of his undignified swearing.

581. *most brave:* really splendid.

583. *Prompted to:* given the cue for. Why does Hamlet mention *hell*?

584. *unpack ... words:* squander my feelings in words (instead of actions).

But in a fiction, in a dream of passion,
Could force his soul so to his own conceit
That from her working all his visage wann'd; 550
Tears in his eyes, distraction in's aspect,
A broken voice, and his whole function suiting
With forms to his conceit? And all for nothing!
For Hecuba!
What's Hecuba to him or he to Hecuba, 555
That he should weep for her? What would he do,
Had he the motive and the cue for passion
That I have? He would drown the stage with tears,
And cleave the general ear with horrid speech;
Make mad the guilty, and appal the free, 560
Confound the ignorant, and amaze indeed
The very faculties of eyes and ears.
Yet I,
A dull and muddy-mettl'd rascal, peak,
Like John-a-dreams, unpregnant of my cause, 565
And can say nothing; no, not for a king
Upon whose property and most dear life
A damn'd defeat was made. Am I a coward?
Who calls me villain, breaks my pate across,
Plucks off my beard and blows it in my face, 570
Tweaks me by the nose, gives me the lie i' th' throat
As deep as to the lungs? Who does me this?
Ha!
'Swounds, I should take it; for it cannot be
But I am pigeon-liver'd and lack gall 575
To make oppression bitter, or ere this
I should 'a fatted all the region kites
With this slave's offal. Bloody, bawdy villain!
Remorseless, treacherous, lecherous, kindless villain!
O, vengeance! 580
Why, what an ass am I! This is most brave,
That I, the son of a dear father murder'd,
Prompted to my revenge by heaven and hell,
Must, like a whore, unpack my heart with words,

585. *fall:* start. *very drab:* real slut. By comparing himself to the worst kind of women, Hamlet implies that his behaviour is effeminate as well as base. *Fie upon't! foh!* means something like 'Ugh, disgusting!'

587. *About:* get to work. *Hum:* hmm . . .

587-97. Hamlet says that the play he is going to have acted the following night, *The Murder of Gonzago*, resembles the circumstances in which his father was killed. He hopes that his uncle's reaction to the play will prove his guilt.

588. *creatures:* people. *sitting at:* attending.

589. *cunning of the scene:* skill of the production.

590. *presently:* on the spot.

591. *proclaim'd their malefactions:* confessed their crimes.

593. *With most miraculous organ:* by most amazing means. This comment, on the way crime inevitably comes to light, echoes Act I, Scene ii, line 256-7.

594. *Play:* act.

596. *tent him to the quick:* probe him where he is sensitive. *If 'a do blench:* if he flinches.

597. *my course:* what to do.

597-603. *The spirit . . . than this:* Hamlet says that as the apparition he saw may not have been his father's ghost, but a devil come to take advantage of his low spirits, trying to deceive him into acting wrongly, he needs further proof of his uncle's guilt. (Has Hamlet's failure to obtain revenge so far been chiefly due to his uncertainty about the ghost's genuineness? If so, the play he is having put on should decide things one way or another.)

599. *T'assume:* disguise itself as. It was believed that devils often masqueraded as innocent ghosts.

600. *weakness:* mental disturbance. *melancholy:* depression.

601. *potent with such spirits:* powerful in such moods.

602. *Abuses:* deceives. *grounds:* motives, proofs.

603. *relative:* definite.

603-4. *The play's the thing . . . King:* Hamlet goes off more cheerful, now that he has a plan. The rhyming couplet with which he sums up his aim, of catching Claudius in the play as in a trap, sounds almost light-hearted.

And fall a-cursing like a very drab,   585
A scullion! Fie upon't! foh!
About, my brains. Hum—I have heard
That guilty creatures, sitting at a play,
Have by the very cunning of the scene
Been struck so to the soul that presently   590
They have proclaim'd their malefactions;
For murder, though it have no tongue, will speak
With most miraculous organ. I'll have these players
Play something like the murder of my father
Before mine uncle. I'll observe his looks;   595
I'll tent him to the quick. If 'a do blench,
I know my course. The spirit that I have seen
May be a devil; and the devil hath power
T' assume a pleasing shape; yea, and perhaps
Out of my weakness and my melancholy,   600
As he is very potent with such spirits,
Abuses me to damn me. I'll have grounds
More relative than this. The play's the thing
Wherein I'll catch the conscience of the King.

Exit

145

ACT THREE

Rosencrantz and Guildenstern, reporting back to Claudius about their interview with Hamlet, have had to confess that they did not get very far in their investigation. Naturally, they suppress the fact that Hamlet saw through their motive for being there. The king, however, is not as angry as they had probably feared: he has another plan up his sleeve, Polonius's suggestion that they should eavesdrop on a conversation between Hamlet and Ophelia.

1. *drift of conference:* leading him on in conversation.
2. It is interesting that Claudius now implies that Hamlet may be putting on something of an act. Guildenstern is quick to pick up the hint in line 8. *confusion:* distracted manner.
3. *Grating:* disturbing.
4. Has Hamlet shown any sign of being violent and dangerous yet? Claudius is cleverly sowing the seeds of the idea that Hamlet is a menace to public safety if he is allowed to go loose, an idea which he exploits fully later on.
5-6. Rosencrantz's statement is accurate as far as it goes. He is eager to show that at least they did get on to the subject of Hamlet's madness, while talking to him.
7-10. Guildenstern makes it clear that their job was not an easy one, and manages a clever compromise between taking the line that Hamlet's behaviour really is mad (though most of their conversation with him was perfectly sane) and agreeing with Claudius that he is putting some of it on, for it would not be good policy to disagree with the king.
7. *forward to be sounded:* easy to question.
8. *crafty:* cunning.
8-10. *keeps aloof . . . state:* manages to avoid our attempts to make him talk about his real state of mind.
10, 14-15. The queen shows more concern than her husband about whether Hamlet seemed happy or not.
11. How far did Hamlet behave like a *gentleman* to them?
12. Guildenstern adds that Hamlet found it an effort to be sociable.
13-14. *Niggard of question . . . reply:* Reluctant to begin any topic of conversation, but quite ready to answer what someone else said. This, of course, is not quite true, as Hamlet asked them persistently why they were at Elsinore.
14-15. *assay him . . . pastime:* try to interest him in some amusement.
16. *fell out:* happened.
17. *o'er-raught:* overtook.

146

ACT THREE

SCENE I—*Elsinore. The Castle*

Enter KING, QUEEN, POLONIUS, OPHELIA,
ROSENCRANTZ *and* GUILDENSTERN

King
    And can you by no drift of conference
    Get from him why he puts on this confusion,
    Grating so harshly all his days of quiet
    With turbulent and dangerous lunacy?

Rosencrantz
    He does confess he feels himself distracted,   5
    But from what cause 'a will by no means speak.

Guildenstern
    Nor do we find him forward to be sounded;
    But, with a crafty madness, keeps aloof
    When we would bring him on to some confession
    Of his true state.

Queen   Did he receive you well?   10

Rosencrantz
    Most like a gentleman.

Guildenstern
    But with much forcing of his disposition.

Rosencrantz
    Niggard of question; but of our demands
    Most free in his reply.

Queen   Did you assay him
    To any pastime?   15

Rosencrantz
    Madam, it so fell out that certain players
    We o'er-raught on the way. Of these we told him;
    And there did seem in him a kind of joy

20. *order:* instructions.

21. *This night:* Hamlet asked for the play to be put on *tomorrow night*, so it seems that this scene takes place on the day after the previous one.

23. *the matter:* what they put on.

24-7. Unsuspectingly, the king leaps at the opportunity to seem the loving step-father.

26. *give him a further edge:* try and make him still more keen.

27. *And drive . . . delights:* Encourage him to take an interest in this kind of entertainment.

28. *Sweet Gertrude:* Claudius at least seems to feel real affection for his wife, and he has the tact (and commonsense) to suggest that she does not make one of the eavesdropping party.

29. *closely:* privately.

30. *as 'twere:* as though.

31. *Affront:* meet face to face, encounter.

32. *lawful espials:* justified spies. Claudius tries to make the undignified ruse appear in a better light. Why doesn't he let Polonius listen in on his own?

33. *bestow:* hide. *seeing unseen:* watching, while ourselves invisible.

34-7. Claudius hopes that they will be able to judge clearly from Hamlet's behaviour during the meeting whether or not it is love-sickness that he suffers from.

38-42. Realizing that in the circumstances Ophelia must feel awkward and miserable, both as the possible cause of the madness of one of the royal family, and as the bait in a trap to catch out the man she loves, the queen has the imagination to reassure her graciously and kindly. She shows that she approves of their love and believes Ophelia herself to be a good person.

39-40. *That your good beauties . . . wildness:* that your virtuous charms are the pleasant reason for Hamlet's strange behaviour.

40-2. Gertrude hopes that Ophelia's good influence will bring him back to his old self, to the credit of both of them.

43. Polonius self-importantly stage-manages the apparently innocent little scene, telling the king to hide with him behind the tapestry (probably behind the curtain of the Elizabethan 'inner stage') while Ophelia walks up and down reading a prayer-book that her father has thoughtfully brought along. *Gracious:* Your Majesty.

44. *bestow:* hide.

To hear of it. They are here about the court,
And, as I think, they have already order   20
This night to play before him.

Polonius   'Tis most true;
And he beseech'd me to entreat your Majesties
To hear and see the matter.

King
With all my heart; and it doth much content me
To hear him so inclin'd.   25
Good gentlemen, give him a further edge,
And drive his purpose into these delights.

Rosencrantz
We shall, my lord.

Exeunt ROSENCRANTZ *and* GUILDENSTERN

King   Sweet Gertrude, leave us too;
For we have closely sent for Hamlet hither,
That he, as 'twere by accident, may here   30
Affront Ophelia.
Her father and myself—lawful espials—
Will so bestow ourselves that, seeing unseen,
We may of their encounter frankly judge,
And gather by him, as he is behav'd,   35
If't be th' affliction of his love or no
That thus he suffers for.

Queen   I shall obey you;
And for your part, Ophelia, I do wish
That your good beauties be the happy cause
Of Hamlet's wildness; so shall I hope your virtues   40
Will bring him to his wonted way again,
To both your honours.

Ophelia   Madam, I wish it may.

Exit QUEEN

Polonius
Ophelia, walk you here.—Gracious, so please you,
We will bestow ourselves.—Read on this book;

45-6. *show . . . loneliness:* your seeming to be engaged in your prayers will explain why you are alone.

47-9. Polonius finds this an opportunity for one of his sententious remarks: people too often cover up their wickedness by pretending to be religious and virtuous.

49-54. Polonius's generalization has struck home; what Claudius says to himself here is the first independent evidence we have that the ghost may have spoken the truth, and that Claudius certainly has a crime on his conscience. He says that what he has done is like an ugly prostitute's face, made to look more attractive by a layer of make-up, just as his own pleasant manner covers up his guilt.

54. *O heavy burden:* Hamlet would be surprised to learn that his uncle is unhappy, too.

56. With his mind for the moment above such things as plotting and deceit, Hamlet comes in deep in thought, and unaware for a while of Ophelia's presence. He is attempting to sort out his feelings about life and death, calmly and dispassionately, in a mood not, as when we last saw him, of anger and hatred, but of quiet despair. Hamlet states the topic he is going to discuss, as though proposing the motion for a philosophical debate. 'Shall I go on living, or not?' he asks. Why does he continue to long for death even though he now has an aim in life (revenge) and a means (the play) of putting it into practice?

57-60. He first asks which is more admirable: to put up with one blow of fate after another (*slings* are catapults used in warfare), or to defy and defeat the overwhelming misery of life by killing oneself. (The idea of fighting with weapons against the sea is found in the well-known Irish legend of Cuchulain, a hero who fought the waves in madness with his sword, until he died. There is also a story about the mad Roman Emperor Caligula fighting a battle against the sea.) *opposing* means at once 'facing up to' and 'fighting against'.

60-4. What is death, after all, asks Hamlet, but a restful sleep?

62-3. *natural shocks . . . heir to:* blows that life inevitably brings to all human beings.

63. *consummation:* satisfying end.

64-82. Maybe death, like sleep, is not untroubled (perhaps we can take Act II, Scene ii, lines 254-6 literally). Why does everyone put up with his suffering in this life if he is not afraid of what might happen to him in the next?

65. *perchance:* perhaps. *rub:* impediment, snag. Hamlet uses a term from the game of bowls, where a *rub* is an unevenness in the ground which prevents a ball rolling smoothly. In this case, it is Hamlet's train of thought that is deflected.

67. *shuffled off . . . coil:* shaken ourselves free of the muddle of this life.

68. *give us pause:* make us hesitate.

68-9. *There's the respect . . . life:* that's why people put up with the misfortune of living a long time.

70-6. Who would put up with all the painful experiences of life when he could find peace in death? The list of these which Hamlet gives shows that he is aware that there are other troubles in the world besides his own, as not all of them apply to him.

70. *scorns of time:* humiliations that time brings.

That show of such an exercise may colour 45
Your loneliness.—We are oft to blame in this:
'Tis too much prov'd, that with devotion's visage
And pious action we do sugar o'er
The devil himself.

King [Aside]   O, 'tis too true!
How smart a lash that speech doth give my conscience! 50
The harlot's cheek, beautied with plast'ring art,
Is not more ugly to the thing that helps it
Than is my deed to my most painted word.
O heavy burden!

Polonius
I hear him coming; let's withdraw, my lord. 55

Exeunt KING *and* POLONIUS
Enter HAMLET

Hamlet
To be, or not to be—that is the question;
Whether 'tis nobler in the mind to suffer
The slings and arrows of outrageous fortune,
Or to take arms against a sea of troubles,
And by opposing end them? To die, to sleep— 60
No more; and by a sleep to say we end
The heart-ache and the thousand natural shocks
That flesh is heir to. 'Tis a consummation
Devoutly to be wish'd. To die, to sleep;
To sleep, perchance to dream. Ay, there's the rub; 65
For in that sleep of death what dreams may come,
When we have shuffled off this mortal coil,
Must give us pause. There's the respect
That makes calamity of so long life;
For who would bear the whips and scorns of time, 70

151

71. *Th' oppressor's wrong:* ill-treatment from tyrants. *contumely:* contempt.

72. *the law's delay:* delay in giving the injured parties their rights.

73. *office:* people in positions of power.

73-4. *the spurns . . . takes:* the contemptuous treatment that good people patiently accept from the bad.

75. *his quietus make:* settle his account.

76. *bodkin:* dagger. *fardels:* burdens.

79-80. Why does Hamlet describe death as a region from which no-one returns? Has he decided the 'ghost' was a devil?

80. *puzzles the will:* makes one uncertain what to do.

83. *conscience:* 'thought', rather than 'a sense of right and wrong' here; Hamlet does not mention the religious objection to suicide that he referred to in Act I, Scene ii, line 131-2. He again accuses himself of cowardice, this time not so much because he has failed to take revenge as because he has not the courage, he says, to do the sensible thing about life: end it.

84-5. 'Like a sick person's face growing increasingly pale, one's determination to do something fades the more one thinks about it.' Hamlet tells himself that all this introspection is unhealthy.

86-8. *enterprises . . . action:* on account of this (thinking too long) the energy needed for undertakings of great importance is sapped away, and they are never carried out. No doubt, Hamlet is referring particularly to his failure to take revenge, which he now puts down to thinking too much (instead of uncertainty about whether the ghost was truthful, as in the last scene).

88-90. As he reaches this depressing conclusion, Hamlet becomes aware of Ophelia's presence, and at first does not seem to remember, if he did overhear it, the plot to spy on him.

88. *Soft you now:* just a moment, what's this?

89-90. *Nymph . . . remember'd:* an elaborate way of saying 'Pretty girl, remember me in your prayers'. Hamlet's tone could either be slightly mocking or entirely serious (he has just been thinking about his 'sins'). Which do you think more likely?

91. Ophelia's greeting, though formal, contains a hint of regret that they have not seen each other for a long time (but this is more her fault than Hamlet's).

92. Here, and in lines 95-6, Hamlet speaks off-handedly, as though he did not want to continue the conversation. In what tone does he repeat the word *well*? His conversation with Polonius in the last scene began very much like this.

93. *remembrances:* souvenirs.

94. *re-deliver:* give back.

95-6. Why does Hamlet say this? Does he do so simply because it would be undignified for him to take back his gifts, or does he mean 'These are not love-tokens, for I don't love you' (see line 115)?

97. Hurt, but still very respectful (as she is throughout the conversation), Ophelia reproaches Hamlet with unkindness.

98. *of so sweet breath compos'd:* sounding so sweet. In the next line she develops the idea into 'smelling sweet'.

Th' oppressor's wrong, the proud man's contumely,
The pangs of despis'd love, the law's delay,
The insolence of office, and the spurns
That patient merit of th' unworthy takes,
When he himself might his quietus make 75
With a bare bodkin? Who would fardels bear,
To grunt and sweat under a weary life,
But that the dread of something after death—
The undiscover'd country, from whose bourn
No traveller returns—puzzles the will, 80
And makes us rather bear those ills we have
Than fly to others that we know not of?
Thus conscience does make cowards of us all;
And thus the native hue of resolution
Is sicklied o'er with the pale cast of thought, 85
And enterprises of great pitch and moment,
With this regard, their currents turn awry
And lose the name of action.—Soft you now!
The fair Ophelia.—Nymph, in thy orisons
Be all my sins remember'd.

Ophelia   Good my lord, 90
How does your honour for this many a day?

Hamlet
I humbly thank you; well, well, well.

Ophelia
My lord, I have remembrances of yours
That I have longed long to re-deliver.
I pray you now receive them.

Hamlet   No, not I; 95
I never gave you aught.

Ophelia
My honour'd lord, you know right well you did,
And with them words of so sweet breath compos'd

100-1. *to the noble mind . . . unkind:* With dignity, Ophelia rejects the idea that she is the sort of girl who would keep expensive presents after a love affair is over. *wax:* grow, become.

103. Something arouses Hamlet's suspicions. Ophelia has been waiting already equipped with the gifts, as though she knew she was going to meet him (though she could, of course, have made a habit of carrying them with her); her last remark sounds prepared (note the rhyme); and perhaps Hamlet becomes aware that they are in the sort of place where they could easily be spied on (and perhaps he *was* in time to hear Polonius's plan in Act II, Scene ii). *Ha, ha!* is an angry exclamation. *honest:* good; it is the very word he attacked Polonius with (Act II, Scene ii, lines 176–9).

105. *fair:* beautiful.

107-8. *your honesty . . . beauty:* 'if you were virtuous you would guard your beauty more carefully.' It is strange that she is wandering around on her own, when recently she has been modestly refusing to see him.

109-10. Though at a loss as to what he means, Ophelia manages to parry his remark with spirit. *commerce:* dealings, connection.

111-13. *the power of beauty . . . likeness:* good looks lead virtuous people astray more easily than people's good qualities transform beauty into a good influence. Hamlet here cynically expresses a view exactly opposite to the queen's (lines 38-42, above), leaving Ophelia with the impression that her beauty has done nothing but harm (she is unaware that he may be thinking of his mother as much as of her). *bawd:* owner of a brothel; Ophelia's beauty arouses lust.

114. *sometime a paradox:* once an apparent contradiction.

114-15. *the time . . . proof:* circumstances prove it true. Ophelia, and the unseen listeners, must be wondering whether he suspects that she is being used as a decoy.

115-19. *I did love you . . . not:* Hamlet bitterly rejects the idea that he ever really loved Ophelia – or perhaps he is deliberately putting an end to their love affair because he feels it is better for her to give up all hope of being involved with him.

117-18. *virtue . . . relish of it:* The metaphor is of grafting 'inoculating' a slip from a cultivated fruit tree on to a wild stock. Hamlet means that the bad blood in his ancestry (or perhaps he means the 'old Adam' in all men) is bound to show itself. *relish:* taste.

120. Ophelia is saddened to find Hamlet saying, like her father, that his vows of love were just the result of physical desire.

121-9. As *nunnery* was a slang word for 'brothel' in Elizabethan times, Hamlet leaves Ophelia uncertain whether he is advising her to retire from the wickedness of the world into a convent, or whether he is saying that she is no better than a prostitute. From the tone of the rest of the remarks in this speech, which do you think more likely?

121-2. *Why . . . sinners:* Give up the idea of marrying me and having my children.

122. *indifferent honest:* not too bad a person.

123-4. *yet . . . borne me:* It is cowardice that we find Hamlet accusing himself of in his soliloquies. Do the adjectives *proud, revengeful* and *ambitious* describe the Hamlet we have seen so far?

As made the things more rich; their perfume lost,
Take these again; for to the noble mind   *100*
Rich gifts wax poor when givers prove unkind.
There, my lord.

Hamlet

Ha, ha! Are you honest?

Ophelia

My lord?

Hamlet

Are you fair?   *105*

Ophelia

What means your lordship?

Hamlet

That if you be honest and fair, your honesty should
admit no discourse to your beauty.

Ophelia

Could beauty, my lord, have better commerce than
with honesty?   *110*

Hamlet

Ay, truly; for the power of beauty will sooner transform honesty from what it is to a bawd than the force
of honesty can translate beauty into his likeness. This
was sometime a paradox, but now the time gives it
proof. I did love you once.   *115*

Ophelia

Indeed, my lord, you made me believe so.

Hamlet

You should not have believ'd me; for virtue cannot so
inoculate our old stock but we shall relish of it. I
loved you not.

Ophelia

I was the more deceived.   *120*

Hamlet

Get thee to a nunnery. Why wouldst thou be a
breeder of sinners? I am myself indifferent honest,
but yet I could accuse me of such things that it were
better my mother had not borne me: I am very proud,

125-7. *with more offences . . . act them in:* 'capable of more crimes than I have time to imagine, plan and carry out.' A vague accusation, which might apply to any human being!

129. *arrant knaves:* out-and-out rascals. Hamlet applied this phrase, by implication, to Claudius in (Act I, Scene v, line 124).

130-3. Hamlet's sudden question, together with the comment that follows it, suggests that by now Hamlet suspects that they are overheard. When Ophelia meets the unexpected attack with a blunt lie, it is the last straw as far as Hamlet is concerned: she too has betrayed him (but what else could she do? She thought she was talking to a potentially dangerous madman). He begins to walk out angrily, but returns three times to hurl further angry remarks at her.

134, 142. Instead of thinking of her own unhappiness, Ophelia prays earnestly (in contrast to the mere pretence of prayer earlier in the scene) for Hamlet to recover from his 'madness'.

135-6. *plague for a dowry:* curse for a wedding present. Hamlet seems to dislike equally the idea of Ophelia marrying himself or someone else!

137. *calumny:* slander. Hamlet echoes what Laertes said in Act I Scene iii, line 38, as though he guesses how important reputation is to the Polonius family.

139. *monsters:* ridiculous, half-human creatures.

143-50. By now, it is not so much Ophelia that Hamlet sees in front of him, as someone that represents what he regards (probably encouraged by his mother's behaviour) as a typical woman: over-made-up, flirtatious, affected, and insincere, and pretending to be innocent while really being coquettish.

143. *paintings:* cosmetics.

145. *jig and amble:* walk in a silly, flirtatious way, mince along.

146. *nickname God's creatures:* give ridiculous names to things. Hamlet has mentioned God twice in this speech, as though he is saying that women are impious in the way they distort what God created.

147. *Go to . . . on't:* that's enough, I'll have no more to do with it.

147-8. *it hath made me mad:* Does Hamlet really believe this, or is he saying it for the benefit of the unseen listeners, to keep alive both the idea that he is mad, and that the cause is Ophelia?

148. *no moe marriage:* no more marriages – in case Ophelia still has not got the message that their love affair is over.

149. *those . . . shall live:* Is this a deliberate threat to the uncle he guesses is hiding behind the arras, or does Hamlet come out with this unintentionally in the heat of the moment?

150. *the rest:* unmarried people, like Ophelia.

151-62. To Ophelia, Hamlet's outburst is completely incomprehensible: he must be quite mad. In spite of the unforgivable things he has said to her, her chief reaction is compassion: she laments the fact that such a gifted, popular prince has come to this – and her words give us an illuminating picture of Hamlet as he was before he became the gloomy person he is now.

152. *The courtier's . . . sword:* he looked, spoke and acted like a perfect courtier, soldier and scholar. Have we had any other evidence of these sides of Hamlet?

revengeful, ambitious; with more offences at my beck *125*
than I have thoughts to put them in, imagination to
give them shape, or time to act them in. What should
such fellows as I do crawling between earth and
heaven? We are arrant knaves, all; believe none of us.
Go thy ways to a nunnery. Where's your father? *130*

Ophelia

At home, my lord.

Hamlet

Let the doors be shut upon him, that he may play the
fool nowhere but in's own house. Farewell.

Ophelia

O, help him, you sweet heavens!

Hamlet

If thou dost marry, I'll give thee this plague for thy *135*
dowry: be thou as chaste as ice, as pure as snow, thou
shalt not escape calumny. Get thee to a nunnery, go,
farewell. Or, if thou wilt needs marry, marry a fool;
for wise men know well enough what monsters you
make of them. To a nunnery, go; and quickly too. *140*
Farewell.

Ophelia

O heavenly powers, restore him!

Hamlet

I have heard of your paintings too, well enough; God
hath given you one face, and you make yourselves
another. You jig and amble, and you lisp, and *145*
nickname God's creatures, and make your wanton-
ness your ignorance. Go to, I'll no more on't; it hath
made me mad. I say we will have no moe marriage:
those that are married already, all but one, shall live;
the rest shall keep as they are. To a nunnery, go. *150*

Exit

Ophelia

O, what a noble mind is here o'erthrown!
The courtier's, soldier's, scholar's, eye, tongue, sword;

153. *Th' expectancy . . . state:* the hope and pride of Denmark.

154-5. *The glass of fashion . . . observers:* everyone copied his clothes and behaviour, and he was courted admiringly by all.

156-62. Ophelia's chief grief is not that she has been insulted and rejected but that the person she loved is changed unrecognizably.

157. This metaphor linking sweetness and sound is similar to the one she used in lines 98-100 above.

159. The 'music' of Hamlet's talk of love has changed to discord.

160-1. *That unmatch'd form . . . ecstasy:* the unequalled beauty of his youth in full bloom is blighted with madness.

161. The contrast between the past and the miserable present has probably reduced Ophelia to tears, but when the king and Polonius creep out from hiding, having made sure that Hamlet really has gone this time, they ignore her completely for a while, as they discuss Hamlet's behaviour.

163-5. Claudius briskly announces that Hamlet is neither in love nor mad. Why is he able to come to a more accurate conclusion than Ophelia and Polonius?

163. *His affections . . . tend:* that is not what is wrong with him.

164. *form:* order, coherence.

166-8. *O'er which . . . danger:* Claudius says Hamlet is hatching some dangerous idea in his mind. His brooding state of mind is compared to a bird sitting on a clutch of eggs.

169-76. Claudius has already begun to put another plan into action: Hamlet needs a change of air, so he must pay a visit to England, ostensibly to collect the tribute owed to Denmark.

169-70. *I have . . . set it down:* making up his mind quickly, Claudius has already written the necessary letter.

172. *Haply:* perhaps.

173. *variable objects:* a change of scene.

174. *something-settled . . . heart:* rather obstinate mood.

175-6. *puts him thus . . . himself:* makes him so unlike himself.

176. *on't:* of it.

177-9. Polonius still believes that it all started with Ophelia!

179-81. Polonius offers no word of comfort to his daughter.

181-6. Polonius, not to be outdone, also has another plan: the queen must try to get Hamlet to confide in her, and once again Polonius will eavesdrop (he seems to have acquired a taste for it!)

182. *the play:* the one Hamlet has commissioned for that evening.

184. *round:* firm.

185-6. *in the ear . . . conference:* where I can hear everything they say.

Th' expectancy and rose of the fair state,
The glass of fashion and the mould of form,
Th' observ'd of all observers—quite, quite down!　155
And I, of ladies most deject and wretched,
That suck'd the honey of his music vows,
Now see that noble and most sovereign reason,
Like sweet bells jangled, out of tune and harsh;
That unmatch'd form and feature of blown youth　160
Blasted with ecstasy. O, woe is me
T' have seen what I have seen, see what I see!

Re-enter KING *and* POLONIUS

King

Love! His affections do not that way tend;
Nor what he spake, though it lack'd form a little,
Was not like madness. There's something in his soul　165
O'er which his melancholy sits on brood;
And I do doubt the hatch and the disclose
Will be some danger; which to prevent
I have in quick determination
Thus set it down: he shall with speed to England　170
For the demand of our neglected tribute.
Haply the seas and countries different,
With variable objects, shall expel
This something-settled matter in his heart
Whereon his brains still beating puts him thus　175
From fashion of himself. What think you on't?

Polonius

It shall do well. But yet do I believe
The origin and commencement of his grief
Sprung from neglected love. How now, Ophelia!
You need not tell us what Lord Hamlet said;　180
We heard it all. My lord, do as you please;
But if you hold it fit, after the play
Let his queen mother all alone entreat him
To show his grief. Let her be round with him;
And I'll be plac'd, so please you, in the ear　185

186. *find him:* find out what is wrong with him.

187. *confine:* lock him up. So this threat also faces Hamlet as a last resort.

189. *Madness . . . go:* Claudius is now firmly taking the attitude that he hinted at at the beginning of the scene: Hamlet may be a dangerous lunatic. Yet a moment ago he said that Hamlet obviously wasn't mad. Why does he contradict himself in this way?

SCENE II

That same evening, Hamlet, in a mood of suppressed excitement, is busy giving last-minute instructions to the players. He stresses the need for true-to-life acting, for, as well as its being preferable anyway to an exaggerated style, it is particularly important that *The Murder of Gonzago*, into which Hamlet has inserted a speech of his own composition, should have a sufficiently powerful effect on Claudius for him to show signs of guilt (preferably in front of the whole court, or at least clear enough to convince Hamlet). Hamlet's way of speaking to the players is so natural that it is hard to believe that only a short while before he was storming at Ophelia.

Nearly all the characters we have met so far are brought together in this, the central scene of the play.

1. *pronounc'd:* recited.

2. *trippingly on the tongue:* fluently, easily. *mouth:* speak with an exaggerated emphasis.

3. *had as lief:* would as soon.

4-5. *saw the air . . . hand:* wave your arms about. Hamlet imitates the gestures of a 'ham' actor.

5. *use all gently:* do everything quietly.

5-8. *for . . . smoothness:* for even the portrayal of intense emotions must be done with restraint, so that it is not in bad taste.

9. *robustious periwig-pated fellow:* loudmouthed fellow with a wig on his head.

10-13. *tear a passion . . . noise:* destroy the feeling of his lines completely by shouting them to impress the lower classes among the audience, who are not capable of appreciating anything but senseless charades or something noisy. *the groundlings* were those who had the cheapest places in an Elizabethan theatre, standing, in what we now call the 'pit', on the ground.

12. *inexplicable dumb-shows:* the practice of having a mime of the story of a play performed before the play itself, like the synopsis of the plot of a novel on the jacket of the book.

14. *Termagant* and *Herod:* always acted as noisy, bragging villains, in early plays.

16. *warrant:* assure.

17. We would say 'either' instead of *neither*, here.

17-18. *let . . . tutor:* use your common-sense.

19. *observance:* precaution.

20. *o'erstep . . . nature:* limit yourself to what is natural.

Of all their conference. If she find him not,
To England send him; or confine him where
Your wisdom best shall think.

King   It shall be so:
Madness in great ones must not unwatch'd go.

Exeunt

SCENE II—*Elsinore. The Castle*

Enter HAMLET *and three of the* PLAYERS

Hamlet
Speak the speech, I pray you, as I pronounc'd it to
you, trippingly on the tongue; but if you mouth it, as
many of our players do, I had as lief the town-crier
spoke my lines. Nor do not saw the air too much with
your hand, thus, but use all gently; for in the very   5
torrent, tempest, and, as I may say, whirlwind of
your passion, you must acquire and beget a temper-
ance that may give it smoothness. O, it offends me to
the soul to hear a robustious periwig-pated fellow
tear a passion to tatters, to very rags, to split the ears   10
of the groundlings, who, for the most part, are
capable of nothing but inexplicable dumb shows and
noise. I would have such a fellow whipp'd for
o'erdoing Termagant; it out-herods Herod. Pray you
avoid it.   15

First Player
I warrant your honour.

Hamlet
Be not tame neither, but let your own discretion be
your tutor. Suit the action to the word, the word to
the action; with this special observance, that you
o'erstep not the modesty of nature; for anything so   20

H.–F   161

21. *o'erdone:* exaggerated. *from:* contrary to. *playing:* acting.

21-5. *whose end . . . pressure:* Shakespeare, through Hamlet, says that the aim of drama has always been to show people what they are really like, as in a mirror, revealing both the good and bad things in human nature and giving a true reflection of the age in which it was written.

24. *scorn:* qualities that deserve scorn.

25. *form and pressure:* shape and impression.

26. *come tardy off:* weakly performed.

26-7. *the unskilful:* ignorant people. *the judicious:* those with good taste.

28-9. *the censure . . . others:* the unfavourable criticism of one of the latter outweighs what a whole theatre-full of the former group says.

31. *not to speak it profanely:* to put it mildly.

32-3. *neither having th'accent of Christians . . . man:* not speaking like a civilized man, or walking like any kind of man at all.

34-6. *some of Nature's journeymen . . . abominably:* they must have been botched up by an inexperienced craftsman, they were so unlike proper men. A journeyman was someone who was not yet a master craftsman, but had served his apprenticeship. (Hamlet's criticisms here of affectation in actors recall the comments he made about women to Ophelia in the last scene.)

37. *reform'd that indifferently:* put that more or less right. As it turns out, the acting in *The Murder of Gonzago* illustrates just the criticisms Hamlet has been making.

39-40. *let . . . set down for them:* make your comedians keep to their script.

41. *of them:* some comedians. *set on:* encourage.

42. *barren:* empty-headed.

43-4. *some necessary question . . . considered:* an important point in the play has to be got across. Hamlet's comments on the irritating habits of comedians suggest that Shakespeare himself suffered from them (they are not at all relevant to the play Hamlet has asked for, which was a tragedy).

46. *uses it:* goes in for it.

47. *my lord:* Polonius. *piece of work:* the play.

49. *presently:* immediately.

o'erdone is from the purpose of playing, whose end,
both at the first and now, was and is to hold, as
'twere, the mirror up to nature; to show virtue her
own feature, scorn her own image, and the very age
and body of the time his form and pressure. Now, 25
this overdone or come tardy off, though it makes the
unskilful laugh, cannot but make the judicious grieve;
the censure of the which one must, in your allowance,
o'erweigh a whole theatre of others. O, there be
players that I have seen play—and heard others praise, 30
and that highly—not to speak it profanely, that,
neither having th' accent of Christians, nor the gait
of Christian, pagan, nor man, have so strutted and
bellowed that I have thought some of Nature's
journeymen had made men, and not made them well, 35
they imitated humanity so abominably.

First Player

I hope we have reform'd that indifferently with us,
sir.

Hamlet

O, reform it altogether. And let those that play your
clowns speak no more than is set down for them; for 40
there be of them that will themselves laugh, to set on
some quantity of barren spectators to laugh too,
though in the meantime some necessary question of
the play be then to be considered. That's villainous,
and shows a most pitiful ambition in the fool that 45
uses it. Go, make you ready.

Exeunt PLAYERS

Enter POLONIUS, ROSENCRANTZ *and* GUILDENSTERN

How now, my lord! Will the King hear this piece of
work?

Polonius

And the Queen too, and that presently.

Hamlet

Bid the players make haste. 50

Exit POLONIUS

51. Seeing Rosencrantz and Guildenstern lingering, no doubt to try further investigations, Hamlet barely politely dismisses them. Perhaps he saw Horatio coming, too, and he wants a private word with him.

53. *What, ho:* hey, there.

54. *sweet lord:* There is affection as well as respect in Horatio's greeting.

55-6. Hamlet abruptly tells his friend that he is as good a man as he has ever met.

57-75. As Horatio modestly begins to disclaim this, Hamlet sharply says that he is not given to flattery; after all, what can he hope to win by it from Horatio, who is not exactly rich? Flattery can be left to those who fawn on pompous people in order to gain something from them.
59. *good spirits:* good-nature.
60. *the poor:* in this case Horatio.
61. *candied tongue:* people who talk in a sugary way. *lick:* like a dog. Pompous people who fall for this sort of thing are ridiculous.
62. *crook . . . knee:* bend their ever-ready knees.
63. *thrift:* financial gain.
64-75. Hamlet says that ever since he was able to judge for himself, and could discriminate between people, he has considered Horatio his best friend. What he values in him is his ability to remain calm whatever the circumstances, and whether it is good or bad luck that comes his way. This is a quality that is enviable, he says (he himself does not possess it), and makes Horatio the kind of friend he needs.
68. Hamlet again refers to the blows of *Fortune* (see Act III, Scene i, line 58).
70. *blood and judgment:* feelings and reason. *comeddled:* harmonized.
71-2. *a pipe . . . please:* this idea of someone like Hamlet being a musical instrument, easily controlled and played upon, is recalled by Hamlet later in the scene.
73. *passion's slave:* easily swayed by his emotions.
75. *Something too much of this:* 'enough of this.' Hamlet does not wish to seem sentimental.
76-88. Getting briskly down to business, Hamlet explains his plan to Horatio, and asks him to watch Claudius carefully. Why does he want an independent witness?
77. *comes near:* resembles.

Will you two help to hasten them?

Rosencrantz

Ay, my lord.

Exeunt they two

Hamlet

What, ho, Horatio!

Enter HORATIO

Horatio

Here, sweet lord, at your service.

Hamlet

Horatio, thou art e'en as just a man   55
As e'er my conversation cop'd withal.

Horatio

O my dear lord!

Hamlet   Nay, do not think I flatter;
For what advancement may I hope from thee,
That no revenue hast but thy good spirits
To feed and clothe thee? Why should the poor be flatter'd?
No, let the candied tongue lick absurd pomp,
And crook the pregnant hinges of the knee
Where thrift may follow fawning. Dost thou hear?
Since my dear soul was mistress of her choice
And could of men distinguish her election,   65
Sh'hath seal'd thee for herself; for thou hast been
As one, in suff'ring all, that suffers nothing;
A man that Fortune's buffets and rewards
Hast ta'en with equal thanks; and blest are those
Whose blood and judgment are so well comeddled   70
That they are not a pipe for Fortune's finger
To sound what stop she please. Give me that man
That is not passion's slave, and I will wear him
In my heart's core, ay, in my heart of heart,
As I do thee. Something too much of this.   75
There is a play to-night before the King;
One scene of it comes near the circumstance

79. *prithee:* beg you. *that act afoot:* that part of the play being performed.

80. *Even . . . soul:* with all your attention.

81. *occulted:* hidden.

82. *unkennel:* reveal. *one speech:* one particular speech, the one Hamlet wrote.

83-5. *It is a damned ghost . . . stithy:* If it is a ghost, it is an evil one and Hamlet's mind is full of vile misconceptions. The Roman blacksmith god, *Vulcan*, was supposed to work inside the volcano Etna, using its fire to forge Jupiter's thunderbolts. Hamlet sees himself as striking down Claudius with his own thunderbolt: the play.

85. *Give him heedful note:* watch him carefully.

87-8. *we will . . . seeming:* we will get together and come to a mutual opinion about his reaction.

89-90. As he often does at a tense moment, Horatio lightens the atmosphere with a joke. *if 'a steal ought:* if he steals anything.

90. *pay:* make good. And as we know, Horatio is not well off!

91-2. As the whole court enters ceremoniously and settles down for the evening's entertainment, Hamlet hastily breaks off the conversation, saying he must behave carelessly.

93. Claudius, probably hoping that this public occasion, unlike the last (Act I, Scene ii), will pass off without Hamlet making it all too clear that his relationship with him is strained, makes a pointedly polite inquiry about his nephew's health. He has learned from the last occasion not to call him 'son'.

94-5. Hamlet, reckless because he feels so near to making a public exposure of his uncle, deliberately misunderstands Claudius's query, taking it to mean 'What are you eating?' *of the chameleon's dish:* This creature was believed to live on air.

95. *promise-cramm'd:* Hamlet is stuffed with empty promises – a remark which the court would take to refer to Hamlet's resentment at being told he is Claudius's heir (Act I, Scene ii, line 109) whereas he could easily have been on the throne himself. A *capon* is a young cock, fattened for eating, and was also a term meaning 'fool'. Hamlet may be hinting that he is not such a fool as to fail to realize that Claudius is plotting to get rid of him. Also, Claudius may well have come straight from one of his many banquets, and Hamlet could be jibing at his interest in food.

96-7. Seeing that Hamlet is in a provocative mood, Claudius tries to dampen down his over-excitement with a repressive remark. *have nothing with:* disown.

98-9. *No, nor mine now:* they have left Hamlet's lips for ever. Having silenced Claudius, Hamlet's restless high spirits lead him to seize on Polonius as the next butt for his wit. *play'd:* acted.

Which I have told thee of my father's death.
I prithee, when thou seest that act afoot,
Even with the very comment of thy soul   80
Observe my uncle. If his occulted guilt
Do not itself unkennel in one speech,
It is a damned ghost that we have seen,
And my imaginations are as foul
As Vulcan's stithy. Give him heedful note;   85
For I mine eyes will rivet to his face;
And, after, we will both our judgments join
In censure of his seeming.

Horatio   Well, my lord.
If 'a steal aught the whilst this play is playing,
And scape detecting, I will pay the theft.   90

*Enter trumpets and kettledrums. Danish march.
Sound a flourish*

Enter KING, QUEEN, POLONIUS, OPHELIA, ROSEN-
CRANTZ, GUILDENSTERN *and other* LORDS *attendant,
with the* GUARD *carrying torches*

Hamlet

They are coming to the play; I must be idle. Get you a
place.

King

How fares our cousin Hamlet?

Hamlet

Excellent, i' faith; of the chameleon's dish. I eat the
air, promise-cramm'd; you cannot feed capons so.   95

King

I have nothing with this answer, Hamlet; these words
are not mine.

Hamlet

No, nor mine now. [*To* POLONIUS] My lord, you
play'd once i' th' university, you say?

Polonius

That did I, my lord, and was accounted a good actor. 100

101. *enact:* act.

102-3. Shakespeare had just written his play *Julius Caesar*, and perhaps was waiting for a suitable opportunity to use the joke that Hamlet goes on to make!

104-5. With a couple of swift puns (Brutus – *brute*, Capitol – *capital*) Hamlet calls this respectable elder statesman a calf. By now, the whole court must be waiting either anxiously, or with eager anticipation, for what Hamlet will say or do next. He does not disappoint them.
106. *stay upon your patience:* Is there a hint of criticism in this remark? *stay upon:* wait for. *patience:* convenience.

108. Hamlet publicly snubs his mother by refusing to sit with her, and going to sit at Ophelia's feet (with whom he quarrelled a few hours earlier). One of his reasons for doing this is, of course, that as the queen must be sitting next to her husband, Hamlet would not be able to watch his face from a seat beside her. Meanwhile, Horatio also must have taken up his position somewhere opposite Claudius. *metal:* stuff (Ophelia is an attractive piece of goods).
109. Polonius triumphantly calls attention to Hamlet's preference for Ophelia, for it supports his theory about Hamlet's 'madness'. He would not have relished Hamlet's treating Ophelia so freely before he hoped something might come of it.
111-19. Ophelia, not knowing what to expect next from her former lover, makes the mistake of seeming prudish, at which Hamlet enjoys embarrassing her further by making improper jokes.
110. *Lady . . . lap:* Hamlet makes the mock-romantic gesture of prostrating himself before his lady.

114. *country matters:* something earthy.

116. *fair:* nice.

Hamlet

What did you enact?

Polonius

I did enact Julius Cæsar; I was kill'd i' th' Capitol;
Brutus kill'd me.

Hamlet

It was a brute part of him to kill so capital a calf
there. Be the players ready? 105

Rosencrantz

Ay, my lord; they stay upon your patience.

Queen

Come hither, my dear Hamlet, sit by me.

Hamlet

No, good mother; here's metal more attractive.

Polonius [*To the* KING]

O, ho! do you mark that?

Hamlet

Lady, shall I lie in your lap? 110

Lying down at OPHELIA's *feet*

Ophelia

No, my lord.

Hamlet

I mean, my head upon your lap?

Ophelia

Ay, my lord.

Hamlet

Do you think I meant country matters?

Ophelia

I think nothing, my lord. 115

Hamlet

That's a fair thought to lie between maid's legs.

Ophelia

What is, my lord?

Hamlet

Nothing.

119. In what tone does Ophelia say this – gaily, or with reproach or surprise? Little does she know the real cause of Hamlet's levity.

122-4. Hamlet replies bitterly that he is the world's jolliest comedian. His mother sets an example of cheerfulness, in spite of the fact that his father has only just died.

125. Ophelia's solemn correction of Hamlet's exaggeration gives us a rough idea of how long ago it was that he saw the ghost, as on that day he said it was less than two months since his father died (Act I, Scene ii, line 138); therefore he has already delayed his revenge for over two months.

126. *So long?* Hamlet is sarcastic: four months is much too long to mourn anybody.

126-7. *Nay then . . . sables:* 'Mourning can go to the devil, I'll dress up in furs like a prosperous elderly gentleman.' By choosing *sables*, a kind of fur associated with old men, Hamlet implies ironically that four months is such a long period that he has grown old in it.

128-30. *there's hope . . . then:* 'If a king whom all admired is remembered for four months, a really great man's memory may last for six – but only if he has made sure of this by building churches' (in which prayers would be said for him, as founder). *by'r lady:* by Our Lady.

130-1. *shall 'a suffer not thinking on:* he will be forgotten.

131. *the hobby-horse:* a carnival horse carried in the Mayday celebrations which the Puritans of Shakespeare's day banned, because they considered them immoral.

132-3. Hamlet sings a line of a popular ballad.

Stage Direction. To the sound of oboes, a mime of the story of the play to follow is performed. The murder shown is exactly like that described by the ghost, except that there is no indication that the killer is the brother of his victim. As Hamlet disparaged dumb-shows earlier in this scene (line 12), and as it gives the whole game away before the play has even started, it seems unlikely that he knew it was going to happen. His next remarks certainly could be taken to mean that he was angry with the players. Claudius, however, says nothing. Perhaps he is not watching yet, but is chatting with the queen or Polonius about Hamlet's behaviour, waiting for the main entertainment to begin. Even if he was looking, the mime may have been so stylized that it was not easy to follow, being, as Hamlet said, *inexplicable. declines:* leans. *makes passionate action:* gestures emotionally. *Mutes:* silent actors.

Ophelia
  You are merry, my lord.
Hamlet
  Who, I?   120
Ophelia
  Ay, my lord.
Hamlet
  O God, your only jig-maker! What should a man do
  but be merry? For look you how cheerfully my
  mother looks, and my father died within's two hours.
Ophelia
  Nay, 'tis twice two months, my lord.   125
Hamlet
  So long? Nay then, let the devil wear black, for I'll
  have a suit of sables. O heavens! die two months ago,
  and not forgotten yet? Then there's hope a great
  man's memory may outlive his life half a year; but,
  by'r lady, 'a must build churches, then; or else shall   130
  'a suffer not thinking on, with the hobby-horse,
  whose epitaph is 'For O, for O, the hobby-horse is
  forgot!'

  The trumpet sounds. Hautboys play. The Dumb
                Show enters
  Enter a KING *and a* QUEEN, *very lovingly; the* QUEEN
  embracing him and he her. She kneels, and makes
  show of protestation unto him. He takes her up, and
  declines his head upon her neck. He lies him down
  upon a bank of flowers; she, seeing him asleep, leaves
  him. Anon comes in a FELLOW, *takes off his crown,*
  kisses it, pours poison in the sleeper's ears, and
  leaves him. The QUEEN *returns; finds the* KING *dead,*
  and makes passionate action. The POISONER, *with*
  some two or three MUTES, *comes in again, seeming to*
  condole with her. The dead body is carried away. The
  POISONER woos the QUEEN *with gifts: she seems harsh*
  awhile, but in the end accepts his love
                Exeunt

134, 136. Ophelia, for one, cannot follow the mime, but guesses that it tells the story of the play.

135. *miching mallecho:* sneaking mischief. This may be a comment either on the actors' giving away the plot, or on the wicked murder and theft of a crown that they have just watched, or both at once.

137. *this fellow:* a slightly contemptuous way of referring to the actor who has stepped forward to introduce the play. Hamlet's affability towards the players has disappeared.

137-8. *keep counsel:* keep a secret. Hamlet seems to be afraid that they are now also going to have a spoken summary of the story, which would spoil his plan, but the prologue's speech is absurdly brief.

143. *naught:* naughty, improper; but Ophelia sounds merrier, as though she is beginning to enjoy Hamlet's teasing. *mark:* attend to.

145. *stooping to your clemency:* throwing ourselves on your mercy.

146. *your hearing:* you to listen to us.

147. Perhaps with relief that the player has said no more than this, Hamlet jeers at the prologue's brevity, comparing it to the sort of trite little motto that used to be inscribed on rings.

149. Just as Ophelia seems to be relaxing in Hamlet's company, he disconcerts her by making a bitter comment on the fickleness of women, directed, perhaps, as much against his mother as her.

150-255. The play that now begins also deals with women's unfaithfulness, but its style contrasts sharply with the dialogue we have just been listening to, and is even more elaborate and longwinded than that of the speech recited in Act II, Scene ii. The rhyming couplets in which it is written add to the impression of artificiality that helps to set this 'play-within-a-play' apart from the rest of the scene. Shakespeare is obviously enjoying parodying the melodramatic style of some other dramatists of his day!

150-5. These lines simply say: 'We have been married for thirty years.' (Hamlet's parents had been married for about that long.) *Phoebus's cart:* the sun, the chariot of Phoebus Apollo. *Neptune:* the god of the sea. *Tellus:* the god of the earth. *Hymen:* the goddess of marriage. These are all figures from Roman mythology.

Ophelia

What means this, my lord?

Hamlet

Marry, this is miching mallecho; it means mischief.　　*135*

Ophelia

Belike this show imports the argument of the play.

Enter PROLOGUE

Hamlet

We shall know by this fellow: the players cannot keep
counsel; they'll tell all.

Ophelia

Will a' tell us what this show meant?

Hamlet

Ay, or any show that you will show him. Be not you　*140*
asham'd to show, he'll not shame to tell you what it
means.

Ophelia

You are naught, you are naught. I'll mark the play.

Prologue　　　*For us, and for our tragedy,*
　　　　　　　Here stooping to your clemency,　　　*145*
　　　　　　　We beg your hearing patiently.

Exit

Hamlet

Is this a prologue, or the posy of a ring?

Ophelia

'Tis brief, my lord.

Hamlet

As woman's love.

Enter the PLAYER KING *and* QUEEN

Player King

Full thirty times hath Phœbus' cart gone round　　*150*
Neptune's salt wash and Tellus' orbed ground,
And thirty dozen moons with borrowed sheen
About the world have times twelve thirties been,

173

156-7. *So many . . . done:* I hope we shall be together for another thirty years.

158-68. The queen in the play says that she is worried about her husband's health lately, but perhaps her love for him makes her over-anxious.

169-73. The 'king' says that he will die soon, and then his wife may remarry someone as loving as himself.

173-6. The player queen interrupts, saying that a woman who remarries must have hated her first husband enough to kill him.

177. *wormwood:* a bitter-tasting plant, used medicinally. Hamlet means 'That's a bitter pill to swallow'. A horrible suspicion must be in his mind; how much did his mother know about the death of his father? How, one wonders, does Gertrude react to what the player queen said? The rest of the court must also be asking themselves this.

180-1. She adds that marrying again, anyway, is as bad as killing one's first husband.

182-95. In a speech that Hamlet must feel is all too true, the actor says that he believes his wife, but so often in this life people fail to live up to something they have promised in the heat of the moment, because the emotion which prompted them to do it has died down. Extremes of either happiness or unhappiness are so similar that a little thing can make one turn into the other.

Since love our hearts and Hymen did our hands
Unite comutual in most sacred bands.   155
Player Queen
So many journeys may the sun and moon
Make us again count o'er ere love be done!
But, woe is me, you are so sick of late,
So far from cheer and from your former state,
That I distrust you. Yet, though I distrust,   160
Discomfort you, my lord, it nothing must;
For women fear too much even as they love,
And women's fear and love hold quantity,
In neither aught, or in extremity.
Now, what my love is, proof hath made you know;   165
And as my love is siz'd, my fear is so.
Where love is great, the littlest doubts are fear;
Where little fears grow great, great love grows there.
Player King
Faith, I must leave thee, love, and shortly too:
My operant powers their functions leave to do;   170
And thou shalt live in this fair world behind,
Honour'd, belov'd; and haply one as kind
For husband shalt thou—
Player Queen   *O, confound the rest!*
Such love must needs be treason in my breast.
In second husband let me be accurst!   175
None wed the second but who kill'd the first.
Hamlet
That's wormwood, wormwood.
Player Queen
The instances that second marriage move
Are base respects of thrift, but none of love.
A second time I kill my husband dead,   180
When second husband kisses me in bed.
Player King
I do believe you think what now you speak;
But what we do determine oft we break.
Purpose is but the slave to memory,

196-211. As life is short, and it is reasonable that one's affections should change with one's circumstances – indeed, they are very closely connected, since those who are prosperous tend to be popular (this reminds one of Hamlet's comments on his father and Claudius) – then his wife may find that fate will cause her to change her mind.

212-19. The player queen swears vehemently that she would deserve the most miserable suffering if she married again.

Of violent birth, but poor validity;   185
Which now, the fruit unripe, sticks on the tree;
But fall unshaken when they mellow be.
Most necessary 'tis that we forget
To pay ourselves what to ourselves is debt.
What to ourselves in passion we propose,   190
The passion ending, doth the purpose lose.
The violence of either grief or joy
Their own enactures with themselves destroy.
Where joy most revels grief doth most lament;
Grief joys, joy grieves, on slender accident.   195
This world is not for aye; nor 'tis not strange
That even our loves should with our fortunes change;
For 'tis a question left us yet to prove,
Whether love lead fortune or else fortune love.
The great man down, you mark his favourite flies;   200
The poor advanc'd makes friends of enemies.
And hitherto doth love on fortune tend;
For who not needs shall never lack a friend,
And who in want a hollow friend doth try,
Directly seasons him his enemy.   205
But, orderly to end where I begun,
Our wills and fates do so contrary run
That our devices still are overthrown;
Our thoughts are ours, their ends none of our own.
So think thou wilt no second husband wed;   210
But die thy thoughts when thy first lord is dead.

Player Queen

Nor earth to me give food, nor heaven light,
Sport and repose lock from me day and night,
To desperation turn my trust and hope,
An anchor's cheer in prison be my scope,   215
Each opposite that blanks the face of joy
Meet what I would have well, and it destroy,
Both here and hence pursue me lasting strife,
If, once a widow, ever I be wife!

H.-G   177

220. Hamlet mockingly hints that the 'queen' may break her word.

221-3. The player king says he wants to be left to go to sleep, and the queen takes a loving farewell of him.

225. Hamlet, in the pause before the 'murderer' enters, pointedly asks his mother what she thinks of the play.

226. Gertrude cautiously says that she thinks her counterpart in the play is too emphatic (she could hardly say she was enjoying herself!)

227. Probably Hamlet stresses the word *she* slightly (though according to the dumb-show the player queen does accept the murderer), implying that his mother is not loyal to her promises.

228-9. Something in Hamlet's manner, together with the sentiments expressed in the play he commissioned, begins to make Claudius uneasy. He asks whether Hamlet has vetted the story of the play to check that there is nothing unsuitable in it.

230-1. 'Oh, no', says Hamlet, 'it's just a comedy.' But he can't resist throwing out the word *poison* to watch Claudius's reaction.

233-9. Hamlet's abrupt, short sentences show how excited he is at the signs of nervousness shown by Claudius's interrogation, and because he knows the crucial part of the play is imminent.

233. The play is the mouse-trap in which Hamlet is going to *catch the conscience of the king* (Act II, Scene ii, line 604). *Marry:* indeed, well. *Tropically:* metaphorically (a 'trope' is a figure of speech); with a pun on 'trap'.

233-4. *This play . . . Vienna:* 'Don't worry,' Hamlet seems to be saying, 'this is nothing to do with Denmark, or you.'

236. *anon:* straight away. *knavish:* wicked.

237-9. *Your Majesty . . . unwrung:* 'that needn't worry innocent people like us – let those who have something on their conscience flinch, like a wretched mare with saddle-sores, for we are unaffected by it.' Some people think that Hamlet is referring to his mother as a *jade*, here, as she certainly has an uneasy conscience.

240. Hamlet's identification of the murderer as *nephew to the King* may relieve Claudius, since it doesn't identify him with the villain (as he may by now have feared), but, on the other hand, the listening court may now see Hamlet as Lucianus, threatening the king, his uncle, through the play, with death if he is not given his dues (the throne). This sort of thing was not unknown in Elizabethan times: Shakespeare's own *Richard II* had been used as a threat against Queen Elizabeth.

Hamlet

  If she should break it now! 220

Player King

  'Tis deeply sworn. Sweet, leave me here awhile;
  My spirits grow dull, and fain I would beguile
  The tedious day with sleep.

[Sleeps]

Player Queen   Sleep rock thy brain,

  And never come mischance between us twain!

[Exit]

Hamlet

  Madam, how like you this play? 225

Queen

  The lady doth protest too much, methinks.

Hamlet

  O, but she'll keep her word.

King

  Have you heard the argument? Is there no offence
  in't?

Hamlet

  No, no; they do but jest, poison in jest; no offence i' 230
  th' world.

King

  What do you call the play?

Hamlet

  'The Mouse-trap.' Marry, how? Tropically. This
  play is the image of a murder done in Vienna:
  Gonzago is the duke's name; his wife, Baptista. You 235
  shall see anon. 'Tis a knavish piece of work; but what
  of that? Your Majesty, and we that have free souls,
  it touches us not. Let the galled jade wince, our
  withers are unwrung.

Enter LUCIANUS

  This is one Lucianus, nephew to the King. 240

241. *a chorus:* a character, or group of characters, who commented o the action of a play, to the audience.

242-3. *I could ... dallying:* I could explain you and your lover to eac other if I could see clearly what was going on. An interpreter used t explain the meaning of puppet shows to the audience. *dallying:* playin around. Hamlet implies that Ophelia's way of being in love (with him is rather mysterious, and perhaps that she treats it as a kind of enter tainment.

244. *keen:* sharp, cruelly witty.

245. Picking up the idea of sharpness, like that of the edge of a knife and pretending that Ophelia also meant 'eager, full of desire', Hamle boldly suggests that he needs to make love to her.

246. Pleasantly shocked, Ophelia says that as Hamlet gets wittier h becomes more improper.

247-8. Reminded, by what she has said, of the marriage service 'take ... for better or for worse' – Hamlet coldly snubs her by implyin, that all marriages are a 'mistake' (perhaps the remark is intended fo his mother to hear). He is too impatient for the play to go on, to tak much interest in this conversation, and tells the actor playing the par of the murderer to stop putting on villainous expressions and begi speaking. He dislikes exaggerated acting.

248-9. *the croaking raven ... revenge;* This is not exactly a prompt being a garbled version of a couple of lines in an old melodrama. Hamle means 'Get on with your ranting.' (But it is interesting that he choose to mention *revenge*, which does not enter into *The Murder of Gonzago)*

250-5. The villain describes with satisfaction how he has the perfec opportunity to commit murder, and how deadly his poison is.

250. *apt:* ready.

251. *Confederate season:* favourable time of day.

252. *of midnight weeds:* from plants gathered at midnight.

253. *With Hecat's ban thrice blasted:* bearing a triple evil curse *Hecate:* the witch goddess.

254. *dire property:* deadly qualities.

255. *On wholesome life usurps:* kills.

256-9. Seeing that the spectacle of someone being poisoned by this very unusual method has been too much for Claudius, who looks very dis- turbed, Hamlet, in wild excitement, interrupts the play, with a summary of the other two relevant features in it, the theft of the victim's property and wife, and reminders that this is just a play after all.

257. *extant:* in existence, in print. *choice:* fine.

261. *false fire:* blank cartridges. Hamlet taunts his normally self- possessed uncle with running off in an undignified way. The queen shows real concern.

Ophelia

You are as good as a chorus, my lord.

Hamlet

I could interpret between you and your love, if I could
see the puppets dallying.

Ophelia

You are keen, my lord, you are keen.

Hamlet

It would cost you a groaning to take off mine edge.   245

Ophelia

Still better, and worse.

Hamlet

So you mis-take your husbands.—Begin, murderer;
pox, leave thy damnable faces and begin. Come; the
croaking raven doth bellow for revenge.

Lucianus

Thoughts black, hands apt, drugs fit, and time agreeing;   250
Confederate season, else no creature seeing;
Thou mixture rank, of midnight weeds collected,
With Hecat's ban thrice blasted, thrice infected,
Thy natural magic and dire property
On wholesome life usurps immediately.   255

[*Pours the poison in his ears*]

Hamlet

'A poisons him i' th' garden for his estate. His name's
Gonzago. The story is extant, and written in very
choice Italian. You shall see anon how the murderer
gets the love of Gonzago's wife.

Ophelia

The King rises.   260

Hamlet

What, frighted with false fire!

Queen   How fares my lord?

Polonius

Give o'er the play.

264. As the evening's entertainment breaks up in confusion, the king calls for the guards with torches to escort him from the room, but somehow it seems also a cry from the heart, for light to relieve his inner darkness.

265-72. Hamlet, forgetting the obligation to avenge his father, now he is sure that Claudius did poison him, is so overjoyed at the success of his plan that he bursts into song, exultantly boasting to Horatio that he is obviously cut out for a dramatic career. He overlooks the fact that Claudius has made no public confession of guilt, and that the court probably attributes his behaviour to disapproval of the tactless theme of the play (the murder of a king, that might well be himself) and of Hamlet's impudent behaviour.

265-8. Hamlet is quoting from some old ballad. The *deer* is Claudius, who will lie awake worrying (*watch*) and the *hart* is Hamlet, who can now have a good sleep.

269-71. *a forest of feathers* and *roses* on *raz'd shoes:* all refer to the gay way Elizabethan actors dressed. The *Provincial roses*, as well as being decorative, covered the tied shoe-laces. *raz'd:* slashed for decoration.

270. *turn Turk:* turn against, let down.

271-2. *a fellowship . . . players:* a partnership in a company of actors.

273. Horatio seems to imply 'Don't be too pleased with yourself yet.'

275-8. Hamlet continues his song, describing how a god-like king (his father) was deposed by – he was going to finish 'an ass' but playfully declines to rhyme.

275. *Damon* and Pythias, like Hamlet and Horatio, were great friends.

278. *paiock:* peacock. The peacock was a symbol of lechery, as well as vanity, in Shakespeare's time. Both qualities, Hamlet thinks, apply to Claudius.

280-1. Hamlet at last calms down sufficiently to say what is in both their minds: he is ready to bet anything that the ghost spoke the truth.

283. *Upon the talk of the poisoning:* Hamlet seems to think that it was when he, or the actor, mentioned poison that Claudius reacted – that is, even before he saw what method of poisoning was employed. We are left still wondering which speech Hamlet actually wrote; could it have been Lucianus's melodramatic description of the poison, or a previous speech, or one that was yet to come when the play was stopped?

285-8. *Come, some music:* To celebrate his triumphant mood, and probably also to cheer up the disappointed players, who must be worried about having displeased the king, Hamlet orders them to provide some music, since their play wasn't popular.

285. In Elizabethan times, *recorders*, an early form of flute, were often used in the theatre and in private entertainments.

King

    Give me some light. Away!

Polonius

    Lights, lights, lights!

Exeunt all but HAMLET *and* HORATIO

Hamlet

    Why, let the strucken deer go weep,   265
    The hart ungalled play;
    For some must watch, while some must sleep;
    Thus runs the world away.
    Would not this, sir, and a forest of feathers—if the
rest of my fortunes turn Turk with me—with two 270
Provincial roses on my raz'd shoes, get me a fellowship in a cry of players, sir?

Horatio

    Half a share.

Hamlet

    A whole one, I.
    For thou dost know, O Damon dear,   275
    This realm dismantled was
    Of Jove himself; and now reigns here
    A very, very—paiock.

Horatio

    You might have rhym'd.

Hamlet

    O good Horatio, I'll take the ghost's word for a 280
thousand pound. Didst perceive?

Horatio

    Very well, my lord.

Hamlet

    Upon the talk of the poisoning.

Horatio

    I did very well note him.

Hamlet

    Ah, ha! Come, some music. Come, the recorders. 285
    For if the King like not the comedy,

287. *belike:* it seems. *perdy:* literally, 'by God'. Perhaps Hamlet is about to say something else about Claudius's dislike of the play, but changes his mind when he sees Rosencrantz and Guildenstern approaching, with a rather self-righteous expression. They, like the rest of the court, have seen nothing odd in the king's behaviour, only in Hamlet's.

289. *vouchsafe:* be so kind as to let me have.

293. Hamlet's manner is irritable. Perhaps he does not care for being addressed as *sir* instead of *my lord*, by someone like Guildenstern.

294-5. Guildenstern meant that Claudius had gone to his room in a very bad mood, but Hamlet blandly chooses the other meaning of *distemper'd* – drunk – mocking Claudius's drinking habits.
295. *choler:* anger. Guildenstern is not amused.

296-299. Hamlet says that it would have been more intelligent to tell the king's doctor that, for if Hamlet tried to cure him Claudius would become even more angry. Hamlet refers to the belief that anger was caused by too much of a certain kind of bile (*choler*) in the body, which could be cured by purging; Hamlet is probably also thinking that Claudius's soul, too, needs purging, but that this would mean his having to face God's anger.
300-1. *put your discourse . . . affair:* speak less incoherently and don't change the subject.

302. *tame:* Hamlet will be no longer 'wild'. *Pronounce:* speak. He refuses to take the conversation seriously, as his next remark also shows.
305. Hamlet pretends he thinks that Guildenstern is some kind of gift.
306-10. Guildenstern complains that Hamlet is being sarcastic, and says that if the prince will give him a sensible answer he will pass on his mother's message; otherwise, he will ask Hamlet's permission to go, and that will be the end of it.

184

Why, then, belike he likes it not, perdy.
Come, some music.

Re-enter ROSENCRANTZ *and* GUILDENSTERN

Guildenstern
Good, my lord, vouchsafe me a word with you.
Hamlet
Sir, a whole history.   *290*
Guildenstern
The King, sir—
Hamlet
Ay, sir, what of him?
Guildenstern
Is, in his retirement, marvellous distemper'd.
Hamlet
With drink, sir?
Guildenstern
No, my lord, rather with choler.   *295*
Hamlet
Your wisdom should show itself more richer to
signify this to his doctor; for for me to put him to
his purgation would perhaps plunge him into far
more choler.
Guildenstern
Good my lord, put your discourse into some frame, *300*
and start not so wildly from my affair.
Hamlet
I am tame, sir. Pronounce.
Guildenstern
The Queen, your mother, in most great affliction of
spirit, hath sent me to you.
Hamlet
You are welcome.   *305*
Guildenstern
Nay, good my lord, this courtesy is not of the right
breed. If it shall please you to make me a wholesome
answer, I will do your mother's commandment; if

313-15. Hamlet makes a sly reference to the fact that he is believed ma (*wholesome:* healthy; *my wit's diseas'd:* 'I have a mental illness'), an then hints that he does not care for their familiar way of calling thei queen simply *your mother.*
314-15. *command:* have.
316. *the matter:* the point.

318. *admiration:* wonder.

319. *stonish:* astonish. *is there no sequel . . . Impart:* 'surely there is some follow-up? Tell me.' Hamlet speaks mockingly in elaborate language

322. *closet:* private room. Polonius, even before Hamlet's provocative behaviour at the play, suggested that Gertrude should interview her son (Act III, Scene i, line 181-6), while he listens.

324. *were she ten times our mother:* Another hint that Rosencrantz and Guildenstern should speak of her more formally.
324-5. *Have you . . . us:* Any more errands? By his choice of the insulting word *trade* and his use of the 'royal plural', Hamlet puts them in their place.
326. Seeing their mistake, Rosencrantz tries to wheedle himself into Hamlet's good books by an appeal to their old friendship, but this is not likely to work, since it is they who have let Hamlet down by spying on him.
327. Hamlet replies facetiously. *pickers and stealers:* hands, from an old prayer, 'Keep our hands from picking and stealing.'
328. *what is . . . distemper?* why are you out of sorts?
329-30. He hints that if Hamlet does not confide in them he may have to be locked up – which was the usual treatment for madmen in those days.
331. To keep them quiet, Hamlet resurrects their theory that he is suffering from thwarted ambition.

332-3. Eagerly, Rosencrantz enquires how Hamlet can be discontented when he has been told that he will become king after Claudius.

not, your pardon and my return shall be the end of
my business.   *310*

Hamlet
Sir, I cannot.

Rosencrantz
What, my lord?

Hamlet
Make you a wholesome answer; my wit's diseas'd.
But, sir, such answer as I can make, you shall command; or rather, as you say, my mother. Therefore *315*
no more, but to the matter: my mother, you say—

Rosencrantz
Then thus she says: your behaviour hath struck her
into amazement and admiration.

Hamlet
O wonderful son, that can so stonish a mother! But
is there no sequel at the heels of this mother's ad- *320*
miration? Impart.

Rosencrantz
She desires to speak with you in her closet ere you go
to bed.

Hamlet
We shall obey, were she ten times our mother. Have
you any further trade with us?   *325*

Rosencrantz
My lord, you once did love me.

Hamlet
And do still, by these pickers and stealers.

Rosencrantz
Good my lord, what is your cause of distemper? You
do surely bar the door upon your own liberty, if you
deny your griefs to your friend.   *330*

Hamlet
Sir, I lack advancement.

Rosencrantz
How can that be, when you have the voice of the King
himself for your succession in Denmark?

334. The proverb finishes 'the horse starves'; it has a similar meaning to 'Hope deferred maketh the heart sick.' *musty:* stale. Hamlet means both that it is a well-worn proverb and that, as fodder to keep his hope alive, it is unattractive.

336-8. As Hamlet speaks to the players, Guildenstern and Rosencrantz may sidle up to each other behind his back to exchange a private word – or perhaps Hamlet just compares them metaphorically to creeping hunters trying to drive their prey into a trap.

336-7. *To withdraw with you:* 'let's go to one side.' It is not clear whether Hamlet says this to an actor or to his 'friends'.

337. *recover the wind of:* 'get downwind from' so that the hunters' presence will not be detected.

338. *toil:* snare.

339-40. Guildenstern replies that if he has too strong a sense of duty Hamlet must attribute it to his affection.

341. *I do not . . . that:* Hamlet implies that he does not know what Guildenstern means by either *duty* or *love*.

342. *this pipe:* the recorder which he has asked to see, with which he demonstrates Rosencrantz and Guildenstern's presumption in thinking they can do what they like with him (see lines 71-2, above).

347. *know no touch of it:* don't know how to, haven't the knack.

348. *It . . . lying:* Hamlet implies that if they can be deceitful they ought to have sufficient skill to play a simple musical instrument. *govern these ventages:* control these openings, or stops.

350. *discourse:* utter. Hamlet probably demonstrates. Most gentlemen in those days had some skill in music. The fact that they seem to have none makes Rosencrantz and Guildenstern look still more stupid.

352-3. Embarrassed, Guildenstern insists that he cannot play any sort of music on the recorder.

354-63. Emphasizing the words *me* and *my*, Hamlet says that in that case they are insulting him if they think that they are clever enough to analyse and manipulate him. Yet, he says, there is much that is worthwhile that they could gain from him, if only they went the right way about it.

356-7. *would pluck out . . . mystery:* want to dig out my inmost secrets. *pluck:* continues the metaphor of a musical instrument, this time a stringed one.

Hamlet

Ay, sir, but 'While the grass grows'—the proverb is
something musty.   335

Re-enter the PLAYERS, *with recorders*

O, the recorders! Let me see one. To withdraw with
you—why do you go about to recover the wind of
me, as if you would drive me into a toil?

Guildenstern

O my lord, if my duty be too bold, my love is too
unmannerly.   340

Hamlet

I do not well understand that. Will you play upon
this pipe?

Guildenstern

My lord, I cannot.

Hamlet

I pray you.

Guildenstern

Believe me, I cannot.   345

Hamlet

I do beseech you.

Guildenstern

I know no touch of it, my lord.

Hamlet

It is as easy as lying: govern these ventages with your
fingers and thumb, give it breath with your mouth,
and it will discourse most eloquent music. Look you, 350
these are the stops.

Guildenstern

But these cannot I command to any utterance of
harmony; I have not the skill.

Hamlet

Why, look you now, how unworthy a thing you make
of me! You would play upon me; you would seem to 355
know my stops; you would pluck out the heart of my
mystery; you would sound me from my lowest note

189

358. *compass:* range.

359. *organ:* This covers the ideas both of a body and a musical instrument.

360. *'Sblood:* God's blood, an angry oath.

362. *fret:* a pun, meaning (*a*) irritate and (*b*) equip a stringed instrument, such as a guitar, with the little metal bars that form the divisions between the notes on the fingerboard.

364. In what tone do you think Hamlet greets Polonius?

365. *would:* wants to.

366. *presently:* immediately. Polonius has come bustling along to see what all the delay is about.

367-8. Hamlet's response to Polonius's peremptory manner is to remind him that he is a lunatic and a prince that must be humoured.

370. *Methinks:* it seems to me.

371. *is back'd:* has a back.

374-6. Having made Polonius agree to nonsense and look thoroughly silly, Hamlet says he will go and see his mother in a little while, that is, in his own good time.

375. *They . . . bent:* They make me play the fool (or, treat me like a fool) to the limit of my endurance.

to the top of my compass; and there is much music,
excellent voice, in this little organ, yet cannot you
make it speak. 'Sblood, do you think I am easier to 360
be play'd on than a pipe? Call me what instrument
you will, though you can fret me, yet you cannot play
upon me.

Re-enter POLONIUS

God bless you, sir!
Polonius
My lord, the Queen would speak with you, and 365
presently.
Hamlet
Do you see yonder cloud that's almost in shape of a
camel?
Polonius
By th' mass, and 'tis like a camel indeed.
Hamlet
Methinks it is like a weasel. 370
Polonius
It is back'd like a weasel.
Hamlet
Or like a whale?
Polonius
Very like a whale?
Hamlet
Then I will come to my mother by and by. [*Aside*]
They fool me to the top of my bent.—I will come by 375
and by.
Polonius
I will say so.

Exit POLONIUS

Hamlet
'By and by' is easily said. Leave me, friends.

Exeunt all but HAMLET

380-90. This exhausting day is not yet over. Hamlet's excitement has
died down during his brush with these irritating men and he is sobered
by the lateness of the hour and the thought of the coming show-down
with his mother. His anger against her has hardened to a point where
he needs to remind himself that he must not harm her. He seems to
have forgotten Claudius for the moment. What was Horatio doing and
thinking while all this was going on?

380. *churchyards yawn:* the dead come out of their graves.

381. *Contagion:* an evil, infectious influence. *Now . . . blood:* Whose
blood? This savage remark is horrifying, coming from the normally
civilized Hamlet.

382-3. *as the day . . . look on:* Hamlet feels he is capable of doing
terrible deeds in the darkness of the night that by day would seem too
horrible.

383. *Soft!* What am I saying? I must pull myself together.

384. *nature:* Hamlet's natural love for his mother.

385. The notorious emperor *Nero* put his own mother to death. *firm
bosom:* steady heart.

386. *unnatural:* see note on nature, above, line 384.

388-90. Hamlet says that he will attack her with words but not with
weapons. He will say things that he must not allow his impulses to act
on. However much he scolds his mother he must not follow up his
words with deeds.

Hamlet's activities really have alarmed Claudius. Without waiting for
the result of the interview with his mother, he decides to pack Hamlet
off to England immediately, taking the line, in public, that Hamlet's
hysterical behaviour, and his obvious hostility towards him personally,
make sending this dangerous madman away the only prudent course.
Claudius does not dare to lock Hamlet up, for reasons which he
explains later, and he does not seem to fear that Hamlet will confide in
Rosencrantz and Guildenstern on the journey, and gain their support:
why not?

1-2. *I like . . . range:* Claudius says that he doesn't like the way Hamlet
is behaving and his own life isn't safe while this madman is roaming
around (which of course it isn't).

3. He says he will get their papers ready immediately (even though it is
the middle of the night).

4. *shall along:* shall go with.

5-7. *The terms . . . brows:* my position as head of state makes it impossible for me to tolerate such immediate danger as Hamlet's looks
threaten.

7. *provide:* get ready.

8-10. Guildenstern obsequiously says how important it is to protect the
many subjects who are dependent on Claudius from losing their king.

11-23. Rosencrantz goes one better, with an elaborate speech on the
same theme. Every ordinary individual, he says, has to use all his wits
to protect himself from harm (self-preservation is certainly uppermost
in his and his partner's minds) but the person on whose well-being so

'Tis now the very witching time of night,
When churchyards yawn, and hell itself breathes out   380
Contagion to this world. Now could I drink hot blood,
And do such bitter business as the day
Would quake to look on. Soft! now to my mother.
O heart, lose not thy nature; let not ever
The soul of Nero enter this firm bosom.   385
Let me be cruel, not unnatural:
I will speak daggers to her, but use none.
My tongue and soul in this be hypocrites—
How in my words somever she be shent,
To give them seals never, my soul, consent!   390

Exit

SCENE III—*Elsinore. The Castle*

Enter KING, ROSENCRANTZ *and* GUILDENSTERN
King
I like him not; nor stands it safe with us
To let his madness range. Therefore prepare you;
I your commission will forthwith dispatch,
And he to England shall along with you.
The terms of our estate may not endure   5
Hazard so near's as doth hourly grow
Out of his brows.
Guildenstern   We will ourselves provide.
Most holy and religious fear it is
To keep those many many bodies safe
That live and feed upon your Majesty.   10
Rosencrantz
The single and peculiar life is bound
With all the strength and armour of the mind
To keep itself from noyance; but much more
That spirit upon whose weal depends and rests
The lives of many. The cease of majesty   15

11-23. many people depend has to be extra careful. When a king dies his death, like a whirlpool, draws everything down with it. The king is like a huge wheel erected on the top of a hill (perhaps at the head of a mine-shaft), which has countless little attachments; when it falls, it drags the whole lot down with it, in terrible confusion. Rosencrantz sums up with a self-satisfied couplet, saying that a king's troubles are shared by everyone.

20. *mortis'd:* firmly fixed.

21. *annexment:* attachment. *petty consequence:* little accessory.

24-6. Claudius has employed flattery too often himself to be much impressed with this. Rather impatiently, he tells them to get ready for the journey, because something must be done to curb the cause of their anxiety, who at the moment can do what he likes.

27-35. In his turn, Polonius is pursuing his plan to investigate Hamlet's madness, unaware that this is already rather out-of-date. He has come straight from his conversation with Hamlet in the last scene.

28. Polonius has found another screen of tapestry (*arras*) in the queen's room, to hide behind.

29. *the process:* what goes on. *tax him home:* scold him severely.

30. *as you said:* Why does Polonius say that the *king* suggested the plan? (See Act III, Scene i, lines 181-6.)

31. *meet:* a good idea. *more audience:* other listener. ·

32. *nature makes them partial:* they are naturally biased.

33. *The speech:* what they say. *of vantage:* from a vantage point.

35-72. Claudius dismisses Polonius calmly, but when he is left alone we see for the first time a resemblance to his nephew: an ability to suppress violent misery under a self-possessed manner when in public. We learn that this apparently confident and imperturbable criminal is in deep and lonely despair, and we cannot help feeling some sympathy for him in this speech, for he seems more troubled about his wickedness than the fact that Hamlet has found him out (if indeed he realizes this).

36-8. Claudius says that he has committed a foul crime, offensive to God and stinking to the skies.

37. *primal eldest:* first and most ancient. Claudius is thinking of the murder of Abel by his brother Cain (a death which he mentioned in Act I, Scene ii, line 105).

38. *A brother's murder:* For the first time, we have definite proof that Claudius did, in fact, murder his brother, so that Hamlet is right in trusting the ghost's word.

38-43. *Pray . . . neglect:* He is troubled (like Shakespeare's Macbeth) by his inability to pray, even though he wishes and tries very hard to do so. His feeling of guilt is so strong that it overrides his efforts to pray, and so, like someone who cannot decide which of two jobs to start on, Claudius does nothing about either his guilt or his prayer. (Hamlet, then, is not the only one who puts things off).

43-51. *What if . . . past:* Claudius says that surely God has enough mercy to forgive even his wickedness, which he feels is clinging to his hand like blood. What is mercy for, he asks, if not to meet the sinner face to face; and hasn't prayer two uses – helping one not only to resist temptation but also to ask for pardon if one has fallen? This gives him renewed hope, as his crime is, after all, in the past.

194

Dies not alone, but like a gulf doth draw
What's near it with it. It is a massy wheel,
Fix'd on the summit of the highest mount,
To whose huge spokes ten thousand lesser things
Are mortis'd and adjoin'd; which when it falls,   20
Each small annexment, petty consequence,
Attends the boist'rous ruin. Never alone
Did the king sigh, but with a general groan.

King

Arm you, I pray you, to this speedy voyage;
For we will fetters put about this fear,   25
Which now goes too free-footed.

Rosencrantz   We will haste us.

    Exeunt ROSENCRANTZ *and* GUILDENSTERN
    Enter POLONIUS

Polonius

My lord, he's going to his mother's closet.
Behind the arras I'll convey myself
To hear the process. I'll warrant she'll tax him home;
And, as you said, and wisely was it said,   30
'Tis meet that some more audience than a mother,
Since nature makes them partial, should o'erhear
The speech, of vantage. Fare you well, my liege.
I'll call upon you ere you go to bed,
And tell you what I know.

King   Thanks, dear my lord.   35

    Exit POLONIUS

O, my offence is rank, it smells to heaven;
It hath the primal eldest curse upon't—
A brother's murder! Pray can I not,
Though inclination be as sharp as will.
My stronger guilt defeats my strong intent,   40
And, like a man to double business bound,
I stand in pause where I shall first begin,
And both neglect. What if this cursed hand

51-64. But, O . . . evidence: Having decided that prayer should do some good, he comes up against the difficulty of not knowing how to start. He can hardly ask for his murder to be pardoned if he refuses to give up what he gained by it: the crown, power, and Gertrude. It is unlikely that he will be let off and allowed to keep the proceeds of the crime. In this wicked world a criminal can buy himself out of trouble, sometimes even with the money he has stolen, but in heaven there is no bribery; there every deed shows itself for what it is, and one has to look one's sins in the face and bear witness to them.

64-9. What then . . . engag'd: In desperation Claudius decides to try to repent, since that is all that is left, and repentance ought to be able to achieve forgiveness. Then he finds that he cannot bring himself to be really sorry, if this means giving up all he has gained. His soul feels like a trapped bird (a sticky substance called bird-lime used to be smeared on branches to catch birds), that becomes more tangled up the more it struggles to get away.

69-72. Help angels . . . well: He tells himself to kneel down and try, making an effort to soften his hard heart and attain the innocence of a child. He tentatively hopes for the best.

73. When Hamlet comes in, on his way to his mother's room, he finds himself with the perfect opportunity to do his duty and obtain his revenge, as Claudius is kneeling down alone with his back to him, unaware of his presence, and has shown by his behaviour at the play that he is guilty. Yet Hamlet spares him, for now. *pat:* easily.

74. And now I'll do't: At this point Hamlet probably draws his sword – and then changes his mind. If he kills his uncle while he is praying, he thinks, Claudius may go straight to heaven, because at that moment his soul will be pure.

75-9. This is not revenge, says Hamlet. This needs to be considered: a wicked man has killed his father and, as a reward, his only son sends the murderer to heaven.

Were thicker than itself with brother's blood,
Is there not rain enough in the sweet heavens   45
To wash it white as snow? Whereto serves mercy
But to confront the visage of offence?
And what's in prayer but this twofold force,
To be forestalled ere we come to fall,
Or pardon'd being down? Then I'll look up;   50
My fault is past. But, O, what form of prayer
Can serve my turn? 'Forgive me my foul murder'!
That cannot be; since I am still possess'd
Of those effects for which I did the murder—
My crown, mine own ambition, and my queen.   55
May one be pardon'd and retain th' offence?
In the corrupted currents of this world
Offence's gilded hand may shove by justice;
And oft 'tis seen the wicked prize itself
Buys out the law. But 'tis not so above: 60
There is no shuffling; there the action lies
In his true nature; and we ourselves compell'd,
Even to the teeth and forehead of our faults,
To give in evidence. What then? What rests?
Try what repentance can. What can it not?   65
Yet what can it when one can not repent?
O wretched state! O bosom black as death!
O limed soul, that, struggling to be free,
Art more engag'd! Help, angels. Make assay:
Bow, stubborn knees; and, heart, with strings of steel,   70
Be soft as sinews of the new-born babe.
All may be well.

Retires and kneels
Enter HAMLET

Hamlet
Now might I do it pat, now 'a is a-praying;
And now I'll do't—and so 'a goes to heaven,
And so am I reveng'd. That would be scann'd: 75
A villain kills my father; and for that,

79. *this is . . . revenge:* that is reward not punishment.

80-2. Claudius killed Hamlet's father when he was unprepared spiritually, after a meal (not fasting in repentance) with all his faults in full bloom, and only God knows what state his soul's account is in. Has Hamlet forgotten the ghost?

83-6. 'According to the beliefs of our religion,' thinks Hamlet, 'He will not be treated lightly. Therefore, it is not revenge to kill Claudius when he is confessing his sins and having them forgiven, so that he is fit and prepared for the afterlife.'

88. Hamlet sheathes his sword again, saying that he will take a more terrible revenge than this. *hent:* grasp (and also, 'seizing of an opportunity').

89. *in his rage:* Wrath was one of the seven deadly sins. Have we ever seen Claudius in a fury?

91. *At game:* gambling.

92. *relish:* flavour, hint.

93-5. *Then trip . . . goes:* 'Catch him out by killing him then, so that he falls headling into hell.' Is this vindictiveness typical of the Hamlet we know? Perhaps he is just finding an excuse for not killing Claudius just now. (How much in character would it be for Hamlet to stab an unarmed man in the back?) On the other hand, compare Act I, Scene ii, line 182-3.

95. *stays:* waits.

96. *This physic . . . days:* Claudius's purging of his soul just enables him to live his wicked life that much longer.

97-8. Ironically, we learn that Claudius has not succeeded in praying properly anyway, so that Hamlet, according to his beliefs, would have sent him to hell after all, if he had killed him then. Both of them, therefore, at the end of this scene, are left dissatisfied.

SCENE IV

Meanwhile, Polonius has hurried to the queen's room, in time to prompt her, with his usual self-importance, in what she has to say. It does not occur to either of them that Hamlet has some scolding to do, too, and that what he has to say to his mother is too intimate for anyone outside the family to overhear.

1. *'A:* he. *lay home:* We would say 'lay into'.

2. *broad:* shameless.

4. *heat:* anger. The fact that the queen has been trying to divert Claudius's anger from Hamlet bears out our impression that she really is fond of her son. Later on, she continues to try to protect him. *I'll . . here:* Polonius indicates the arras behind which he will hide.

I, his sole son, do this same villain send
To heaven.
Why, this is hire and salary, not revenge.
'A took my father grossly, full of bread,   80
With all his crimes broad blown, as flush as May;
And how his audit stands who knows save heaven?
But in our circumstance and course of thought
'Tis heavy with him; and am I then reveng'd
To take him in the purging of his soul,   85
When he is fit and season'd for his passage?
No.
Up, sword, and know thou a more horrid hent.
When he is drunk asleep, or in his rage,
Or in th' incestuous pleasure of his bed;   90
At game, a-swearing, or about some act
That has no relish of salvation in't—
Then trip him, that his heels may kick at heaven,
And that his soul may be as damn'd and black
As hell, whereto it goes. My mother stays.   95
This physic but prolongs thy sickly days.

Exit

King [Rising]
  My words fly up, my thoughts remain below.
  Words without thoughts never to heaven go.

Exit

SCENE IV—*The Queen's closet*
              Enter QUEEN *and* POLONIUS

Polonius
  'A will come straight. Look you lay home to him;
  Tell him his pranks have been too broad to bear with,
  And that your Grace hath screen'd and stood between
  Much heat and him. I'll silence me even here.

5. *round:* firm. In what tone does Hamlet call to his mother?

6. The queen tells Polonius not to worry – she will do as he says.

8. Hamlet's abruptness should have been a warning to his mother that he is not in a very docile mood.

9-10. The queen could hardly have chosen her words more unfortunately, for Hamlet is able to twist them quickly to refer not to Claudius but to his real father, whom his mother has let down.

11. *idle:* foolish.

12. *Go, go:* Hamlet mockingly picks up his mother's *Come, come.*

13. The queen is startled, as well as shocked, by her son's use of the word *wicked.* Hamlet does not conceal his impatience with her.

14. The queen asks indignantly if he has forgotten that he is speaking to his mother. *rood:* cross.

17. Finding that any authority she ever had over Hamlet has gone, and quite unable to cope with his unexpected rudeness and defiance (particularly embarrassing to her because she knows Polonius is listening), the queen moves to call for someone, probably Claudius, who will be able to manage Hamlet – 'Your father will have to deal with you', she implies.

18-20. Hamlet grabs her and forces her into a chair so roughly that the queen is terrified: perhaps Hamlet really is a violent madman. He says she will have to listen to what he tells her of her real nature (his image of holding up a mirror in front of her is similar to the way he described the rôle of drama in Act III, Scene ii, line 23).

Pray you be round with him.

Hamlet [*Within*]   Mother, mother, mother!   5

Queen

I'll warrant you. Fear me not. Withdraw, I hear him
coming.

POLONIUS *goes behind the arras*
Enter HAMLET

Hamlet

Now, mother, what's the matter?

Queen

Hamlet, thou hast thy father much offended.

Hamlet

Mother, you have my father much offended.   10

Queen

Come, come, you answer with an idle tongue.

Hamlet

Go, go, you question with a wicked tongue.

Queen

Why, how now, Hamlet!

Hamlet   What's the matter now?

Queen

Have you forgot me?

Hamlet   No, by the rood, not so:

You are the Queen, your husband's brother's wife;   15
And—would it were not so!—you are my mother.

Queen

Nay then, I'll set those to you that can speak.

Hamlet

Come, come, and sit you down; you shall not budge.
You go not till I set you up a glass
Where you may see the inmost part of you.   20

Queen

What wilt thou do? Thou wilt not murder me?
Help, help, ho!

23-5. Instead of rushing to his queen's rescue like a loyal subject, Polonius cowers in his hiding place, also squeaking for help. Not knowing who it is, but sure that anyone hiding in the queen's private room is up to no good, and no better than vermin, Hamlet swiftly runs the sword that a few minutes before spared Claudius, through the tapestry, and into Polonius, who has eavesdropped once too often.

26-7. When he finds that the queen, instead of being relieved by his prompt dealing with some sort of treachery, is dismayed, Hamlet is disconcerted. Then for a moment he has a wild hope: could it be Claudius, the only person with any business there? If so, he would certainly not have died in a state of grace. (In the heat of the moment, Hamlet does not remember that he left Claudius praying a moment before.)

29-30. In his confusion and anger that she blames him for a quite understandable action, Hamlet comes out with the terrible suspicion that he has been harbouring, but has been reluctant to recognize (see Act III, Scene ii, line 177 and note): she may have connived at his father's death.

31. Gertrude is genuinely startled, and the rest of the play suggests that she is innocent of this guilt (though we never have definite proof). She may think that Hamlet is threatening to kill her present husband, until she takes in the second half of the sentence. *it was my word:* that's what I said.

32-3. *Thou . . . better:* Finding it is only the pathetic old busybody Polonius whom he killed, Hamlet wryly dismisses him with the comment that he thought he was his superior, the king; then, as though this incident were a casual interruption, he turns back to the queen.

34. *busy:* busybody-like.

35-9. Telling the queen, who is no doubt crying, to sit down again, Hamlet says that he intends to make her really upset, if she is still capable of feeling.

37. *it . . . stuff:* any impression can be made on it.

38. *damned custom:* wicked habits. *braz'd:* hardened, made her 'as bold as brass'.

39. *proof:* armour. *bulwark:* barrier. *sense:* proper feeling.

40. *wag thy tongue:* speak.

41-6. *Such an act . . . oaths:* Something, says Hamlet, that shames her modesty, makes any virtue she possesses seem hypocritical, destroys the beauty of her innocent love for her father, and brands her as a harlot (these, when convicted, were branded on the forehead), showing her marriage vows to have been empty promises. Hamlet is tormented by the idea that even while his father was alive Gertrude was corrupt.

Polonius [*Behind*]
  What, ho! help, help, help!
Hamlet [*Draws*]
  How now! a rat? Dead, for a ducat, dead!

Kills POLONIUS *with a pass through the arras*

Polonius [*Behind*]
  O, I am slain!   25
Queen
  O me, what hast thou done?
Hamlet   Nay, I know not:
  Is it the King?
Queen
  O, what a rash and bloody deed is this!
Hamlet
  A bloody deed!—almost as bad, good mother,
  As kill a king and marry with his brother.   30
Queen
  As kill a king!
Hamlet   Ay, lady, it was my word.

Parting the arras

  Thou wretched, rash, intruding fool, farewell!
  I took thee for thy better. Take thy fortune;
  Thou find'st to be too busy is some danger.
  Leave wringing of your hands. Peace; sit you down,   35
  And let me wring your heart; for so I shall,
  If it be made of penetrable stuff;
  If damned custom have not braz'd it so
  That it be proof and bulwark against sense.
Queen
  What have I done that thou dar'st wag thy tongue   40
  In noise so rude against me?
Hamlet   Such an act
  That blurs the grace and blush of modesty;
  Calls virtue hypocrite; takes off the rose
  From the fair forehead of an innocent love,

46-52. Her act took the whole meaning out of her marriage contract, and desecrated its religious significance. The very sky blushes above the earth with a hot face, as though the Day of Judgment were coming, and it is disgusted by what she has done. (Whether a storm is actually brewing outside or not, one certainly takes place in this scene between mother and son, and clears the air.)

52-3. *Ay me . . . index?* What are you working up to by all this shouting? By using the word *thunders*, Gertrude also picks up Hamlet's description of a storm approaching.

54-68. *Look here . . . moor:* Hamlet makes his mother look at the contrast between two pictures, one of his father and the other of his uncle, which may be hanging on the wall of the queen's room, or worn as miniatures around their necks, or perhaps they are purely imaginary.

55. *counterfeit presentment:* portraits.

56. *this brow:* his father's.

57. *Hyperion* was the sun-god, with whom Hamlet compared his father in Act I, Scene ii, line 140. *front of Jove:* the forehead of the king of the gods, with whom Hamlet identified his father in Act III, Scene ii, line 277.

58. *Mars:* the Roman god of war.

59. *A station . . . Mercury:* he holds himself like the graceful messenger of the gods.

60. *lighted:* alighted. *heaven-kissing:* high.

61-3. *A combination . . . man:* an outward appearance that seemed to combine the attributes of all the gods, as though to say 'This is what a man should be like.'

64. The word *was* is stressed.

65. *Here is your husband:* Claudius.

65-6. *like . . . brother:* infecting his healthy brother like a diseased ear of corn.

67. *this fair mountain:* the older Hamlet.

68. *batten:* eat gluttonously. *moor*, being an undistinguished stretch of wasteland, contrasts with the *fair mountain*, but it also probably refers to Claudius's dark complexion, whereas *fair*, together with the references to Hyperion, suggests that Hamlet's father was light-skinned (therefore more good-looking, according to Elizabethan standards). *Ha!* is an angry exclamation.

69-71. *You cannot . . . judgment:* Hamlet says his mother's reason for marrying again cannot have been love, for, at her age, physical passion is more amenable to being restrained by common-sense. What could be more insulting to a woman than to call her middle-aged, and imply that she is 'past it'?

71-82. *and what judgment . . . mope:* He says that she must have some sort of perception, or she wouldn't be alive, but it must be paralysed, for even a lunatic would not make such a mistake. No-one's common-sense has ever been so completely overcome by madness that it would not have been able to discriminate between two such different men. She must have been deceived in a game of blind-man's buff with the devil, then, because even if she lacked one, or nearly all, of her five senses, or only had part of one left, she could not have acted so stupidly. She should have been able to smell out the truth about Claudius.

And sets a blister there; makes marriage-vows 45
As false as dicers' oaths. O, such a deed
As from the body of contraction plucks
The very soul, and sweet religion makes
A rhapsody of words. Heaven's face does glow
O'er this solidity and compound mass 50
With heated visage, as against the doom—
Is thought-sick at the act.

Queen   Ay me, what act,
That roars so loud and thunders in the index?

Hamlet

Look here upon this picture and on this,
The counterfeit presentment of two brothers. 55
See what a grace was seated on this brow;
Hyperion's curls; the front of Jove himself;
An eye like Mars, to threaten and command;
A station like the herald Mercury
New lighted on a heaven-kissing hill— 60
A combination and a form indeed
Where every god did seem to set his seal,
To give the world assurance of a man.
This was your husband. Look you now what follows:
Here is your husband, like a mildew'd ear 65
Blasting his wholesome brother. Have you eyes?
Could you on this fair mountain leave to feed,
And batten on this moor? Ha! have you eyes?
You cannot call it love; for at your age
The heyday in the blood is tame, it's humble, 70
And waits upon the judgment; and what judgment
Would step from this to this? Sense, sure, you have,
Else could you not have motion; but sure that sense
Is apoplex'd; for madness would not err,
Nor sense to ecstasy was ne'er so thrall'd 75
But it reserv'd some quantity of choice
To serve in such a difference. What devil was't
That thus hath cozen'd you at hoodman-blind?
Eyes without feeling, feeling without sight,

80. *sans:* without.

83-9. *Rebellious hell . . . will:* If wicked impulses can cause such a revolution in the character of a middle-aged woman, young people might as well let their virtue go up in flames. We can't criticize behaviour prompted by youthful vitality, when older people are just as lustful, and allow their reason to condone their doing what they fancy.

89-92. Hamlet's tirade against his mother, unlike what he said to Ophelia in Act III, Scene i, seems to be founded on truth, for Gertrude acknowledges with distress that she has deeply ingrained and indelible faults.

92-5. Hardly hearing her, Hamlet goes on to express his disgust for the sexual side of her marriage with Claudius.

93. *rank:* foul. *enseamed:* greasy.

94. *Stew'd in corruption:* wallowing in rottenness. *honeying:* billing and cooing.

95. *Over the nasty sty:* like disgusting pigs.

96. *These words like daggers:* compare *I will speak daggers* (Act III, Scene ii, line 387). Hamlet has achieved his aim.

97-102. Hamlet, completely carried away by the relief of being able to say what he has been bottling up for so long, does not realize he has gone far enough, and continues abusing his uncle.

98. *tithe:* tenth part.

99. *precedent lord:* first husband. *a vice of kings:* a character like Vice, in the old religious plays, who used to wear a fool's parti-coloured costume (compare *shreds and patches*, line 103).

100-2. *A cutpurse . . . pocket:* someone who stole the kingdom, the power and the crown like a furtive pickpocket. Unexpectedly, the ghost enters, dressed not in armour this time, but in ordinary, everyday clothes.

103-5. At first, Hamlet does not notice the apparition, but when he does, awe and shame suddenly overwhelm him.

103. *of shreds and patches:* wearing a professional fool's motley costume.

104-5. *Save me . . . guards:* As when he first saw the ghost, Hamlet asks the angels to protect him, but after his moment of surprise and fear, he addresses it reverently.

106. Seeing her son speaking to what looks like empty air, the queen, like Ophelia, forgets her own misery in compassion.

107-10. Hamlet's guilty feelings about his delay in taking revenge lead him to guess correctly part of the reason why the ghost has come.

107. *tardy:* slow, lazy.

Ears without hands or eyes, smelling sans all,   *80*
Or but a sickly part of one true sense
Could not so mope. O shame! where is thy blush?
Rebellious hell,
If thou canst mutine in a matron's bones,
To flaming youth let virtue be as wax   *85*
And melt in her own fire; proclaim no shame
When the compulsive ardour gives the charge,
Since frost itself as actively doth burn,
And reason panders will.

Queen   O Hamlet, speak no more!
Thou turn'st my eyes into my very soul;   *90*
And there I see such black and grained spots
As will not leave their tinct.

Hamlet   Nay, but to live
In the rank sweat of an enseamed bed,
Stew'd in corruption, honeying and making love
Over the nasty sty!

Queen   O, speak to me no more!   *95*
These words like daggers enter in my ears;
No more, sweet Hamlet.

Hamlet   A murderer and a villain!
A slave that is not twentieth part the tithe
Of your precedent lord; a vice of kings;
A cutpurse of the empire and the rule,   *100*
That from a shelf the precious diadem stole
And put it in his pocket!

Queen
No more!

           Enter GHOST

Hamlet   A king of shreds and patches—
Save me, and hover o'er me with your wings,   *104*
You heavenly guards! What would your gracious figure?

Queen
Alas, he's mad!

Hamlet
Do you not come your tardy son to chide,

207

108. *laps'd . . . passion:* letting opportunities slip by and the wish for revenge to die down. *lets go by:* puts off.

110-11. The ghost renews its instruction to *remember me* and says it has come to renew Hamlet's determination to take revenge. *whet:* sharpen.

112-15. It shows it has also come to prevent Hamlet upsetting his mother further (compare its command in Act I, Scene v, lines 85-8), and asks him to reassure her now that she sees her son apparently having an hallucination.

112. *amazement:* bewilderment, confusion (not just surprise).

114. *Conceit:* imagination.

116. Hamlet speaks perhaps rather absent-mindedly, but in a much gentler, more courteous tone to her.

116-24. The queen, still unable to see anything, remains very anxious about her son's apparent fit of madness.

117. *bend your eye:* gaze. *vacancy:* empty space.

118. *with . . . discourse:* talk to bodiless, insubstantial air.

119-22. *Forth . . . end:* She says that he is staring wildly and that his hair is standing on end.

120. *as . . . alarm:* like sleeping soldiers jumping up when an alarm is sounded.

121. *bedded:* lying flat. In Elizabethan times, such things as fingernails and hair were referred to as *excrements*.

123-4. *Upon . . . patience:* try to calm down. *distemper:* mental disturbance.

126-7. *His form . . . capable:* his ghostly appearance, together with his reason for coming, would move even a stone.

127-30. Speaking again to the ghost, Hamlet says that if it continues to look so sadly at him, it may soften his heart to a point where his firm resolution will disintegrate, and he will weep instead of killing Claudius.

130. *want true colour:* lack its proper character.

That, laps'd in time and passion, lets go by
Th' important acting of your dread command?
O, say!

Ghost

             Do not forget; this visitation   *110*
Is but to whet thy almost blunted purpose.
But look, amazement on thy mother sits.
O, step between her and her fighting soul!
Conceit in weakest bodies strongest works.
Speak to her, Hamlet.   *115*

Hamlet

How is it with you, lady?

Queen   Alas, how is't with you,
That you do bend your eye on vacancy,
And with th' incorporal air do hold discourse?
Forth at your eyes your spirits wildly peep;
And, as the sleeping soldiers in th' alarm,   *120*
Your bedded hairs like life in excrements
Start up and stand an end. O gentle son,
Upon the heat and flame of thy distemper
Sprinkle cool patience! Whereon do you look?

Hamlet

On him, on him! Look you how pale he glares.   *125*
His form and cause conjoin'd, preaching to stones,
Would make them capable.—Do not look upon me,
Lest with this piteous action you convert
My stern effects; then what I have to do
Will want true colour—tears perchance for blood.   *130*

Queen

To whom do you speak this?

Hamlet

Do you see nothing there?

Queen

Nothing at all; yet all that is I see.

Hamlet

Nor did you nothing hear?

137. *in his habit as he liv'd:* in his everyday clothes.

138. *portal:* door.

139-41. *This is . . . cunning in:* The more emphatic Hamlet becomes, following with his eyes the movement of what to her is an illusion, the more convinced the queen becomes that he is mad. She says that this is something invented by his mind, and that madness often causes convincing hallucinations. As Shakespeare has given the ghost lines to speak, he obviously wishes us to believe in the ghost's reality. Why, then, has the queen not seen it, when even Horatio, etc., did?

141. *Ecstasy!* Madness!

142-3. *temperately keep time . . . music:* beats as steadily and healthily.

144. *Bring me to the test:* Try me.

145-6. Hamlet says he will repeat word for word what went on, which would not be possible for a madman. *gambol:* shy away.

147-51. *Lay not . . . unseen:* Don't soothe your soul with a lie, telling yourself that it is not you who are sinful but I who am mad, as though you were applying an ointment to a sore, which will just cover up a foul, rotting ulcer that eats away at you invisibly.

151-4. For Gertrude, as well as for Claudius, the only way out is to repent and resolve to behave better in future.

153-4. *do not . . . ranker:* Hamlet means that if the queen conceals her guilt from herself she will just be encouraging her sins to flourish. This image of rank weeds is similar to what Hamlet said of the world in general in Act I, Scene ii, lines 135-7, but there, too, it was really his mother's behaviour that was at the root of it. Similarly, the image of rottenness has already occurred several times.

154. *Forgive . . . virtue:* I am sorry to sound so self-righteous.

155-6. Hamlet says that in these lax, unhealthy times (*fat and pursy:* out of condition, physically) even really good people have to apologize and plead for an opportunity of helping sinners to improve.

158. *cleft:* broken. *twain:* two.

159-61. *O . . . Good night:* Seeing that his mother really has taken to heart what he has said, Hamlet begins to leave her, but several times, as with his interview with Ophelia in Act III, Scene i, thinks of something else he must say while he has the opportunity.

161. *but . . . bed:* The reason for this is not just that Claudius is not worthy of the wife of Hamlet's father, but that, strictly speaking, their marriage was incestuous.

162. *Assume:* act as though you possess.

163-7. *That monster . . . put on:* habit is a queer thing – it can behave like a devil when it takes away one's consciousness of doing wrong, yet it is like an angel when it holds out, like a ready-to-wear garment (punning with another meaning of *habit*) an easy way of doing the right thing.

Queen

  No, nothing but ourselves.   *135*

Hamlet

  Why, look you there. Look how it steals away.

  My father, in his habit as he liv'd!

  Look where he goes even now out at the portal.

Exit GHOST

Queen

  This is the very coinage of your brain.

  This bodiless creation ecstasy   *140*

  Is very cunning in.

Hamlet   Ecstasy!

  My pulse as yours doth temperately keep time,

  And makes as healthful music. It is not madness

  That I have utter'd. Bring me to the test,

  And I the matter will re-word which madness   *145*

  Would gambol from. Mother, for love of grace,

  Lay not that flattering unction to your soul,

  That not your trespass but my madness speaks:

  It will but skin and film the ulcerous place,

  Whiles rank corruption, mining all within,   *150*

  Infects unseen. Confess yourself to heaven;

  Repent what's past; avoid what is to come;

  And do not spread the compost on the weeds,

  To make them ranker. Forgive me this my virtue;

  For in the fatness of these pursy times   *155*

  Virtue itself of vice must pardon beg,

  Yea, curb and woo for leave to do him good.

Queen

  O Hamlet, thou hast cleft my heart in twain.

Hamlet

  O, throw away the worser part of it,

  And live the purer with the other half.   *160*

  Good night—but go not to my uncle's bed;

  Assume a virtue, if you have it not.

  That monster custom, who all sense doth eat,

167-9. Hamlet says that if his mother does not go to bed with Claudius that night she will begin to find it increasingly easy to refrain.

170-2. *For use . . . potency:* Habit can almost change one's personality, and restrain, or even remove, evil, remarkably effectively. (Why is Hamlet such an expert on the effect of habit?)

172-4. *Once more . . . of you:* Once again turning back as he is about to go, Hamlet, now with all his anger departed, adds a consoling word: when his mother has fully repented, he will again be the respectful, loving son.

174-7. Looking down at the almost forgotten body of Polonius, he soberly says that he is sorry that he killed him, but fate seems to have chosen to make this man a nuisance to him, and vice versa, using Hamlet as an instrument of justice.

178. *bestow:* hide, get rid of. *answer well:* take the responsibility for.

180-1. Hamlet says that he has only hurt her for her own good, and that, though life may not be pleasant from now on, at least it was worse before.

182. By now, Gertrude shows a rather touching dependence on her son's advice.

183-90. Hamlet paints an ironic picture of how his mother is not to behave: she is not to be wheedled by Claudius into telling him that Hamlet is, in fact, not mad, but just pretending to be.

184. *bloat:* bloated. Hamlet dislikes what he considers his uncle's gluttonous habits.

185. *wanton:* sexily. *mouse:* an affectionate term, like 'pet'.

186. *reechy:* filthy.

188. *ravel:* unravel, reveal.

189. *essentially:* really. *in madness:* insane.

190. *mad in craft:* feigning madness for a purpose. *'Twere good:* 'That would be a splendid idea,' says Hamlet, sarcastically.

191. *but:* just. *fair, sober, wise:* Hamlet now tries to bolster up his mother's self-respect.

192. *paddock:* toad. *gib:* tom cat. These, and bats, were considered evil creatures in Shakespeare's time.

193. *dear concernings:* important personal matters.

194-8. No, let the cat out of the bag, by all means, Hamlet scoffs. He refers to a story where an ape, who finds that some birds, which it accidentally releases from a basket on a roof-top, can fly, tries jumping out of the basket itself, but of course, it falls and breaks its neck. Hamlet means that his mother will only cause trouble for herself if she tries seeing what happens if she confided in her husband. *To try conclusions:* as an experiment.

Of habits devil, is angel yet in this,
That to the use of actions fair and good   165
He likewise gives a frock or livery
That aptly is put on. Refrain to-night;
And that shall lend a kind of easiness
To the next abstinence; the next more easy;
For use almost can change the stamp of nature,   170
And either curb the devil, or throw him out,
With wondrous potency. Once more, good night;
And when you are desirous to be blest,
I'll blessing beg of you. For this same lord
I do repent; but Heaven hath pleas'd it so,   175
To punish me with this, and this with me,
That I must be their scourge and minister.
I will bestow him, and will answer well
The death I gave him. So, again, good night.
I must be cruel only to be kind;   180
Thus bad begins and worse remains behind.
One word more, good lady.

Queen   What shall I do?
Hamlet
    Not this, by no means, that I bid you do:
Let the bloat King tempt you again to bed;
Pinch wanton on your cheek; call you his mouse;   185
And let him, for a pair of reechy kisses,
Or paddling in your neck with his damn'd fingers,
Make you to ravel all this matter out,
That I essentially am not in madness,
But mad in craft. 'Twere good you let him know;   190
For who that's but a queen, fair, sober, wise,
Would from a paddock, from a bat, a gib,
Such dear concernings hide? Who would do so?
No, in despite of sense and secrecy,
Unpeg the basket on the house's top,   195
Let the birds fly, and, like the famous ape,
To try conclusions, in the basket creep
And break your own neck down.

199-201. The queen promises that she will keep his secret. *breath of life:* breath and life are inseparable.

202. Satisfied that his mother is on his side, Hamlet prepares to trust her with another secret: that he knows the trip to England (who told him of it?) is just a cover for some sort of plot against him; but he intends to go one better than Claudius.

202-3. In spite of the harsh, almost unforgivable things Hamlet has said to her, the queen's reaction is one of genuine regret. She and her son are all the closer for their quarrel, probably understanding each other better than they have for a long time; and now they must part.

204. *There's letters seal'd:* Claudius wrote them only that evening. *my two school-fellows:* Rosencrantz and Guildenstern.

205. *adders fang'd:* They are no better than poisonous snakes.

206. *bear the mandate:* are briefed for the journey. *sweep:* clear, prepare.

207. *marshal me to knavery:* escort me into danger.

208-11. *For 'tis . . . moon:* Beginning to exult at the opportunity for definite action at last, Hamlet says that it is a good game, blowing up a mining expert with his own explosives. (He is comparing their plots and counterplots to laying mines in a battlefield; it is now almost open war, and his enemy is experienced in this sort of thing.) With any luck, Hamlet will be able to dig a tunnel and lay a charge underneath theirs, and blow them sky-high (i.e. he has a plot of his own that will ruin theirs).

211. *O, 'tis most sweet:* Hamlet is really beginning to enjoy the prospect.

212. *When . . . meet:* When two plots clash head-on.

213. Hamlet realizes that Claudius will use the killing of Polonius as an excuse for packing off Hamlet immediately.

214. *lug the guts:* He sees no reason for being sentimental about Polonius's corpse. *neighbour:* next.

215-19. With a jest about how Polonius has been improved by death, for he has acquired the secrecy, discretion and gravity he should have had when alive (he puns on *still* and *grave*; also, *to draw . . . you:* to finish both with Polonius and with the conversation) Hamlet matter-of-factly drags the body out, saying goodbye to his mother for the fifth, and last, time. He leaves us with the impression that, unlike the inconclusive interview with Ophelia, this talk has allowed him to go away with a lighter heart than he has had for a long time.

Stage Direction. *severally:* separately.

Queen

   Be thou assur'd, if words be made of breath
   And breath of life, I have no life to breathe   *200*
   What thou hast said to me.

Hamlet

   I must to England; you know that?

Queen   Alack,

   I had forgot. 'Tis so concluded on.

Hamlet

   There's letters seal'd; and my two school-fellows,
   Whom I will trust as I will adders fang'd—   *205*
   They bear the mandate; they must sweep my way
   And marshal me to knavery. Let it work;
   For 'tis the sport to have the engineer
   Hoist with his own petar; and't shall go hard
   But I will delve one yard below their mines   *210*
   And blow them at the moon. O, 'tis most sweet
   When in one line two crafts directly meet.
   This man shall set me packing.
   I'll lug the guts into the neighbour room.
   Mother, good night. Indeed, this counsellor   *215*
   Is now most still, most secret, and most grave,
   Who was in life a foolish prating knave.
   Come, sir, to draw toward an end with you.
   Good night, mother.

     Exeunt severally; HAMLET *tugging in* POLONIUS

ACT FOUR

SCENE I

That same night, almost immediately after her conversation with Hamlet, the queen encounters her husband; either she went to find him, or he came to discover why Polonius had not come back to report to him. She is in a difficult position: she has to choose between keeping her promises to her son, and her loyalty to her husband, with the added knowledge that they are bitter enemies, and plotting ruthlessly against each other. She cannot reject Claudius completely, even if she wants to, for they are bound together, not just by marriage, but by their joint responsibility towards Denmark. No wonder she is in a distracted state, which the king immediately notices. Gertrude shows, however, that she has more intelligence than we might give her credit for, when her son's safety is at stake.

1. *matter:* some meaning.
2. *translate:* explain. *'tis fit . . . them:* 'I must know what it is all about.' Claudius takes an uncompromising tone with his wife, implying that he does not like hysterical women; perhaps she is turning away, and refusing to speak to him.
3. He guesses that it is something to do with Hamlet.
4. *Bestow . . . us:* leave us alone. (Why were Rosencrantz and Guildenstern with the king, and why does the queen want them to go?)
5. *mine own lord:* Gertrude gives the impression that she is turning to Claudius for comfort. This seems to cause him to soften his tone.
7. The queen's first word shows that Hamlet's secret is safe.
7-8. *the sea . . . mightier:* in a storm. *lawless fit:* insane frenzy.
9-12. The queen distorts the incident very slightly, giving the impression that Hamlet had a mad suspicion (*brainish apprehension*) that there was a rat behind the tapestry, and slew it. (Even a madman would hardly believe that a so-called 'rat' would call for help, as Polonius did, so she carefully suppresses this fact.)
12-23. Unfortunately, her attempt to excuse Hamlet's killing of Polonius, on the grounds that it was partly an accident and partly due to the fact that he was not responsible for his actions at the time, misfires, for Claudius, after a characteristic remark that it was just as well that he himself wasn't there too, uses the incident as further evidence that Hamlet should not be allowed to roam around freely. (Hamlet had foreseen this – Act III, Scene iv, line 213).
12. *heavy:* unfortunate.
15. *to us:* to me – the royal plural, used even to his wife, shows how pompous Claudius is. Unaware of how much his wife now knows, Claudius tries to convert her to the idea that Hamlet is dangerous.
16-19. *Alas . . . young man:* Another thought strikes him, which genuinely worries him: people will blame him for Polonius's death, since he did not keep a watch on his mad step-son, and keep him shut away.

ACT FOUR

SCENE I—*Elsinore. The Castle*
    Enter KING, QUEEN, ROSENCRANTZ *and* GUILDENSTERN

King

  There's matter in these sighs, these profound heaves,
  You must translate; 'tis fit we understand them.
  Where is your son?

Queen

  Bestow this place on us a little while.

    Exeunt ROSENCRANTZ *and* GUILDENSTERN

  Ah, mine own lord, what have I seen to-night!   *5*

King

  What, Gertrude? How does Hamlet?

Queen

  Mad as the sea and wind, when both contend
  Which is the mightier. In his lawless fit,
  Behind the arras hearing something stir,
  Whips out his rapier, cries 'A rat, a rat!'   *10*
  And in this brainish apprehension kills
  The unseen good old man.

King   O heavy deed!
  It had been so with us had we been there.
  His liberty is full of threats to all—
  To you yourself, to us, to every one.   *15*
  Alas, how shall this bloody deed be answer'd?
  It will be laid to us, whose providence
  Should have kept short, restrain'd, and out of haunt,

19-23. *But so much . . . life:* Claudius hypocritically tells his wife that he was so fond of Hamlet that he refused to admit what he should be doing, but put off dealing with him till it was too late, like someone with a horrible disease, who tries to cover it up while it slowly kills him.

24. *draw apart:* remove.

25-7. Still trying to protect Hamlet, the queen tells a flat lie, saying that even in his madness he shows himself to be good at heart (like gold ore showing up in a mixed sample of minerals) because he is weeping over Polonius's body. In fact, Hamlet's last words were a joke.

29. *The sun . . . touch:* at dawn. By now it is probably past midnight.

30. *ship him hence:* send him to England. *this vile deed:* the killing of Polonius.

32. *countenance and excuse:* recognize, and offer excuses for.

33. *both go join . . . aid:* go and get some assistance.

36. *fair:* politely.

38. *call up:* wake up.

40. *untimely:* at the wrong time. i.e. Polonius's death.
40-4. *so haply . . . air:* So that, with any luck, slanderous rumours – which everywhere in the world find and destroy their victims, like guns hitting their targets – will not hurt me, or indeed anyone.

45. This is only partly true, for even though Claudius is unhappy in himself, and is worried about the repercussions from Polonius's death, he must be glad that now he has one more weapon to use against Hamlet, who is becoming more and more of a threat.

This mad young man. But so much was our love,
We would not understand what was most fit;   20
But, like the owner of a foul disease,
To keep it from divulging, let it feed
Even on the pith of life. Where is he gone?

Queen

To draw apart the body he hath kill'd;
O'er whom his very madness, like some ore   25
Among a mineral of metals base,
Shows itself pure: 'a weeps for what is done.

King

O Gertrude, come away!
The sun no sooner shall the mountains touch
But we will ship him hence; and this vile deed   30
We must with all our majesty and skill
Both countenance and excuse. Ho, Guildenstern!

Re-enter ROSENCRANTZ *and* GUILDENSTERN

Friends, both go join you with some further aid:
Hamlet in madness hath Polonius slain,
And from his mother's closet hath he dragg'd him;   35
Go seek him out; speak fair, and bring the body
Into the chapel. I pray you haste in this.

Exeunt ROSENCRANTZ *and* GUILDENSTERN

Come, Gertrude, we'll call up our wisest friends
And let them know both what we mean to do
And what's untimely done; so haply slander—   40
Whose whisper o'er the world's diameter,
As level as the cannon to his blank,
Transports his poison'd shot—may miss our name,
And hit the woundless air. O, come away!
My soul is full of discord and dismay.   45

Exeunt

SCENE II

A few moments later, Rosencrantz and Guildenstern find Hamlet coming away from the place where he has hidden Polonius's body, and, probably feeling that it is now they who have the upper hand, abruptly ask him where it is.

1. There is a note of satisfaction in Hamlet's words. Why has he hidden the body away?

3. *soft:* what's this?

6. Hamlet means that he has sent Polonius to his death ('ashes to ashes, dust to dust') and probably also that he has pushed it into a dusty corner. *Compounded:* mingled. *kin:* related.

9. Hamlet deliberately disconcerts them by changing the subject.

11. *counsel:* secret. Hamlet says that if he can keep their secret – that he saw through their plan to spy on him, a fact which no doubt they have concealed from Claudius – he can keep a secret of his own: where the body is.

12-13. *Besides . . . king:* Anyway, why should a prince condescend to reply to something a sponge asks him? Hamlet hints that they should speak more politely to him, but they, like Polonius when he was called a fishmonger, just think this is another sign that Hamlet is mad, a fact which leads them to feel they need not bother to show him any respect.

15-20. Hamlet shows that he knows very well what he meant: they have 'sucked up' to the king, seeking favour, rewards and power. But the king gets more out of them, in the end, than they do out of him, for they will be flattered (*mouth'd*) until he needs something from them, and then he will act ruthlessly, taking everything he wants from them, and leaving them nothing.

SCENE II—*Elsinore. The Castle*

Enter HAMLET

Hamlet
Safely stow'd.
Gentlemen [*Within*]
Hamlet! Lord Hamlet!
Hamlet
But soft! What noise? Who calls on Hamlet? O, here
they come!

Enter ROSENCRANTZ *and* GUILDENSTERN

Rosencrantz
What have you done, my lord, with the dead body?   5
Hamlet
Compounded it with dust, whereto 'tis kin.
Rosencrantz
Tell us where 'tis, that we may take it thence
And bear it to the chapel.
Hamlet
Do not believe it.
Rosencrantz
Believe what?   10
Hamlet
That I can keep your counsel, and not mine own.
Besides, to be demanded of a sponge—what replica-
tion should be made by the son of a king?
Rosencrantz
Take you me for a sponge, my lord?
Hamlet
Ay, sir; that soaks up the King's countenance, his   15
rewards, his authorities, But such officers do the King
best service in the end: he keeps them, like an ape an
apple in the corner of his jaw; first mouth'd to be last
swallowed; when he needs what you have glean'd, it is
but squeezing you and, sponge, you shall be dry again.   20

21. Even if Rosencrantz does understand what Hamlet means, he finds it a safer policy to pretend not to.

22. *knavish:* mischievous. *sleeps:* is not understood.

24-5. Irritated by the fact that he has just been called a fool, and ignoring the warning that they are not wise to rely so much on Claudius's gratitude, Rosencrantz continues to adopt a rather high-handed attitude to the prince (saying *you must*) forgetting Claudius's instruction to *speak him fair.*

26-7. Hamlet means that Polonius is now with King Hamlet, in the afterlife, but the other king, Claudius, can't find his body.

28. Nothing shocks Guildenstern so much as disrespectful comments about his patron.

29. *Of nothing:* worth nothing. *Hide fox, and all after:* 'Let's play hide-and-seek.' Possibly he runs off, to support their belief (which they must have felt was borne out by this conversation) that he is mad. Possibly he just means that the whole situation is a game of concealment and tracking down.

SCENE III

It is still the middle of the same night, or rather the small hours of the next morning. Claudius has woken up some attendants and courtiers (see Act IV, Scene i, lines 38-40) in order to have witnesses of what he hopes will seem his firm but merciful treatment of Hamlet. The whole set-up must look rather like a hasty court-martial to Hamlet, when he enters. Both he and Claudius must by now be very tired after a day full of crises, but Hamlet shows by his manner that he does not intend to make things too easy for his uncle, though he realizes that, at the moment, Claudius has the upper hand.

1-11. The king is outlining his policy concerning Hamlet, in an official statement to those around: Hamlet is a public menace, but he cannot be punished by the full force of the law because he is popular with the ordinary, misled mass of people, who admire someone because they like the look of him, rather than because he deserves it, and, when this is the case, they object to the punishment, rather than the crime. Therefore, to cope with the situation effectively, the step of sending Hamlet away must seem like a deliberate manoeuvre. Serious diseases can only be dealt with by drastic measures. (In this last remark the king is referring not only to Hamlet's 'insanity' but to the situation as a whole.)

11. *what hath befall'n?* what's happened? Seeing Rosencrantz without Hamlet, Claudius fears something has gone wrong.

Rosencrantz
  I understand you not, my lord.

Hamlet
  I am glad of it; a knavish speech sleeps in a foolish
  ear.

Rosencrantz
  My lord, you must tell us where the body is, and go
  with us to the King.   25

Hamlet
  The body is with the King, but the King is not with
  the body. The King is a thing—

Guildenstern
  A thing, my lord!

Hamlet
  Of nothing. Bring me to him. Hide fox, and all after.

                      Exeunt

SCENE III—*Elsinore. The Castle*

          Enter KING, *attended*

King
  I have sent to seek him, and to find the body.
  How dangerous is it that this man goes loose!
  Yet must not we put the strong law on him:
  He's lov'd of the distracted multitude,
  Who like not in their judgment but their eyes;   5
  And where 'tis so, th' offender's scourge is weigh'd,
  But never the offence. To bear all smooth and even,
  This sudden sending him away must seem
  Deliberate pause. Diseases desperate grown
  By desperate appliance are reliev'd,   10
  Or not at all.

          Enter ROSENCRANTZ

      How now! what hath befall'n?

12. *bestow'd:* hidden.

14. *Without:* outside. *guarded:* Rosencrantz and Guildenstern were taking no chances this time, and have given themselves the pleasure of escorting in the prisoner, in style.

16. *the lord:* not 'the prince'.

17-19. The king tries to take a direct, no-nonsense line with the 'lunatic', but finds it difficult to deal with his nephew's cryptic reply.

20-6. In spite of the facetiousness of Hamlet's tone, he touches on a serious topic he has been contemplating for some time: worldly ambition is futile, for in death, to which everyone must come, all men are equal, whether they are kings, like Claudius, or beggars. (Compare what he said in Act II, Scene ii, lines 263-4.)

20-1. *Not . . . at him:* worms are making a meal of Polonius, all gathered together as at a political conference (one actually took place at the town of Worms, in Shakespeare's time, so this is a topical joke that would amuse his audience).

21-4. *Your worm . . . maggots:* Worms get better food than anyone else, for human beings feed other animals so that they can eat them, but meanwhile they are just fattening themselves for the worms that will eat them when they die. (These comments may be partly aimed at the *politic worms* standing round, the courtiers, who are feasting on the spectacle of a prince in disgrace.)

24. *your fat king:* probably a dig at Claudius's figure; he certainly seems fond of feasting! *your* is used in a general sense, simply meaning 'a.'

25. *variable service:* different courses. *one table:* Hamlet is referring in a macabre way to the fate of all dead bodies, being eaten.

27. 'How sad!' Claudius seems to imply. 'Hamlet has gone quite mad.'

28-32. Hamlet suggests that, as a beggar might well eat a fish that had eaten a maggot that had fed on a king's corpse, a bit of a king could easily suffer the humiliation of going through the digestive system of a beggar (*progress:* formal procession). Hamlet's unspoken message is: you may think yourself important and powerful now, but some day you will be worth nothing at all – a mere beggar may get the better of you. (Perhaps Hamlet refers to himself here; see *beggar that I am* in Act II, Scene ii, line 272.)

Rosencrantz

    Where the dead body is bestow'd, my lord,

    We cannot get from him.

King   But where is he?

Rosencrantz

    Without, my lord; guarded, to know your pleasure.

King

    Bring him before us.   *15*

Rosencrantz

    Ho, Guildenstern! bring in the lord.

Enter HAMLET *and* GUILDENSTERN

King

    Now, Hamlet, where's Polonius?

Hamlet

    At supper.

King

    At supper! Where?

Hamlet

    Not where he eats, but where 'a is eaten; a certain *20*
    convocation of politic worms are e'en at him. Your
    worm is your only emperor for diet: we fat all
    creatures else to fat us, and we fat ourselves for
    maggots; your fat king and your lean beggar is but
    variable service—two dishes, but to one table. That's *25*
    the end.

King

    Alas, alas!

Hamlet

    A man may fish with the worm that hath eat of a
    king, and eat of the fish that hath fed of that worm.

King

    What dost thou mean by this?   *30*

Hamlet

    Nothing but to show you how a king may go a
    progress through the guts of a beggar.

33-5. Claudius seems to realize that something unpleasant has just been implied, for he quickly changes the subject back to Polonius, and, though Hamlet knows that he can't put the question off for ever, he mockingly suggests that, if Polonius can't be found in heaven, Claudius himself is the one to look him out in hell.

37. *nose:* smell.

40. *stay:* wait. Having had to give Claudius an answer, Hamlet keeps his end up with a grim joke.

41. *especial:* own.

42. *we do tender:* I cherish. *as:* while, at the same time. *dearly:* sincerely. This, of course, is for the benefit of the listeners.

43-4. *must . . . quickness:* makes your going away urgently necessary.

45. *bark:* boat. *at help:* favourable.

46. *Th'associates tend:* Your companions (Rosencrantz and Guildenstern) are waiting. *bent:* ready.

47-9. Why does Hamlet pretend to be surprised? His *Good!* must disconcert Claudius, who probably expects some sort of objection – but Hamlet is not going to give him this satisfaction.

48. *our purposes:* my reasons.

49. *I see . . . them:* My guardian angel is aware of them. Hamlet hints that he knows that Claudius intends him no good. Even if this puts Claudius on his guard, Hamlet can't bear to seem such a fool as to be completely unsuspicious. Besides, a number of the courtiers are there to receive the hint, too.

50. *Farewell, dear mother:* Does Hamlet say these words mockingly to Claudius, or sadly, to himself?

51. Claudius seizes another opportunity to impress the court with his patient treatment of his lunatic step-son.

52-3. The fact that Hamlet can now make an almost light-hearted joke about the strange closeness of the relationship that once repelled him, suggests that his talk with his mother has cleared the air considerably for him.

53-4. *Come, for England:* Hamlet's exit line enables him to leave with dignity, as though voluntarily, instead of being escorted by guards.

King

Where is Polonius?

Hamlet

In heaven; send thither to see; if your messenger find
him not there, seek him i' th' other place yourself. 35
But if, indeed, you find him not within this month,
you shall nose him as you go up the stairs into the
lobby.

King [*To* ATTENDANTS]

Go seek him there.

Hamlet

'A will stay till you come. 40

Exeunt ATTENDANTS

King

Hamlet, this deed, for thine especial safety—
Which we do tender, as we dearly grieve
For that which thou hast done—must send thee hence
With fiery quickness. Therefore prepare thyself;
The bark is ready, and the wind at help, 45
Th' associates tend, and everything is bent
For England.

Hamlet   For England!

King   Ay, Hamlet.

Hamlet   Good!

King

So is it, if thou knew'st our purposes.

Hamlet

I see a cherub that sees them. But, come; for England!
Farewell, dear mother. 50

King

Thy loving father, Hamlet.

Hamlet

My mother: father and mother is man and wife; man
and wife is one flesh; and so, my mother. Come, for
England.

Exit

227

55. *at foot:* close on his heels. *tempt:* entice. Claudius knows that there would be trouble if any of his ordinary subjects saw Hamlet being deported by force.

58. *else . . . affair:* otherwise needs to be done.

59-69. Now that Claudius is alone we learn exactly what his plan is: the king of England, whose country has recently been conquered by the Danes, has been told, in the sealed letters which Rosencrantz and Guildenstern are carrying, to put Hamlet to death, on pain of incurring Claudius's displeasure (a veiled threat of further war).

61. *cicatrice:* scar.

62-3. *thy free awe . . . us:* The king of England has voluntarily acknowledged Claudius as his overlord. *coldly set:* calmly set aside.

64. *sovereign process:* royal command. *imports at full:* gives full instructions.

65. *congruing . . . effect:* indicating.

67. *hectic:* fever. Another occasion (see lines 9-11, above) where Claudius refers to Hamlet's existence as a disease he must deal with, just as Hamlet referred to Gertrude's guilt in this way. On this occasion, Claudius visualizes the old-fashioned cure: blood-letting.

69. *Howe'er my haps . . . begun:* Whatever happens to me, I shall be miserable. Now Claudius, like Hamlet, is obsessed by the need to get rid of his enemy.

SCENE IV

For the first time in the play, we leave Elsinore, and what has become its suffocating atmosphere of suspicion and intrigue, and move with Hamlet out into the open air. We meet the Fortinbras whom we heard of at the beginning of the play, passing his army through Denmark on his way to fight in Poland. Here is a young prince in a similar position to Hamlet: his father is dead, his uncle on the throne, and he himself filled with restless high spirits; but unlike Hamlet, he does not hesitate for a moment about what he should be doing, and Hamlet cannot help being struck by the contrast.

2. *licence:* permission.

3. *Craves . . . march:* Asks for a safe conduct.

5-6. *If . . . in his eye:* If Claudius wishes to see me I shall pay my respects to him in person. Unlike Hamlet, Fortinbras makes a habit of using the royal plural. The general impression we have of him from this brief glimpse is that he is decisive, authoritative, and, in spite of his youth, an efficient organizer.

8. *softly:* slowly. He is speaking to the rest of the army.

King

    Follow him at foot; tempt him with speed aboard;   55
    Delay it not; I'll have him hence to-night.
    Away! for everything is seal'd and done
    That else leans on th' affair. Pray you make haste.

Exeunt all but the KING

    And, England, if my love thou hold'st at aught—
    As my great power thereof may give thee sense,   60
    Since yet thy cicatrice looks raw and red
    After the Danish sword, and thy free awe
    Pays homage to us—thou mayst not coldly set
    Our sovereign process; which imports at full,
    By letters congruing to that effect,   65
    The present death of Hamlet. Do it, England:
    For like the hectic in my blood he rages,
    And thou must cure me. Till I know 'tis done,
    Howe'er my haps, my joys were ne'er begun.

Exit

SCENE IV—*A plain in Denmark*

Enter FORTINBRAS *with his* ARMY *over the stage*

Fortinbras

    Go, Captain, from me greet the Danish king.
    Tell him that by his licence Fortinbras
    Craves the conveyance of a promis'd march
    Over his kingdom. You know the rendezvous.
    If that his Majesty would aught with us,   5
    We shall express our duty in his eye;
    And let him know so.

Captain   I will do't, my lord.

Fortinbras

    Go softly on.

9. Hamlet naturally takes an interest in anything that seems to affect his kingdom, and, though he has just missed Fortinbras, is in time to meet the captain, who is on his way to Elsinore.

10. *are of:* belong to.

11. *How purpos'd?* Where are they marching to?

12. *Against:* to fight.

15. *main:* whole.

17. *addition:* exaggeration.

19. *no profit but the name:* no value at all.

20. *To pay . . . farm it:* I would not rent it even for only five ducats.

22. *A ranker rate . . . fee:* More money, even if it were sold outright. No doubt the captain is glad to have a sympathetic listener for opinions he dares not voice to Fortinbras.

26. *debate . . . straw:* settle this trifling matter.

27-9. *This is . . . dies:* Hamlet says that the absurd quarrel is caused by the countries concerned having too much prosperity and peace, so that they become secretly restless for action, and so destroy themselves. He compares the situation with an internal abscess or tumour, secretly developing and finally killing.

230

Exeunt all but the CAPTAIN
Enter HAMLET, ROSENCRANTZ, GUILDENSTERN *and*
OTHERS

Hamlet
Good sir, whose powers are these?
Captain
They are of Norway, sir.   10
Hamlet
How purpos'd, sir, I pray you?
Captain
Against some part of Poland.
Hamlet
Who commands them, sir?
Captain
The nephew to old Norway, Fortinbras.
Hamlet
Goes it against the main of Poland, sir,   15
Or for some frontier?
Captain
Truly to speak, and with no addition,
We go to gain a little patch of ground
That hath in it no profit but the name.
To pay five ducats, five, I would not farm it;   20
Nor will it yield to Norway or the Pole
A ranker rate should it be sold in fee.
Hamlet
Why, then the Polack never will defend it.
Captain
Yes, it is already garrison'd.
Hamlet
Two thousand souls and twenty thousand ducats   25
Will not debate the question of this straw.
This is th' imposthume of much wealth and peace,
That inward breaks, and shows no cause without
Why the man dies. I humbly thank you, sir.

231

30. *God buy you:* good-bye. *Will't please you go, my lord?* Rosencrantz is mindful of Claudius's exhortations to hurry, but is now more respectful in his manner to Hamlet.

31. *before:* ahead.

32-66. As after he heard the chief player recite an emotional speech in Act II, Scene ii, Hamlet is struck by the difference between other people's reactions and his own, and makes another resolution not to waste any more time in hesitating about whether to take revenge.

32. *occasions:* incidents, encounters. *inform against:* accuse.

33. *And spur . . . revenge:* Urging me not to be so apathetic about taking revenge.

33-5. *What . . . no more:* Again contemplating the nature and purpose of human existence, Hamlet says that surely man was not intended to live like a mere animal, making the satisfaction of his bodily needs the chief aim and business of his life.

36-9. *Sure . . . unus'd:* Surely God did not give man his intellect, his divine ability to contemplate and reason about both past and future (the causes and the consequences of things) in order to let it moulder away, unused. Hamlet tries to justify his habit of spending so much time just thinking.

39-46. *Now . . . to do't:* Hamlet cannot decide whether his reason for not having taken revenge yet is that he cannot keep his mind on anything longer than an animal could (*oblivion:* forgetfulness) or, on the contrary, because of a timid hesitation caused by analysing the possible consequences of his actions too fully – an activity which is 75 % due to cowardice rather than common sense. He can't make out why he has not taken revenge yet, as he has had the motive, the determination, the ability and the opportunity to do it.

46. *Examples . . . me:* I am set examples which I cannot ignore. *gross:* blatantly obvious.

47. *Witness:* for instance. *of such mass and charge:* so large and expensive to run.

48. *delicate and tender:* fine and youthful. Hamlet's generosity of mind is shown in that he admires rather than feels jealous of Fortinbras.

49. *puff'd:* filled, made buoyant and active. Why does Hamlet call ambition *divine* here, but satirizes it in Act II, Scene ii, lines 252-65?

50. *Makes mouths at:* jeers at, defies. *event:* outcome (of the battle).

51-3. *Exposing . . . egg-shell:* 'Risking his and his army's lives, and tempting fate, for something quite worthless.'

53-6. *Rightly . . . stake:* Still, as in his *To be or not to be* speech (Act III, Scene i), Hamlet asks himself what the noblest and most honourable way of behaving is. True nobility, he says, does not consist in taking offence at, and fighting over, every little thing, but in being ready to avenge the least real insult to one's honour.

56-65. *How . . . the slain:* Hamlet says what an ignoble position he is in, in that case, as his father has been murdered, his mother dishonoured, his mind and his feelings stirred up by what Claudius has done, and yet he has let everything slide, while, here in front of him, a huge army goes to face death willingly, for the sake of a scrap of ground so small that there will hardly be room to fight on it or to bury the slain; all this because of a daydream of achieving a little honour, reputation and glory.

Captain
  God buy you, sir.

                              Exit

Rosencrantz   Will't please you go, my lord?   30
Hamlet
  I'll be with you straight. Go a little before.

                    Exeunt all but HAMLET

  How all occasions do inform against me,
  And spur my dull revenge! What is a man,
  If his chief good and market of his time
  Be but to sleep and feed? A beast, no more!   35
  Sure he that made us with such large discourse,
  Looking before and after, gave us not
  That capability and godlike reason
  To fust in us unus'd. Now, whether it be
  Bestial oblivion, or some craven scruple   40
  Of thinking too precisely on th' event—
  A thought which, quarter'd, hath but one part wisdom
  And ever three parts coward—I do not know
  Why yet I live to say 'This thing's to do',
  Sith I have cause, and will, and strength, and means,   45
  To do't. Examples gross as earth exhort me:
  Witness this army, of such mass and charge,
  Led by a delicate and tender prince,
  Whose spirit, with divine ambition puff'd
  Makes mouths at the invisible event,   50
  Exposing what is mortal and unsure
  To all that fortune, death, and danger dare,
  Even for an egg-shell. Rightly to be great
  Is not to stir without great argument,
  But greatly to find quarrel in a straw,   55
  When honour's at the stake. How stand I, then,
  That have a father kill'd, a mother stain'd,
  Excitements of my reason and my blood,
  And let all sleep, while to my shame I see

65-6. Hamlet concludes by saying that he is determined to be ruthless from now on. He has said this more than once before, however, and will have to act quickly before Claudius's plot, to have him put to death in England, comes off.

SCENE V

For a while we see nothing more of Hamlet, and we hardly have time to wonder how he is getting on, for those still at Elsinore are occupied with their own troubles: Ophelia, who shows no signs of knowing the real circumstances of her father's death (they have been hushed up) is only aware that she has been suddenly deprived not only of her brother but of her father and her lover, all of whom she depended upon as well as loved. This, together with the accumulated strain, unhappiness and guilt caused by her father's conflicting attitudes to her love-affair with Hamlet, and her firm belief that she has driven her lover mad, has caused her to suffer a complete mental breakdown, taking refuge in madness from an intolerable situation.

1. Why does the queen at first refuse to speak to Ophelia, though earlier on she was kind to her?
2. *importunate:* insistent. *distract:* distracted.
3. *What . . . have?* What does she want?
5. *tricks:* treachery. *hems:* coughs.
6. *Spurns . . . straws:* reacts angrily to trifles. *speaks . . . doubt:* makes ambiguous remarks, without a clear meaning.
7. *nothing:* meaningless.
8-10. *Yet . . . thoughts:* But those who hear her make an effort to put her incoherent words together, gape at what she says, and fit it together roughly to correspond with their own ideas of what she means.

11-13. *Which . . . unhappily:* Ophelia's expressions and gestures give the impression that there is thought behind what she says, but it is so confused that one can only be sure that she is unhappy.
14-15. Horatio, in spite of the fact that he knows Claudius is a murderer, stays on at the court (probably he thinks he can be of more use to Hamlet there than anywhere else) and shows a real concern for Denmark's stability, taking it upon himself to advise the queen to see Ophelia, because otherwise she will start awkward rumours.

The imminent death of twenty thousand men   60
That, for a fantasy and trick of fame,
Go to their graves like beds, fight for a plot
Whereon the numbers cannot try the cause,
Which is not tomb enough and continent
To hide the slain? O, from this time forth,   65
My thoughts be bloody, or be nothing worth!

Exit

SCENE V—*Elsinore. The Castle*

Enter QUEEN, HORATIO *and a* GENTLEMAN

Queen

I will not speak with her.

Gentleman

She is importunate, indeed distract.
Her mood will needs be pitied.

Queen   What would she have?

Gentleman

She speaks much of her father; says she hears
There's tricks i' th' world, and hems, and beats her
    heart;   5
Spurns enviously at straws; speaks things in doubt,
That carry but half sense. Her speech is nothing,
Yet the unshaped use of it doth move
The hearers to collection; they yawn at it,
And botch the words up fit to their own thoughts;   10
Which, as her winks and nods and gestures yield them,
Indeed would make one think there might be thought,
Though nothing sure, yet much unhappily.

Horatio

'Twere good she were spoken with; for she may strew
Dangerous conjectures in ill-breeding minds.   15

17-20. The queen, her eyes opened to her weaknesses by Hamlet, says that her conscience, as is always the case with someone who has sinned, makes her feel that every little thing is leading to something terrible. Guilt is so full of absurd suspicions that its presence is revealed by its very anxiety to avoid notice.

Stage Direction. *distracted:* revealing by her manner that she is mad.

21. This exaggerated greeting is hardly the way in which the meek Ophelia would have addressed the queen, when she was sane. In a way, she may also be implying 'What has become of the Denmark that was once so splendid?' After this opening sentence, she doesn't seem to have a very clear idea to whom she is speaking, or what she has come to say.

22. *How now . . . !* 'What's this?' or 'Pull yourself together.'

23. The queen may have thought that Ophelia was going to make some awkward comments on her father's death, but instead she breaks into song – not of the sophisticated kind that must have been popular at court, but one of the ballads that were enjoyed by the humbler people (how might she have come to know them?), with their typical themes of death and love, topics very much in Ophelia's mind just now. The first song is about a loved one who died while away on a pilgrimage. For all Ophelia knows, Hamlet may be dead by now – or perhaps she is confused as to who it is who has died.

25-6. A hat with a *cockle*-shell badge was worn by pilgrims making a journey to a shrine, and they also carried a *staff* and wore *sandals*.

27. *imports:* means.

33. *O, ho!* Is this a sigh, a mad laugh, or what?
Nay, but . . . The queen makes a vain attempt to get through to Ophelia.

34. Perhaps Ophelia was present at her father's secret funeral.

35. Even now Gertrude turns to her husband for support in this sort of crisis.

Queen
    Let her come in.

                Exit GENTLEMAN

    [*Aside*] To my sick soul, as sin's true nature is,
    Each toy seems prologue to some great amiss.
    So full of artless jealousy is guilt,
    It spills itself in fearing to be spilt.   20

            Enter OPHELIA *distracted*

Ophelia
    Where is the beauteous Majesty of Denmark?
Queen
    How now, Ophelia!
Ophelia   [*Sings*]
       How should I your true love know
          From another one?
       By his cockle hat and staff,   25
          And his sandal shoon.
Queen
    Alas, sweet lady, what imports this song?
Ophelia
    Say you? Nay, pray you mark.
           [*Sings*]
       He is dead and gone, lady,
          He is dead and gone;
       At his head a grass-green turf,   30
          At his heels a stone.
    O, ho!
Queen   Nay, but, Ophelia—
Ophelia   Pray you mark.
           [*Sings*]
       White his shroud as the mountain snow—

             Enter KING

Queen
    Alas, look here, my lord.   35

36. *Larded:* Garlanded.

39. *pretty:* dear, good. Awkwardly, Claudius also tries to make contact with her, but all he gathers from her reply is that she is thinking of her father (line 45).

40. *Well, God dild you:* I'm all right, thank you. *God dild:* God reward.

40-1. *They say the owl was a baker's daughter:* Ophelia refers to an old folk-tale about a baker's daughter who was turned into an owl, no longer able to speak but only to hoot, for behaving ungenerously to Jesus. Though at first it seems a completely unrelated remark for her to make, and the listeners probably see it as lunatic nonsense, it does make some sense. Ophelia, too, has undergone a terrible change, and is no longer able to talk sensibly, and she, too, feels dimly that in some way it must be her fault. She cannot, she vaguely thinks, have been kind enough to Hamlet, if he went mad for love of her.

41-2. *Lord . . . may be:* The change that has come over her, and the uncertainty about what she is to do with the rest of her life, make Ophelia feel insecure.

42. *God be at your table:* A benediction, probably addressed to Claudius.

43. The king, at least, realized that Ophelia identified herself with the baker's daughter.

44. *Pray . . . of this:* Please don't let's talk of this any more.

46-64. Ophelia's second song is about a girl (with whom Ophelia again obviously identifies herself) who offered her love to someone who then seduced her on a false promise of marriage. Is she letting out in her madness a secret about her relationship with Hamlet (this would throw a new light on what he said to her in the lobby and during the play), or have her father's and brother's cynical warnings about Hamlet's intentions convinced her that what they suggested has actually happened? Perhaps neither of these is the case, and she just expresses the feeling that, because Hamlet apparently rejected her and betrayed her trust in his love (Act III, Scene i, lines 115-19), she has lost all her happiness and innocence.

46. *St. Valentine's day:* the day on which sweethearts traditionally declared their love.

47. *betime:* early.

51. *dupp'd:* raised the latch of, opened.

54. Is the king shocked by what she has just implied? Her next remark does suggest that he tried to stop her going on.

55. *make an end on't:* finish it.

56. *Gis:* Jesus.

58. *will do't . . . to't:* will seduce girls if they have a chance.

59. *By Cock:* by God. This distortion, like *Gis*, and many other oaths and swear-words, was invented to avoid blaspheming.

64. *An . . . bed:* If you had not offered yourself to me.

Ophelia   Larded with sweet flowers;
    Which bewept to the grave did not go
    With true-love showers.

King

How do you, pretty lady?

Ophelia

Well, God dild you! They say the owl was a baker's   40
daughter. Lord, we know what we are, but know not
what we may be. God be at your table!

King

Conceit upon her father.

Ophelia

Pray let's have no words of this; but when they ask
you what it means, say you this: 45

    [*Sings*]

    To-morrow is Saint Valentine's day,
      All in the morning betime,
    And I a maid at your window,
      To be your Valentine.
    Then up he rose, and donn'd his clothes,   50
      And dupp'd the chamber-door;
    Let in the maid, that out a maid
      Never departed more.

King

Pretty Ophelia!

Ophelia

Indeed, la, without an oath, I'll make an end on't.   55

    [*Sings*]

    By Gis and by Saint Charity,
      Alack, and fie for shame!
    Young men will do't, if they come to't;
      By Cock, they are to blame.
    Quoth she 'Before you tumbled me,   60
      You promis'd me to wed'.
He answers:
    'So would I 'a done, by yonder sun,
      An thou hadst not come to my bed'.

65. This must be the first Claudius has heard of Ophelia's mental condition.

66. *I hope all will be well:* Is it a past or present worry that is on Ophelia's mind? Something, perhaps, to do with Hamlet?

66-8. *I cannot . . . ground:* Again, her father's death comes back to her.

68-71. *My brother . . . good night:* With a sudden firmness, she threatens to tell Laertes what has been going on (this is just what the king and queen, and even Horatio, must fear), and, putting on a royal air, she dismisses her imaginary attendants and departs in a non-existent coach, letting us have a pathetic glimpse of the day-dreams she must once have had, of being Hamlet's wife, the future queen.

72. Why does Claudius want a watch kept on Ophelia?

73-4. *O, this is the poison . . . death:* For once, Claudius sounds as though temporarily he has felt real sympathy for someone else; but he over-simplifies the reason for Ophelia's breakdown.

76-7. *When sorrows . . . battalions:* Troubles tend to come all at once, rather than one at a time (*spies:* advance scouts). Beginning to talk of Ophelia's troubles, Claudius goes on to describe his own.

78. *your son gone:* Claudius is no longer so eager to acknowledge Hamlet as his son!

78-9. *he most violent . . . remove:* it was his fault, because he behaved violently, that he had to be sent away.

79-81. *the people . . . Polonius' death:* unpleasant, unhealthy rumours about Polonius's death are being circulated among the people. (What sort of rumours?)

81-2. *and we . . . inter him:* It was not wise to have him buried furtively.

83. *Divided . . . judgment:* Who is no longer herself, and has lost her sanity.

84. *pictures:* only outwardly human beings. *or mere beasts:* It is interesting that Claudius is expressing exactly the same idea as Hamlet in the last scene (lines 33-5).

85. *as much . . . these:* as important as the other misfortunes put together.

87-8. *Feeds . . . ear:* Laertes (having probably received a message that his father was dead) is brooding on his grief, shrouding himself in gloom, and is surrounded by gossips who whisper scandalous tales to him about his father's death, finding it necessary, in the absence of real evidence, to name the king as the guilty party.

92. *O my dear Gertrude:* Claudius is beginning, in his anxiety and unhappiness, to lean on his wife for moral support even more than she on him.

King

How long hath she been thus? 65

Ophelia

I hope all will be well. We must be patient; but I cannot choose but weep to think they would lay him i' th' cold ground. My brother shall know of it; and so I thank you for your good counsel. Come, my coach! Good night, ladies; good night, sweet ladies, 70 good night, good night.

Exit

King

Follow her close: give her good watch, I pray you.

Exeunt HORATIO *and* GENTLEMAN

O, this is the poison of deep grief; it springs
All from her father's death. And now behold—
O Gertrude, Gertrude! 75
When sorrows come, they come not single spies,
But in battalions! First, her father slain;
Next, your son gone, and he most violent author
Of his own just remove; the people muddied,
Thick and unwholesome in their thoughts and whispers 80
For good Polonius' death; and we have done but
      greenly
In hugger-mugger to inter him; poor Ophelia
Divided from herself and her fair judgment,
Without the which we are pictures, or mere beasts;
Last, and as much containing as all these, 85
Her brother is in secret come from France;
Feeds on his wonder, keeps himself in clouds,
And wants not buzzers to infect his ear
With pestilent speeches of his father's death;
Wherein necessity, of matter beggar'd, 90
Will nothing stick our person to arraign
In ear and ear. O my dear Gertrude, this,

93. *a murd'ring piece:* a cannon loaded with bits and pieces of iron that inflicted unpleasant wounds.

94. *Gives . . . death:* kills me several times over.

96. *Attend!* Come here, someone!

97. *Switzers:* Swiss hired guards, at one time employed by many rulers in Europe.

98-108. In a panic, the gentleman tells the king to escape. Laertes, with a group of sympathizers, is sweeping towards him like a strong tide. *overpeering of his list:* rising above its usual level.

100. *Eats . . . haste:* Is not more ruthless in the way it rushes over and floods the low-lying land.

101. *in a riotous head:* with a rebellious force.

102. *O'erbears:* overwhelms.

102-8. *The rabble . . . king:* The ordinary people call Laertes their lord and, throwing aside all the considerations of precedent and history that make such decisions constitutional, and, as though there were no such thing as tradition, they say they will elect their king for themselves, and he will be Laertes. (He was not even of the royal family.)

107. *Caps . . . clouds:* They throw their caps in the air, clap, and cheer their decision.

109-10. As the mob outside batters at the locked doors, having overcome the guard, the queen compares them to dogs, in full cry on a false scent, going in completely the wrong direction (*counter*). She means that they are behaving treacherously, hunting down Claudius, the actual king, instead of the rebellious Laertes. In spite of the fact that Hamlet's talk with her must have made her have second thoughts about her marriage, she has not a moment's hesitation in supporting her husband, as the properly elected king, against a rebel.

112-14. As Laertes, with drawn sword, and his supporters, burst in, it looks for a moment as though they are about to lynch Claudius, but Laertes's temporary popularity with them (and therefore his dangerous power) is shown by the way they willingly obey him. What, do you think, has made him so popular with them, suddenly?

112. *this king:* this so-called king. *without:* outside.

Like to a murd'ring piece, in many places
Gives me superfluous death.

A noise within

Queen
  Alack, what noise is this?   95
King
  Attend!

Enter a GENTLEMAN

Where are my Switzers? Let them guard the door.
What is the matter?
Gentleman   Save yourself, my lord:
  The ocean, overpeering of his list,
  Eats not the flats with more impitious haste   100
  Than young Laertes, in a riotous head,
  O'erbears your officers. The rabble call him lord;
  And, as the world were now but to begin,
  Antiquity forgot, custom not known,
  The ratifiers and props of every word,   105
  They cry 'Choose we; Laertes shall be king'.
  Caps, hands, and tongues, applaud it to the clouds,
  'Laertes shall be king, Laertes king'.
Queen
  How cheerfully on the false trail they cry!

Noise within

  O, this is counter, you false Danish dogs!   110
King
  The doors are broke.

Enter LAERTES, *with* OTHERS, *in arms*

Laertes
  Where is this king?—Sirs, stand you all without.
All
  No, let's come in.
Laertes   I pray you give me leave.

115. *Keep:* guard.

115-16. Laertes's fierce accusation of Claudius, assuming that he is responsible for Polonius's death, though he has no definite proof, contrasts strongly with Hamlet's hesitation to take action about his father's death, even when he had convincing evidence of his guilt.

116. The queen is quick here, and in line 128, to put in a placating word.

117-20. Laertes says that no real son could be calm in these circumstances.

118. *cuckold:* a man whose wife was unfaithful to him. *brands the harlot:* See note on Act III, Scene iv, lines 42-7.

119. *Even here:* Laertes emphasizes his meaning by pointing to his own forehead. *unsmirched:* innocent.

120-27. Up to now in the play, Claudius has managed to avoid angry scenes and violence (in his handling both of family and political affairs, such as the Fortinbras threat), but now that he is faced with personal danger he copes with the situation calmly and with dignity, quickly re-establishing his authority over the slightly hysterical young man who threatens to kill him at any moment.

121. *giant-like:* powerful and threatening.

122. *Let him go, Gertrude:* The queen is courageously risking danger herself by attempting to hold back Laertes with her own hands.

122-6. Claudius says that Gertrude need not worry about his safety, for an anointed king is surrounded by divine protection, as by a hedge, which prevents traitors getting further than contemplating the harm they want to do. (This belief used to be so strongly held, by some, that it is not entirely absurd for Claudius to make this claim, however wicked he may be, as he had been duly appointed king with, no doubt, all the appropriate religious ceremonies. His confidence certainly sobers Laertes a little.)

128. *Dead:* Claudius shrewdly realizes that any attempt at an indirect answer would only exasperate Laertes more.

129. By insisting that Laertes should say all he wants to, Claudius cleverly takes some of the wind out of his sails.

130. *juggled with:* played with, made a fool of.

131-6. *To hell . . . father:* Laertes says that he doesn't care if he goes to hell for breaking his oath of loyalty to the king, and his conscience and virtues can go there too. His standpoint is this: he doesn't care what happens in this world or the next, provided he obtains full revenge for his father's death. Unlike Hamlet, Laertes has no scruples about the rights or wrongs of the revenge he wants to take. *throughly:* thoroughly.

137. *Who shall stay you?* Who is trying to stop you? *My will . . . world's:* The opposition of the whole world will not prevent me doing what I want to do.

All

    We will, we will.

                Exeunt

Laertes

    I thank you. Keep the door.—O thou vile king,   115

    Give me my father!

Queen   Calmly, good Laertes.

Laertes

    That drop of blood that's calm proclaims me bastard;

    Cries cuckold to my father; brands the harlot

    Even here, between the chaste unsmirched brow

    Of my true mother.

King   What is the cause, Laertes,   120

    That thy rebellion looks so giant-like?

    Let him go, Gertrude; do not fear our person:

    There's such divinity doth hedge a king

    That treason can but peep to what it would,

    Acts little of his will. Tell me, Laertes,   125

    Why thou art thus incens'd. Let him go, Gertrude.

    Speak, man.

Laertes

    Where is my father?

King   Dead.

Queen   But not by him.

King

    Let him demand his fill.

Laertes

    How came he dead? I'll not be juggled with.   130

    To hell, allegiance! Vows, to the blackest devil!

    Conscience and grace, to the profoundest pit!

    I dare damnation. To this point I stand,

    That both the worlds I give to negligence,

    Let come what comes; only I'll be reveng'd   135

    Most throughly for my father.

King

    Who shall stay you?

138. *means:* resources. *husband:* economize with.

139. *They . . . little:* They will go a long way, though they are limited. (Compare Act IV, Scene iv, lines 45-6.)

140-41. *the certainty . . . father:* exactly what happened to your father.

141-3. *is't writ . . . loser:* are you determined to make a clean sweep of everyone, friend and enemy, those on your side and those against? Claudius compares Laertes to a gambler ruthlessly collecting his winnings.

144. *Will . . . then?* 'May I tell you who they are, then?' Claudius, having got Laertes to listen to him at last, has regained control of the situation, for all he now has to do is to channel Laertes's anger in the right direction – against Hamlet.

145-7. Spreading out his arms with another melodramatic gesture, Laertes compares himself to a pelican, feeding its young (as it was believed to do in those days) with its own blood, from its torn breast. (In fact, these birds feed their offspring on half-digested fish, stored in their throats, so it is easy to see how the legend arose.) Laertes means that he would do anything for his father's true friends. *kind:* devoted to its family.

147-52. *Why . . . eye:* Ignoring the crudeness of Laertes's exaggerated language, Claudius smoothly compliments him on the appropriateness of what he has said. *good child:* dutiful son.

149-52. Claudius tells him that he will soon see, as clear as daylight, that he himself is not to blame, and indeed sincerely grieves about Polonius's death. Before Claudius goes on to say that it was Hamlet who killed Polonius (no doubt, Gertrude is waiting anxiously to see if he is going to blame her son), a commotion outside heralds Ophelia, who wanders vaguely in, the rabble at the door making way for her.

154-63. As soon as he sees her distracted appearance, Laertes realizes what has happened and, moved to tears, he vows, now more soberly, to avenge the double injury done to his family. He assumes, like Claudius, that her madness was caused by her father's death.

154-5. Laertes asks his anger to take away his consciousness of what he sees, and his tears to blind him. *sense and virtue:* power of perception.

156-7. *thy madness . . . beam:* 'I will make the man who drove you mad pay for it more than thoroughly.' Laertes's image is of Ophelia's madness and the punishment for it being weighed by a pair of scales.

157. By describing his sister as a *rose of May*, Laertes conjures up an impression of the fresh, springlike beauty that was once hers.

160. *be as mortal:* die as easily.

161-3. Affection for one's family is a noble kind of love, and at its best it sacrifices something precious (in this case, Ophelia's sanity) when a loved one dies. Even at such a moment, Laertes, like his father, cannot resist an opportunity to make a little speech.

Laertes   My will, not all the world's.
  And for my means, I'll husband them so well
  They shall go far with little.
King   Good Laertes,
  If you desire to know the certainty   *140*
  Of your dear father, is't writ in your revenge
  That, swoopstake, you will draw both friend and foe,
  Winner and loser?
Laertes   None but his enemies.
King
  Will you know them, then?
Laertes
  To his good friends thus wide I'll ope my arms   *145*
  And, like the kind life-rend'ring pelican,
  Repast them with my blood.
King   Why, now you speak
  Like a good child and a true gentleman.
  That I am guiltless of your father's death,
  And am most sensibly in grief for it,   *150*
  It shall as level to your judgment 'pear
  As day does to your eye.

                [A noise within: 'Let her come in.']

Laertes
  How now! What noise is that?

                Re-enter OPHELIA

  O, heat dry up my brains! tears seven times salt
  Burn out the sense and virtue of mine eye!   *155*
  By heaven, thy madness shall be paid with weight
  Till our scale turn the beam. O rose of May!
  Dear maid, kind sister, sweet Ophelia!
  O heavens! is't possible a young maid's wits
  Should be as mortal as an old man's life?   *160*
  Nature is fine in love; and where 'tis fine
  It sends some precious instance of itself
  After the thing it loves.

                247

164-7. Again, Ophelia's song is about a funeral, though when she adds the words *Fare you well, my dove*, the phrase sounds more appropriate to Hamlet than Polonius. She shows no sign of recognizing her brother.

168-9. Laertes says that if she had begged him to take revenge when she was sane it could not move him as much as this pathetic madness.

170-71. *You must sing . . . a-down-a:* Ophelia seems to be reproving Laertes for interrupting her song, and tells him to sing the chorus.

171. *O, how the wheel becomes it!* The most probable meaning of this is that the chorus of the song is appropriate to the rest of it (as Polonius and the *tears* referred to are *down* in the grave). Other possibilities are that she refers to the humming of an imaginary spinning wheel that forms a suitable accompaniment to her song, or that she dances about.

171-2. *It is . . . daughter:* Perhaps Ophelia is describing the story of the song she is singing; anyway, the situation is again in some ways like hers – she is a daughter who has been deceived, as she sees it, in love. Hamlet, however, was Polonius's *master*, not the other way round.

173. The disjointedness of her remarks, Laertes says, is more touching than a sensible way of speaking would be.

174-83. Ophelia now distributes flowers among those present, apparently under the impression that she is at a funeral or a wedding (whose wedding?), or a combination of both. All the ones she mentions had symbolic meanings in Elizabethan times. Do you think they are real or imaginary flowers? Which would be the more effective?

174-6. She explains the significance of *rosemary* and *pansies*, both of which she gives to the same person, whom she calls *love*. Is it the absent Hamlet, to whom both remembrance and thoughts are appropriate, or perhaps Laertes, who, she dimly feels, must do her remembering (of her father) and thinking for her?

177. *A document in madness:* even in her madness, she makes sense.

179. *There's fennel . . . columbines:* These plants stood for flattery and deceit, with a hint of adultery – obviously Claudius is the person for whom they are intended.

179-81. *There's rue . . . a Sundays:* Rue, otherwise known as *herb of grace*, was a symbol of repentance and sorrow. The first meaning is appropriate to the queen, and the second to herself.

181-2. *O, you must . . . difference:* Ophelia hints that the meaning of the plant is different for each of them.

182. *daisy:* another symbol of deceit. It is probably Laertes's turn by now. He has not tried to deceive anyone yet, as far as we know, but does so later on in the play.

183. *violets:* symbol of faithfulness. These would certainly be appropriate to Laertes, who should try to remain faithful to his father's memory. (On the other hand, this also could be intended for Hamlet, who Ophelia believes has been faithless to her; compare also, Act I, Scene iii, line 7.) Since her father died, however, she says, all faithfulness seems to have disappeared from the world.

184. *They say . . . end:* Either someone has told her, or she is trying to persuade herself, that Polonius died well, whereas, in fact, his was an undignified and cowardly end.

185. Ophelia sings a snatch of another half-remembered love-song.

Ophelia   [*Sings*]

    They bore him barefac'd on the bier;

    Hey non nonny, nonny, hey nonny;   *165*

    And in his grave rain'd many a tear—

Fare you well, my dove!

Laertes

Hadst thou thy wits, and didst persuade revenge,

It could not move thus.

Ophelia

You must sing 'A-down, a-down', and you call him *170*
a-down-a. O, how the wheel becomes it! It is the false
steward, that stole his master's daughter.

Laertes

This nothing's more than matter.

Ophelia

There's rosemary, that's for remembrance; pray you,
love, remember. And there is pansies, that's for *175*
thoughts.

Laertes

A document in madness—thoughts and remembrance
fitted.

Ophelia

There's fennel for you, and columbines. There's rue
for you; and here's some for me. We may call it herb *180*
of grace a Sundays. O, you must wear your rue with a
difference. There's a daisy. I would give you some
violets, but they wither'd all when my father died.
They say 'a made a good end.

        [*Sings*]

    For bonny sweet Robin is all my joy.   *185*

186-7. *Thought . . . prettiness:* She transforms ideas, grief, intense emotion, even evil, into something graceful and attractive. *favour* might also refer to the tokens, in the form of flowers, that she has given them to wear.

188-97. Ophelia's last song is again about a death, this time clearly that of an old man.

194. *poll:* head.

196. *cast away moan:* grieve in vain.

198. Adding that she prays God to have mercy on everyone, and bidding them all goodbye (literally, 'God be with you') Ophelia leaves us with the impression that even in her madness she has the remains of a simple piety and charitableness.

199. Even Laertes is nearly reduced to speechlessness.

200-10. *Laertes . . . content:* Deciding to strike while the iron is hot, Claudius suggests that the two of them get together with a few of Laertes's friends to arbitrate the question of responsibility for Polonius's death. If Claudius is proved guilty he will resign his kingdom, his possessions, even his life to Laertes, but, if not, Laertes must help him to punish the real culprit.

200. *commune with:* share.

201. *Go but apart:* Just go away on your own.

202. *Make choice . . . will:* Choose any sensible friends you wish.

204. *by direct . . . hand:* either directly or indirectly.

205. *us touch'd:* me guilty.

207. *in satisfaction:* as recompense.

208. *lend your patience to us:* listen to me patiently.

209. *we shall . . . soul:* I shall help you to achieve what you want.

210-15. Laertes, more quietly than when he first appeared, but still showing that he is determined to obtain satisfaction, replies with the questions he wants answered: how Polonius was killed and why he was buried without any of the ceremony that an eminent statesman generally has.

212. *hatchment:* coat of arms. *o'er his bones:* on his tomb.

213. *ostentation:* pomp and ceremony.

214. Polonius's voice, says his son, is heard, as it were, calling from the other world for vengeance (as Hamlet's father, too, did. We are again reminded of the parallel between the situations of the two young men).

Laertes

    Thought and affliction, passion, hell itself,

    She turns to favour and to prettiness.

Ophelia   *[Sings]*

        And will 'a not come again?

        And will 'a not come again?

           No, no, he is dead,   *190*

           Go to thy death-bed,

        He never will come again.

        His beard was as white as snow,

        All flaxen was his poll;

           He is gone, he is gone,   *195*

           And we cast away moan:

        God-a-mercy on his soul!

    And of all Christian souls, I pray God. God buy you.

                      Exit

Laertes

    Do you see this, O God?

King

    Laertes, I must commune with your grief,   *200*

    Or you deny me right. Go but apart,

    Make choice of whom your wisest friends you will,

    And they shall hear and judge 'twixt you and me.

    If by direct or by collateral hand

    They find us touch'd, we will our kingdom give,   *205*

    Our crown, our life, and all that we call ours,

    To you in satisfaction; but if not,

    Be you content to lend your patience to us,

    And we shall jointly labour with your soul

    To give it due content.

Laertes   Let this be so.   *210*

    His means of death, his obscure funeral—

    No trophy, sword, nor hatchment, o'er his bones,

    No noble rite nor formal ostentation—

    Cry to be heard, as 'twere from heaven to earth,

216. *where th' offence is . . . fall:* the guilty man will be punished with death. Claudius now has a second line of attack against Hamlet: if the English plot miscarries, he can use Laertes's desire for revenge against him.

SCENE VI

Horatio, isolated amid the intrigues and unsettled atmosphere of the court, is probably relieved to hear from Hamlet, though, typically, he makes no comment about his feelings.

1. *What:* what sort of people. *would:* want to.

8. *'A shall . . . Him:* God will, if he pleases. In spite of his rough appearance, the sailor's hearty manner seems to please Horatio; his directness is certainly a refreshing contrast to the polished insincerity of the court.

9-10. *th'ambassador . . . England:* The sailor does not seem to know who the writer really is. Why should Hamlet wish to remain incognito?

10-11. *let to know:* led to believe.

12-29. Hamlet's letter is in a hurried but straightforward style, very different from that of the one he wrote to Ophelia (Act II, Scene ii, lines 109–24).

12. *overlook'd:* read.

13. *means to:* access to.

14. *Ere . . . sea:* Before we had been at sea two days.

That I must call't in question.

King   So you shall;   215
And where th' offence is, let the great axe fall.
I pray you go with me.

Exeunt

SCENE VI—*Elsinore. The Castle*

Enter HORATIO *with an* ATTENDANT

Horatio
What are they that would speak with me?

Attendant
Sea-faring men, sir; they say they have letters for you.

Horatio
Let them come in.

Exit ATTENDANT

I do not know from what part of the world
I should be greeted, if not from Lord Hamlet.   5

Enter SAILORS

Sailor
God bless you, sir.

Horatio
Let Him bless thee too.

Sailor
'A shall, sir, an't please Him. There's a letter for you,
sir; it came from th' ambassador that was bound for
England—if your name be Horatio, as I am let to   10
know it is.

Horatio [*Reads*]
'Horatio, when thou shalt have overlook'd this, give
these fellows some means to the King: they have
letters for him. Ere we were two days old at sea, a

253

15. *appointment:* equipment.

16-17. *put on a compelled valour:* were forced to put up a fight.

17. *in the grapple:* while the ships were grappled together.

19-20. *They have dealt . . . mercy:* Though pirates, they have treated me well.

21. *good turn:* probably some form of ransom.

22. *repair:* come.

23-5. *I have words . . . matter:* Hamlet says he has something to tell Horatio that will horrify him, and even then what he says will hardly convey the full significance of the matter. It seems that Hamlet has discovered the plot to murder him.

25-6. *These good fellows:* the pirates.

26. *where I am:* Why doesn't Hamlet commit to paper either what he has to say about the plot against his life or where he is to be found?

27. *hold their course:* continue their journey.

29. *He . . . thine:* This warm greeting bears out what Hamlet said at the beginning of Act III, Scene ii, about his respect and affection for Horatio.

30. *give you way for:* enable you to deliver.

31-2. *And do't . . . them:* And do it all the more quickly if you will show me where I can find the person who sent them.

SCENE VII

Laertes is now satisfied, after the proposed investigation has taken place, not only that Claudius is innocent of Polonius's death but that Hamlet was plotting to kill the king, too. Claudius is careful to base his misrepresentation of Hamlet on as much truth as possible, but he has no real evidence for the second charge.

1. *Now . . . seal:* You must agree that I am clear of the crime.

2. *put me in your heart:* consider me.

3. *Sith:* since. *with a knowing ear:* are convinced.

5. *Pursu'd:* attempted to take. (Claudius, of course, is unaware that Hamlet actually had the chance to kill him.) *well appears:* certainly seems so.

6. *proceeded not against these feats:* took no steps to punish what he did.

7. *crimeful:* criminal. *capital in nature:* punishable by death.

8-9. *As by . . . stirr'd up:* As your safety, common-sense and every other consideration should have urgently prompted you to do.

pirate of very warlike appointment gave us chase. 15
Finding ourselves too slow of sail, we put on a compelled valour; and in the grapple I boarded them. On
the instant they got clear of our ship; so I alone
became their prisoner. They have dealt with me like
thieves of mercy; but they knew what they did: I am 20
to do a good turn for them. Let the King have the
letters I have sent; and repair thou to me with as
much speed as thou would'st fly death. I have words
to speak in thine ear will make thee dumb; yet are
they much too light for the bore of the matter. These 25
good fellows will bring thee where I am. Rosencrantz
and Guildenstern hold their course for England; of
them I have much to tell thee. Farewell.

He that thou knowest thine, HAMLET.'
Come, I will give you way for these your letters, 30
And do't the speedier that you may direct me
To him from whom you brought them.

Exeunt

SCENE VII—*Elsinore. The Castle*

Enter KING *and* LAERTES

King
Now must your conscience my acquittance seal,
And you must put me in your heart for friend,
Sith you have heard, and with a knowing ear,
That he which hath your noble father slain
Pursu'd my life.
Laertes   It well appears. But tell me 5
Why you proceeded not against these feats,
So crimeful and so capital in nature,
As by your safety, wisdom, all things else,
You mainly were stirr'd up.

10. *unsinew'd:* weak, lame.

11. *th'are:* they are.

11-16. The first reason he gives is that Gertrude is devoted to Hamlet, and Claudius himself is so fond of her that he could not go contrary to her wishes, regardless of whether it is a good thing or not (*My virtue or my plague*) that he feels like this about her.

14. *so conjunctive . . . soul:* so much a part of my life.

15-16. *as the star . . . her:* Claudius compares himself following his wife's wishes to a star pursuing its one and only path.

17. *Why . . . go:* Why I could not make him account for himself in public.

18. *general gender:* common people.

19-21. *dipping . . . graces:* Claudius compares the way that the public would regard any punishment imposed on Hamlet (*gyves:* fetters) as cause for sympathy rather than a disgrace, to the way a certain spring was said to be able to change wood into stone.

21-4. *so that . . . them:* Using another metaphor, Claudius says that an attack on Hamlet would have only done harm to himself through his flying in the face of public opinion, as though he had tried to shoot light-weight arrows against a strong wind that just blew them back in his face.

25-9. *And so . . . perfections:* Laertes asks whether he just has to put up with all the wrongs that Hamlet has done him, passively.

26. *desp'rate terms:* a hopeless state of insanity.

27-9. *Whose worth . . . perfections:* Whose qualities, if one can describe her as she once was, not as she is now, exalted her above everyone else in her generation. Then Laertes adds that all the same he will find an opportunity some day to take revenge. This is just what Claudius wanted to hear: that Laertes does not see the law as the only way of obtaining 'justice'.

30. *Break . . . that:* You don't need to lose any sleep over that.

30-3. *You . . . pastime:* Having spoken as man to man up to now in this scene, Claudius reverts to the royal plural, to give an impression of his kingly dignity as he tells Laertes that he is not one to ignore an impudent threat to his safety.

34. By this mixture of pronouns *I* and *we*, Claudius implies that as a private individual he was fond of Polonius, and as a king he realizes his duty to protect himself.

35-6. Just as he is about to say how much he too wants to punish Hamlet, a letter from him (mentioned in the last scene) arrives. *teach . . . imagine:* enable you to realize.

37. *this to the Queen:* We never hear any more of this letter.

38. Claudius is disconcerted. Hamlet should either be still at sea or, if he has landed in England, dead by now; in neither case should he be able to send a letter.

King   O, for two special reasons,
  Which may to you, perhaps, seem much unsinew'd,   10
  But yet to me th'are strong. The Queen his mother
  Lives almost by his looks; and for myself,
  My virtue or my plague, be it either which—
  She is so conjunctive to my life and soul
  That, as the star moves not but in his sphere,   15
  I could not but by her. The other motive,
  Why to a public count I might not go,
  Is the great love the general gender bear him;
  Who, dipping all his faults in their affection,
  Work like the spring that turneth wood to stone,   20
  Convert his gyves to graces; so that my arrows,
  Too slightly timber'd for so loud a wind,
  Would have reverted to my bow again,
  But not where I have aim'd them.

Laertes
  And so have I a noble father lost;   25
  A sister driven into desp'rate terms,
  Whose worth, if praises may go back again,
  Stood challenger on mount of all the age
  For her perfections. But my revenge will come.

King
  Break not your sleeps for that. You must not think 30
  That we are made of stuff so flat and dull
  That we can let our beard be shook with danger,
  And think it pastime. You shortly shall hear more.
  I lov'd your father, and we love our self;
  And that, I hope, will teach you to imagine—   35

Enter a MESSENGER *with letters*

  How now! What news?
Messenger   Letters, my lord, from Hamlet:
  These to your Majesty; this to the Queen.
King
  From Hamlet! Who brought them?

39. The pirates obviously thought it was better not to risk being cross-examined by the king.

43-7. In striking contrast with the one Horatio received, this letter is haughty and mysterious in tone, hinting defiance, with a strange undercurrent of excitement.

43. The contemptuous *High and Mighty*, parodying the way a letter to a king should begin, is followed by an abrupt announcement that Hamlet has returned to Denmark. *naked* (see line 52) sets the king thinking; does Hamlet mean that he is destitute – an implied criticism of Claudius – or is he saying that now there will be no more pretence but, like a naked sword, he is ready to act?

44-5. *shall I . . . eyes:* a sarcastic way of saying that he will ask for an audience with the king.

45-6. *first asking . . . thereunto:* with your kind permission. Again the politeness is mockingly exaggerated.

46. *recount the occasion of:* explain the reason for.

48-9. For once Claudius is at a loss, for the letter is so ambiguous that he has little idea of how much Hamlet knows or what his intentions are.

48. *all the rest:* Rosencrantz and Guildenstern in particular.

49. *abuse:* trick, forgery.

50. *hand:* hand-writing.

51. *character:* way of writing.

52-3. Studying the letter again, Claudius notices another disconcerting word. Does *alone* mean just that Hamlet has returned alone, or that he wishes to see Claudius on his own, the next day? The latter possibility sounds rather ominous to Claudius, no doubt.

53. *devise me?* make any suggestion?

54. *I am lost in it:* 'I can make nothing of it.' Laertes goes on to say that Hamlet cannot return soon enough for him, for he is longing to relieve his feelings by telling him what he thinks of him.

57-9. Claudius cautiously begins to sound Laertes's reaction to an underhand plot he has just formulated.

58. *As . . . otherwise?* And how else could you feel? (or, possibly, 'How could he have come back, and, if he has, how else can we act?')

60. *o'errule . . . peace:* force me to make it up with him.

61. *To thine own peace:* Claudius means that he is just encouraging Laertes to do something for his own peace of mind.

62. *As checking at:* because he took against. Claudius uses a falconer's term for a hawk that turns aside from its proper prey. *that:* because.

63-5. *I will work . . . fall:* I shall entice him by a plan I have just matured in my mind, to which he is bound to succumb.

Messenger

    Sailors, my lord, they say; I saw them not.

    They were given me by Claudio; he receiv'd them   40

    Of him that brought them.

King   Laertes, you shall hear them.

    Leave us.

Exit MESSENGER

    [*Reads*] 'High and Mighty. You shall know I am set

    naked on your kingdom. To-morrow shall I beg leave

    to see your kingly eyes; when I shall, first asking your   45

    pardon thereunto, recount the occasion of my sudden

    and more strange return. HAMLET.'

    What should this mean? Are all the rest come back?

    Or is it some abuse, and no such thing?

Laertes

    Know you the hand?   50

King

    'Tis Hamlet's character. 'Naked'!

    And in a postcript here, he says 'alone'.

    Can you devise me?

Laertes

    I am lost in it, my lord. But let him come;

    It warms the very sickness in my heart   55

    That I shall live and tell him to his teeth

    'Thus didest thou'.

King   If it be so, Laertes—

    As how should it be so, how otherwise?—

    Will you be rul'd by me?

Laertes   Ay, my lord;

    So you will not o'errule me to a peace.   60

King

    To thine own peace. If he be now return'd,

    As checking at his voyage, and that he means

    No more to undertake it, I will work him

    To an exploit now ripe in my device,

    Under the which he shall not choose but fall;   65

66-8. Hamlet's death (this is the first time he has said in so many words that he wants to kill his nephew; he drops the word casually) will be so arranged that, even to his mother, it will look like an accident, with no-one at all to blame.

68. *be rul'd:* do what you say. Laertes is replying to Claudius's request in line 59.

69-70. *The rather . . . organ:* all the more readily if you could arrange for me to be the instrument of his death.

70. *It falls right:* that fits in with my plan.

71-106. Claudius seems to change the subject, describing at length the wonderful reports he has had of Laertes's skill in fencing.

73-6. *Your sum . . . siege:* He envied this one accomplishment of yours more than all the rest put together, and yet, in my opinion, it is the least important of your good points. (Claudius introduces a little discreet flattery and, at the same time, gives the impression that Hamlet does not appreciate Laertes's best qualities.)

76. *part:* attribute, quality.

77. *A very . . . youth:* The sort of accomplishment that gives an extra attraction to a gay young man.

78. *needful:* useful, acting as an asset.

78-81. *for youth . . . graveness:* it suits a young man (like Laertes) to dress – and live – gaily, just as it is fitting for an older man to wear fur-trimmed dark clothes (i.e. behave soberly). Claudius is suggesting that it is not suitable for someone of his age to indulge in the sort of pastime that a young man like Laertes can; this is in case Laertes feels that Claudius is taking a cowardly way out in getting him to carry out the dangerous part of the plan.

81. *since:* ago.

82. *Here:* at the Danish court.

84-5. *they can . . . witchcraft in't:* they can all ride well, but this gentleman was a wizard at it.

85. *grew unto his seat:* seemed part of the saddle.

86-8. *And . . . beast:* He got his horse to do such wonderful things that the two of them seemed to be one creature.

88-90. *topp'd my thought . . . did:* what he did exceeded my wildest imaginings.

93-4. *the brooch . . . nation:* 'he is an ornament to France.' Claudius is getting Laertes into the right frame of mind by quoting real or imaginary praise from an eminent sportsman, though what he is going to suggest is most unsportsmanlike.

And for his death, no wind of blame shall breathe;
But even his mother shall uncharge the practice
And call it accident.
Laertes   My lord, I will be rul'd
The rather, if you could devise it so
That I might be the organ.
King   It falls right.   70
You have been talk'd of since your travel much,
And that in Hamlet's hearing, for a quality
Wherein they say you shine. Your sum of parts
Did not together pluck such envy from him
As did that one; and that, in my regard,   75
Of the unworthiest siege.
Laertes   What part is that, my lord?
King
A very riband in the cap of youth,
Yet needful too; for youth no less becomes
The light and careless livery that it wears
Than settled age his sables and his weeds,   80
Importing health and graveness. Two months since
Here was a gentleman of Normandy—
I have seen myself, and serv'd against, the French,
And they can well on horseback; but this gallant
Had witchcraft in't; he grew into his seat,   85
And to such wondrous doing brought his horse,
As he had been incorps'd and demi-natur'd
With the brave beast. So far he topp'd my thought,
That I, in forgery of shapes and tricks,
Come short of what he did.
Laertes   A Norman was't?   90
King
A Norman.
Laertes
Upon my life, Lamord.
King   The very same.
Laertes
I know him well. He is the brooch indeed

261

95-8. *He made . . . especial:* He said what a wonderful knowledge of the theory and practice of personal combat you have, particularly of swordsmanship.

100. *If one . . . you:* To watch you fencing against someone of your own standard. *scrimers of their nation:* French fencers.
101. *had neither . . . eye:* could not attack, defend or aim properly.

103. *Did Hamlet . . . envy:* Filled Hamlet with such poisonous jealousy. (Is this a characteristic we have ever seen in Hamlet?)

105. *Your . . . o'er:* That you should travel here immediately.

106. After his long digression, Claudius seems to hesitate before coming to the point, but is eagerly prompted by Laertes.

107-9. *Laertes . . . heart?* Claudius deliberately re-arouses Laertes's anger against Hamlet because he is still afraid that Laertes's sense of honour or the sportsmanship which he has just been praising will lead him to react with disgust to what he is suggesting.
108. *the painting of a sorrow:* just outwardly grieving.

110-13. Hastily, Claudius says that he doesn't doubt Laertes's affection for his father – it is just that experience has proved to him (*in passages of proof*) that, just as love has a beginning, it has an end: time diminishes and kills it, just as the flame of a candle is dimmed by its own burnt-out wick. (Could Claudius be thinking of his own marriage here?)

116-23. *And nothing . . . easing:* Developing his thought to a sad generalization about life (much as Hamlet might), he says that nothing good stays the same always, for even goodness in excess destroys itself by its own bulk. When we want to do something we should do it immediately, otherwise our wish to do it becomes fainter, and we are put off by every word, action or chance occurrence until it becomes a painful duty, sapping one's strength, as extravagant sighing was supposed to do. (Since life consists of breath, sighs, being a waste of breath, were thought to use up a bit of one's life.) What has Claudius himself been putting off, until the idea has become more and more painful?
123. *But . . . ulcer:* Continuing the imagery of illness, Claudius tells himself to come to the point, painful though it is, and deal with what is causing the trouble.
124. *undertake:* do.
125. *deed:* actions.

And gem of all the nation.

King

He made confession of you;   95
And gave you such a masterly report
For art and exercise in your defence,
And for your rapier most especial,
That he cried out 'twould be a sight indeed
If one could match you. The scrimers of their nation   100
He swore had neither motion, guard, nor eye,
If you oppos'd them. Sir, this report of his
Did Hamlet so envenom with his envy
That he could nothing do but wish and beg
Your sudden coming o'er, to play with you.   105
Now, out of this—

Laertes   What out of this, my lord?

King

Laertes, was your father dear to you?
Or are you like the painting of a sorrow,
A face without a heart?

Laertes   Why ask you this?

King

Not that I think you did not love your father;   110
But that I know love is begun by time,
And that I see, in passages of proof,
Time qualifies the spark and fire of it.
There lives within the very flame of love
A kind of wick or snuff that will abate it;   115
And nothing is at a like goodness still;
For goodness, growing to a pleurisy,
Dies in his own too much. That we would do,
We should do when we would; for this 'would' changes,
And hath abatements and delays as many   120
As there are tongues, are hands, are accidents;
And then this 'should' is like a spendthrift's sigh
That hurts by easing. But to the quick of th' ulcer:
Hamlet comes back; what would you undertake
To show yourself in deed your father's son   125

126. *More than:* not just. *To cut . . . church:* Laertes's brutal reply bears out what he said earlier (Act IV, Scene v, lines 133–5), that he is prepared to risk damnation and act completely ruthlessly, if only he can obtain revenge. (Even a convicted criminal used to be able to claim sanctuary in a church.)

127-8. *No place . . . bounds:* If Claudius is shocked, he does not show it: a murderer himself, he blandly agrees that while murder is wrong anywhere, revenge is above such laws.

129. *Keep close:* Stay hidden. Why doesn't Claudius want Laertes and Hamlet to meet until his plan (see below) is ready to be put into action?

131. *We'll . . . excellence:* I'll get people to praise your skill highly.

132. *set a double varnish on the fame:* put the finishing touches to the reputation.

133. *in fine:* in short. *together:* to fight.

134. *wager on your heads:* By laying bets about the result of the fencing match, Claudius will make people think it is just a game.

134-9. *He, being remiss . . . father:* Claudius explains that, as Hamlet will be off his guard, and is by nature magnanimous and not given to deception himself (an interesting tribute from Hamlet's enemy) he will not examine the fencing swords; it will then be easy for Laertes, with a little trickery if necessary, to pick out a sharpened blade from among the blunted ones, and to take his revenge with it on Hamlet. *a pass of practice* means both 'a practice bout' and 'a treacherous stroke' – Claudius is making a grim joke.

139-48. Laertes does not seem to hesitate for a moment in agreeing to this underhand plan; in fact, he now goes one better, saying that, to make doubly sure, he will put a deadly poison on his sword, one scratch from which will be enough to kill Hamlet.

140. *anoint:* apply something to.

141. *unction:* potion. *mountebank:* quack.

142. *mortal:* deadly.

143. *cataplasm so rare:* costly poultice.

144-5. *Collected . . . moon:* made up from extracts of all the healing plants in the world.

146. *withal:* with it. *point:* sword.

147. *contagion:* poison. *gall:* graze.

148-54. Claudius feels that it will be fatal if their plan misfires and their guilt is revealed, so they must have a reserve scheme ready.

149-50. *Weigh . . . shape:* Decide what is the best time and method for putting our plan into practice.

150-4. *If this . . . proof:* He compares the plan to a cannon bursting when it is being tested. *Soft:* wait a minute.

155. *We'll:* Claudius will. *cunnings:* respective skill.

156. *ha't:* have it.

157-62. *When . . . hold there:* Having spent a few moments visualizing a typical fencing match, Claudius hits on a clever idea: when, after playing for a while, they are hot and thirsty – and with this end in mind, Laertes is to keep the pace up – Hamlet will ask for a drink, and Claudius will have one offered to him which will have been specially prepared for the occasion. If Hamlet has managed to avoid a poisoned thrust from Laertes their aim will still be achieved, because if he just

More than in words?
Laertes   To cut his throat i' th' church.
King
No place, indeed, should murder sanctuarize;
Revenge should have no bounds. But, good Laertes,
Will you do this? Keep close within your chamber.
Hamlet return'd shall know you are come home.   *130*
We'll put on those shall praise your excellence,
And set a double varnish on the fame
The Frenchman gave you; bring you, in fine, together,
And wager on your heads. He, being remiss,
Most generous, and free from all contriving,   *135*
Will not peruse the foils; so that with ease
Or with a little shuffling, you may choose
A sword unbated, and, in a pass of practice,
Requite him for your father.
Laertes   I will do't;
And for that purpose I'll anoint my sword.   *140*
I bought an unction of a mountebank,
So mortal that but dip a knife in it,
Where it draws blood no cataplasm so rare,
Collected from all simples that have virtue
Under the moon, can save the thing from death   *145*
That is but scratch'd withal. I'll touch my point
With this contagion, that, if I gall him slightly,
It may be death.
King   Let's further think of this;
Weigh what convenience both of time and means
May fit us to our shape. If this should fail,   *150*
And that our drift look through our bad performance,
'Twere better not assay'd, therefore this project
Should have a back or second, that might hold
If this did blast in proof. Soft! let me see.
We'll make a solemn wager on your cunnings—   *155*
I ha't.
When in your motion you are hot and dry—
As make your bouts more violent to that end—

157-62- sips from the cup (which will be poisoned, too) he will die Hamlet can hardly avoid succumbing to one of these three plans, for the fact that Claudius and Laertes are both prepared to go to any lengths to kill him (poison was regarded with great horror in Elizabethan days, much as germ warfare is in our time) puts him at a disadvantage, as his sense of honour is much stricter than theirs.

162. A noise, perhaps of weeping and/or shouting outside, indicates to Claudius that there is yet another crisis.

163-4. *One woe . . . follow:* The queen's words echo what her husband said to her (Act IV, Scene v, lines 76-7); both of them are beginning to feel overwhelmed with troubles.

165. *O, where?* Laertes is so stunned by the latest tragedy that has struck his family, that he can only ask a rather pointless question; however, the queen answers him literally.

166-83. This description of Ophelia's death gives the impression that, sad as it was, there was something peaceful and even beautiful about it. Ophelia has not exactly committed suicide, for she was too disturbed to know exactly what was happening or to take responsibility for her actions; nor was she the victim of an unpleasant accident, for we are made to feel that she went to her death willingly, almost happily, accompanied by the music and flowers with which we have come to associate her.

166. *willow:* a well-known symbol of rejected love, so it is particularly fitting here. *aslant:* leaning across.

167. *hoar:* silvery.

168. *Therewith:* using sprigs of willow; perhaps somewhere in her mind she recalled the tree's associations.

169. *crowflowers:* buttercups. *long purples:* purple orchids.

170. *liberal:* free-spoken, uninhibited. *grosser:* coarser. (One of the nicknames of this plant was the 'Rampant Widow', a term which Gertrude might well be sensitive about!)

171. *cold:* prim. *dead men's fingers:* describes the palm-shaped roots of the orchid.

172-5. *There . . . brook:* As Ophelia climbed along the tree to hang her garlands of weeds on the overhanging branches, a treacherous twig broke and she and her flowers fell in the stream.

177. *Which time:* as long as she floated. *lauds:* hymns.

178. *incapable of:* unable to grasp.

179-80. *a creature . . . element:* a creature that normally lives in the water, and is used to it.

182. *lay:* song. Ophelia provided for herself the hymns and wreaths of a funeral, so that we feel her death was not without a touch of the appropriate dignity and ceremony (perhaps the queen, with the tact we have seen her to possess, is emphasizing the romantic side of his sister's death to soften the blow for Laertes).

185-89. *Too much . . . out:* Laertes says he does not want to add his tears to the water that has drowned Ophelia, and yet he cannot help giving in to his natural feelings, however embarrassing he may find it. He apologizes for crying, saying that in a moment he will behave in a more manly way.

And that he calls for drink, I'll have preferr'd him
A chalice for the nonce; whereon but sipping,   160
If he by chance escape your venom'd stuck,
Our purpose may hold there. But stay; what noise?

Enter QUEEN

Queen
One woe doth tread upon another's heel,
So fast they follow. Your sister's drown'd, Laertes.
Laertes
Drown'd? O, where?   165
Queen
There is a willow grows aslant the brook
That shows his hoar leaves in the glassy stream;
Therewith fantastic garlands did she make
Of crowflowers, nettles, daisies, and long purples
That liberal shepherds give a grosser name,   170
But our cold maids do dead men's fingers call them.
There, on the pendent boughs her coronet weeds
Clamb'ring to hang, an envious sliver broke;
When down her weedy trophies and herself
Fell in the weeping brook. Her clothes spread wide 175
And, mermaid-like, awhile they bore her up;
Which time she chanted snatches of old lauds,
As one incapable of her own distress,
Or like a creature native and indued
Unto that element; but long it could not be   180
Till that her garments, heavy with their drink,
Pull'd the poor wretch from her melodious lay
To muddy death.   Alas, then she is drown'd!
Laertes
Queen
Drown'd, drown'd.
Laertes
Too much of water hast thou, poor Ophelia,   185
And therefore I forbid my tears; but yet

190-1. *I have ... douts it:* I am burning with anger that I long to express, but my tears prevent me. *dout:* put out, quench.

191-4. How typical of Claudius to comment on the inconvenience rather than the sadness of Ophelia's death! However, though perhaps he is afraid that this last disaster may provoke Laertes into acting rashly, and not keeping to their plan, it is for the queen's benefit that he says he has been trying to pacify Laertes: he must not let her suspect that, in fact, he has been inciting Laertes to kill Hamlet. If he had any doubts about whether Laertes would do so, they are probably dispelled now.

It is our trick; nature her custom holds,
Let shame say what it will. When these are gone,
The woman will be out. Adieu, my lord.
I have a speech o' fire that fain would blaze   190
But that this folly douts it.

Exit

King   Let's follow, Gertrude.
How much I had to do to calm his rage!
Now fear I this will give it start again;
Therefore let's follow.

Exeunt

269

ACT FIVE

SCENEI

We are kept in suspense for a while about whether Hamlet will manage to escape the three-fold trap that awaits him while, like him, we have a change of scene. Though it is a graveyard where we now meet Hamlet (perhaps it is here, or near here, that he arranged to meet Horatio), the atmosphere at the beginning of the scene is comparatively clear and fresh, for, as in Act IV Scene iv, for a little while we escape from the gloom of Elsinore. Hamlet has clearly benefited from the change of air: he gives the impression of having lost for good the doubt and depression that weighed him down until the night he left home. After the interview with his mother he seems on a much more even keel. All trace of madness, real or put on, has left him, and he seems much more mature.

The scene opens with a conversation between two comic yokels (*clown*, in Shakespearian plays, means both 'rustic' and 'comedian') who seem quite unaffected by the gloomy side of their occupation – digging Ophelia's grave (for which the trap-door in the Elizabethan stage would come in useful). On the contrary, they crack cheerful jokes about it. 'Beggars' like these are certainly better off than kings (see Act II, Scene ii, lines 263–84 and Act IV, Scene iii, lines 24–32)!

1-2. The gravedigger sounds surprised that Ophelia is going to be buried in a churchyard because suicides were not supposed to be buried in consecrated ground. His phrase for killing oneself, however, is absurd, because, if Ophelia has found *salvation* then she is in heaven, and there is no need to treat her like a criminal.
3-5. *straight:* immediately (with a pun, meaning 'narrow'). *crowner:* coroner. The reason behind this decision, we learn later, is that Claudius insisted on it – no doubt to avoid further trouble with Laertes.
6-7. The speaker knows something about the law, and remembers that killing someone in self-defence is not a crime. But suicide can hardly be considered self-defence!
8. *found:* the coroner decided.
9. The clown is trying to say 'se defendendo', Latin for 'in self-defence'; what he has actually said means 'injuring oneself', the very opposite. He is showing off his slight knowledge of the sort of legal terms that would have been bandied about at the inquest.
9-10. *here lies the point:* this is the argument. Shakespeare bases this deliberately garbled account of legal proceedings on a well-known law-suit of his own times, also concerning suicide by drowning.
10-12. *if I drown . . . wittingly:* Giving an impression of developing a watertight argument, the clown, in fact, says nothing that makes any real sense. *wittingly:* deliberately, consciously. *argal:* another misheard Latin word. The word which the clown intended to say was 'ergo', meaning 'therefore'.
13. *hear you:* listen. *Goodman Delver:* Mr. Digger.

ACT FIVE

SCENE I—*Elsinore. A churchyard*

Enter two CLOWNS *with spades and picks*

First Clown

Is she to be buried in Christian burial when she
wilfully seeks her own salvation?

Second Clown

I tell thee she is; therefore make her grave straight.
The crowner hath sat on her, and finds it Christian
burial. 5

First Clown

How can that be, unless she drown'd herself in her
own defence?

Second Clown

Why, 'tis found so.

First Clown

It must be 'se offendendo'; it cannot be else. For here
lies the point: if I drown myself wittingly, it argues an 10
act; and an act hath three branches—it is to act, to
do, to perform; argal, she drown'd herself wittingly.

Second Clown

Nay, but hear you, Goodman Delver.

271

14. *Give me leave:* wait till I finish. *good:* right.

16. *it is, will he . . . goes:* it is his own choice whether he drowns himself or not.
17-19. *but if . . . life:* The gravedigger again triumphantly concludes with an obvious truth. (The argument he was trying to remember was based on the idea that the man concerned – whose relatives did not want his property to go to the crown, which it would if he were proved a suicide – was not his normal self when he died).
20. The other clown might well be puzzled!

21. *marry is't:* indeed it is. *quest:* inquest.

22. *ha:* have. *an't:* about it. As 'common' people, these two speak more carelessly than more educated characters.
23-4. *out a Christian burial:* in unconsecrated ground.

25. *there thou say'st:* you're right there.
25-7. *the more pity . . . Christen:* it's not fair for important people to have more right to kill themselves than their fellow-Christians.

28-30. Taking up his spade, and perhaps reminded by its shield-like shape of a coat of arms, he thinks of a joke. 'Everyone who digs', he begins, 'is the earliest kind of gentleman, because he does what Adam did.'

33. The other gravedigger falls into the trap, taking his mate to mean 'possessing a coat of arms' (which only gentlemen were allowed to have).
34-5. *What . . . the Scripture?* With mock horror, he suggests that the other man doesn't know his Bible.
34-8. Having dispatched this joke successfully, with a pun on *arms*, he goes on to another. *to the purpose:* correctly. *confess thyself:* a proverbial saying, finishing 'and be hanged'.

39. *Go to:* get along with you.

First Clown

Give me leave. Here lies the water; good. Here
stands the man; good. If the man go to this water   15
and drown himself, it is, will he, nill he, he goes—
mark you that; but if the water come to him and
drown him, he drowns not himself. Argal, he that is
not guilty of his own death shortens not his own life.

Second Clown

But is this law?   20

First Clown

Ay, marry, is't; crowner's quest law.

Second Clown

Will you ha' the truth an't? If this had not been a
gentlewoman, she should have been buried out a
Christian burial.

First Clown

Why, there thou say'st; and the more pity that great   25
folk should have count'nance in this world to drown
or hang themselves more than their even Christen.
Come, my spade. There is no ancient gentlemen but
gard'ners, ditchers, and grave-makers; they hold up
Adam's profession.   30

Second Clown

Was he a gentleman?

First Clown

'A was the first that ever bore arms.

Second Clown

Why, he had none.

First Clown

What, art a heathen? How dost thou understand the
Scripture? The Scripture says Adam digg'd. Could   35
he dig without arms? I'll put another question to
thee. If thou answerest me not to the purpose,
confess thyself—

Second Clown

Go to.

273

40. *What is he:* what kind of man is it?

42. This time the other fellow is not to be outdone, and finds an answer, though not the right one. *that frame:* the gallows. The *tenants* are, of course, the people who are hanged on it (perhaps the idea was put into his mind by the unfinished proverb in line 38).

44. *I like . . . well:* you've got the right idea. *in good faith:* upon my word.

45-8. *but how . . . well to thee:* He manages to twist the other's words to indicate that, because the gallows do a good job for criminals, the other gravedigger had better be careful in saying it is stronger than anything else, even the church, otherwise he may find himself on the gallows. *To't again, come:* come on, have another go.

51. *unyoke:* get it off your chest.

52. *Marry, now I can tell:* It's on the tip of my tongue!

53. *To't:* go on.

54. *Mass:* 'by the Mass', a mild oath.

55-6. *Cudgel . . . beating:* Give up making the effort to think – however much you punish a stupid donkey he won't go any faster.

57-8. *the houses . . . doomsday:* A grave lasts longer than a gallows or anything else, because the person buried in it will stay there till the Day of Judgment.

58-9. *get thee to Yaughan:* go along to the pub. *stoup of liquor:* flagon of drink.

60. At last this workman really manages to get down to his work, and even then only because he is able to look forward to having a drink when he has finished! To help himself along he cheerfully sings a garbled version of an old ballad, as he briskly digs through the much-used soil of the churchyard, throwing out the bones of the former tenants of the grave. The song he vaguely remembers is about a man who renounces love to prepare for death – Hamlet, who by now is listening, may feel it is particularly apt in his own case.

62. *contract-o-the time for-a:* The extra syllables are added by the clown to fit the notes of the tune, and possibly also represent his grunts as he digs.

First Clown

What is he that builds stronger than either the mason,   40
the shipwright, or the carpenter?

Second Clown

The gallows-maker; for that frame outlives a
thousand tenants.

First Clown

I like thy wit well; in good faith the gallows does
well; but how does it well? It does well to those that   45
do ill. Now thou dost ill to say the gallows is built
stronger than the church; argal, the gallows may do
well to thee. To 't again, come.

Second Clown

Who builds stronger than a mason, a shipwright, or
a carpenter?   50

First Clown

Ay, tell me that, and unyoke.

Second Clown

Marry, now I can tell.

First Clown

To 't.

Second Clown

Mass, I cannot tell.

Enter HAMLET *and* HORATIO, *afar off*

First Clown

Cudgel thy brains no more about it, for your dull ass   55
will not mend his pace with beating; and when you
are ask'd this question next, say 'a grave-maker': the
houses he makes lasts till doomsday. Go, get thee to
Yaughan; fetch me a stoup of liquor.

Exit SECOND CLOWN
[*Digs and sings*]

In youth, when I did love, did love,   60
   Methought it was very sweet,
To contract-o-the time for-a my behove,
   O, methought there-a-was nothing-a meet.

64-5. To Hamlet, it is strange that someone with such a job should not feel, as he would, something of the awe of death.

66. *Custom . . . easiness:* 'He's got used to it through doing it so often,' says Horatio, in his matter-of-fact way.

67-8. *'Tis e'en so . . . sense:* 'That's true – a hand that is not hardened by work is more sensitive.' Hamlet perhaps implies that delicacy of feeling, such as his, is something of a luxury, only possessed by those who have leisure to cultivate it.

69-78. Continuing his muddled song (*intil:* into) he throws a skull out of the grave, which starts a train of thought in Hamlet's mind that has occurred to him before (see Act IV, Scene iii, lines 20-5): death reduces everyone, however important, to the same level.

74. *jowls:* throws.

76. *pate:* head. *politician:* In Shakespeare's time this was someone who occupied himself in the intrigue of court life rather than, as now, one concerned with the business of government.

76-7. *which . . . o'erreaches:* whom this fool now gets the better of. *circumvent:* get round, deceive.

80. *a courtier:* (like Rosencrantz or Guildenstern) is always ready to flatter someone who might be able to do something for him, says Hamlet.

82. *Such-a-one:* So-and-so.

83. *beg:* borrow.

85. *e'en:* just. *my Lady Worm's:* he belongs to the worms. *chapless:* having lost his bottom jaw.

86. *mazard* was a slang word for 'head'.

87. *fine revolution:* wonderful change. *an:* if. *trick:* knack.

88-9. *Did . . . them?* What a waste of money and effort go into bringing up a human being, if his bones are just going to end up being used as skittles (perhaps the skull has been bowled against some of them).

89. *Mine:* his own bones. *ache . . . on't:* The thought of the futility of human achievement makes Hamlet sad.

Hamlet

Has this fellow no feeling of his business, that 'a sings
in grave-making?   65

Horatio

Custom hath made it in him a property of easiness.

Hamlet

'Tis e'en so; the hand of little employment hath the
daintier sense.

First Clown   [*Sings*]

     But age, with his stealing steps,
       Hath clawed me in his clutch,   70
     And hath shipped me intil the land,
       As if I had never been such.

Throws up a skull

Hamlet

That skull had a tongue in it, and could sing once.
How the knave jowls it to the ground, as if 'twere
Cain's jawbone, that did the first murder! This might   75
be the pate of a politician, which this ass now
o'erreaches; one that would circumvent God, might
it not?

Horatio

It might, my lord.

Hamlet

Or of a courtier; which could say 'Good morrow,   80
sweet lord! How dost thou, sweet lord?' This might
be my Lord Such-a-one, that praised my Lord Such-
a-one's horse, when 'a meant to beg it—might it not?

Horatio

Ay, my lord.

Hamlet

Why, e'en so; and now my Lady Worm's, chapless,   85
and knock'd about the mazard with a sexton's spade.
Here's fine revolution, an we had the trick to see't.
Did these bones cost no more the breeding but to
play at loggats with them? Mine ache to think on't.

95-108. Hamlet makes fun of the pompous complications of legal language and practice – they seem so superficial when they are compared with the simple reality of death.

95. *quiddities* and *quillets:* distorted Latin words; Hamlet means 'What is the use of all that hair-splitting?'

96. *tenures:* ownership of property.

97. *rude knave:* rough rascal. *sconce:* another slang word for 'head'.

98-9. *and will not . . . battery:* without saying he will sue him for assault. *in's:* in his. Hamlet passes on from the lawyer to the sort of man who tries to acquire as much property as possible during his lifetime.

100. *statutes and recognizances:* statutes and bonds.

101. *fines, vouchers* and *recoveries:* legal terms connected with buying land.

101-3. *Is this the fine . . . dirt?* Hamlet makes a wry joke about the pointlessness of a dead man having spent his life collecting something he cannot take with him, and of all his self-importance being lost in the indignity of decay. He uses the word *fine* in four senses: (i) end, (ii) the legal meaning just mentioned, (iii) splendid, and (iv) powdery. *recovery of his recoveries:* another pun, meaning 'all he gets back from his acquisition of land'.

103-4. *vouchers* and *vouch:* 'guarantees' and 'allow' – another pun.

104. *double ones:* double vouchers.

105-6. *the length and breadth of a pair of indentures:* Hamlet means a piece of ground (the man's grave) no bigger than the two halves of a legal document, of the kind written in duplicate and then torn in half (so that, by matching up the two halves later, each half could be proved genuine, and forgery was impossible). It is tempting to see in the word *indentures* a reference also to the teeth of the skull – but 'dentures' is a modern word!

106. *conveyances:* title deeds.

107. *this box:* the coffin, which is hardly big enough to hold all the dead man's documents.

107-8. *must th'inheritor . . . more:* The man who comes into possession of all that land will have to end up shut in a coffin. *ha?* means 'eh?'

112-13. *They are . . . assurance in that:* Hamlet means that people who try to give themselves a sense of security by acquiring a lot of legal documents (which were written on *parchment*) are fools.

114. *sirrah:* the way in which inferiors, like servants or children, were addressed. It means roughly 'my man'.

First Clown   [*Sings*]   90
    A pick-axe and a spade, a spade,
      For and a shrouding sheet:
    O, a pit of clay for to be made
      For such a guest is meet.

Throws up another skull

Hamlet
  There's another. Why may not that be the skull of a
  lawyer? Where be his quiddities now, his quillets, his   95
  cases, his tenures, and his tricks? Why does he suffer
  this rude knave now to knock him about the sconce
  with a dirty shovel, and will not tell him of his action
  of battery? Hum! This fellow might be in's time a
  great buyer of land, with his statutes, his recogni-   100
  zances, his fines, his double vouchers, his recoveries.
  Is this the fine of his fines, and the recovery of his
  recoveries, to have his fine pate full of fine dirt? Will
  his vouchers vouch him no more of his purchases,
  and double ones too, than the length and breadth of   105
  a pair of indentures? The very conveyances of his
  lands will scarcely lie in this box; and must th'
  inheritor himself have no more, ha?

Horatio
  Not a jot more, my lord.

Hamlet
  Is not parchment made of sheep-skins?   110

Horatio
  Ay, my lord, and of calves' skins too.

Hamlet
  They are sheep and calves which seek out assurance
  in that. I will speak to this fellow. Whose grave's
  this, sirrah?

First Clown
  Mine, sir.   [*Sings*]   115
    O, a pit of clay for to be made
      For such a guest is meet.

118. Though Hamlet did not get the reply he expected, he is ready with an answer to it, using *liest* in both its senses – (i) 'are not telling the truth', and, (ii) 'are situated' (not necessarily, in Elizabethan days, 'lying down').

119. The gravedigger quickly picks up Hamlet's pun, and goes one better. *You lie out on't:* This means both 'You are telling a fib' and 'You are standing outside the grave.' He obviously has no idea whom he is speaking to so disrespectfully.

120. *I do not lie in't . . . mine:* I am telling the truth in it, and it is mine because I have dug it.

121-2. Hamlet tries establishing the truth in words of one syllable. *quick:* living.

125. Even here, the clown has an answer. Promptly he puns with *quick*, saying that the accusation of being a liar will rebound back to Hamlet (because it fits him better).

128. Hamlet has met his match. He tries putting his question in what he thinks is a foolproof way, but in vain.

131-2. *How . . . undo us:* Amused by this labourer's quick wit, Hamlet comments to Horatio that he is a very literal rogue (perhaps he also means that he is a 'complete' rogue, too!) and they will have to speak very precisely (*by the card*) or they will be caught out by double meanings (*equivocation*).

133-6. *the age . . . kibe:* Hamlet remarks that these days, when everyone is so refined, the lower classes are following in the footsteps of the courtiers closely enough to chafe the chilblains on their heels. He is referring to the fashion for witty backchat.

137. *came to't:* started on the job.

137-8. *the day . . . Fortinbras:* See Act I, Scene i, lines 80–95, for the story.

Hamlet

I think it be thine indeed, for thou liest in't.

First Clown

You lie out on't, sir, and therefore 'tis not yours. For
my part, I do not lie in't, yet it is mine.   *120*

Hamlet

Thou dost lie in't, to be in't and say it is thine; 'tis for
the dead, not for the quick; therefore thou liest.

First Clown

'Tis a quick lie, sir; 'twill away again from me to you.

Hamlet

What man dost thou dig it for?

First Clown

For no man, sir.   *125*

Hamlet

What woman, then?

First Clown

For none neither.

Hamlet

Who is to be buried in't?

First Clown

One that was a woman, sir; but, rest her soul, she's
dead.   *130*

Hamlet

How absolute the knave is! We must speak by the
card, or equivocation will undo us. By the Lord,
Horatio, this three years I have took note of it: the
age is grown so picked that the toe of the peasant
comes so near the heel of the courtier, he galls his *135*
kibe. How long hast thou been a grave-maker?

First Clown

Of all the days i' th' year, I came to't that day that
our last King Hamlet overcame Fortinbras.

Hamlet

How long is that since?

First Clown

Cannot you tell that? Every fool can tell that: it was *140*

281

143. Hamlet thinks he will try a little detective work, to find out what sort of rumours are going around about him, but he does not get very far.

144. '*a*: he.

147-8. *seen*: noticed. *there . . . as he:* The joke about the madness of Englishmen is an old one!

149. Hamlet asks a question to which he must be eager to hear the answer.

151. Just as Hamlet thinks he is on to something, the clown catches him out again.

154. *Why, here in Denmark:* Hamlet meant 'For what reason?' but the gravedigger chooses to take him literally.

155. This can only mean that Hamlet is now thirty years old (see line 141 above). Is this what you expected?

156. With a complete change of subject, Hamlet decides to seize the opportunity to get a few facts about death straight.

158. *pocky corses:* of men who had had the pox (syphilis).

158-9. *scarce hold the laying-in:* hardly keep together long enough to be buried.

163-4. *your:* used in a general sense, simply meaning 'a' 'the'. *sore:* serious.

that very day that young Hamlet was born—he that
is mad, and sent into England.

Hamlet

Ay, marry, why was he sent into England?

First Clown

Why, because 'a was mad: 'a shall recover his wits
there; or, if 'a do not, 'tis no great matter there.   145

Hamlet

Why?

First Clown

'Twill not be seen in him there: there the men are as
mad as he.

Hamlet

How came he mad?

First Clown

Very strangely, they say.   150

Hamlet

How strangely?

First Clown

Faith, e'en with losing his wits.

Hamlet

Upon what ground?

First Clown

Why, here in Denmark. I have been sexton here, man
and boy, thirty years.   155

Hamlet

How long will a man lie i' th' earth ere he rot?

First Clown

Faith, if 'a be not rotten before 'a die—as we have
many pocky corses now-a-days that will scarce hold
the laying in—'a will last you some eight year or nine
year. A tanner will last you nine year.   160

Hamlet

Why he more than another?

First Clown

Why, sir, his hide is so tann'd with his trade that 'a
will keep out water a great while; and your water is a

164. *whoreson:* literally meaning 'son of a prostitute', is here just used vaguely, like most swear words, for emphasis.
165. *lien:* lain.

171. *A pestilence on him . . . rogue:* he was a crazy rogue, curse him. *'A:* he.
172. *Rhenish:* Rhine wine (it seems to be the standard drink at Elsinore – see Act I, Scene iv, line 10).
173. *Yorick:* Since he died when Hamlet was only seven, he must have been employed by Hamlet's father, not Claudius.
174. Hamlet is shaken to find what he has been discussing so lightly brought home to him in a personal way. His satirical descriptions of the imaginary owners of the skulls seem callous now that he finds this one belongs to someone he admired and loved.
175. *E'en that:* that very one.
176-208. Looking the fact of death literally in the face, Hamlet is awed by the completeness with which it reduces to nothing, not only worldly ambition and empty pomp but the good things of life – gaiety and friendship. Even the attraction that the once familiar Yorick had for him is destroyed because he is repelled by his skull. He moves on to imply, however, that awareness of this may help one to gain a sense of proportion.
178. *fancy:* imagination, wit.
180. *my gorge . . . it:* it makes my stomach turn over.
182. *gambols:* capers.
184. *on a roar:* roaring with laughter.
184-5. *Not one . . . chap-fall'n?* Hamlet asks whether Yorick has nothing funny to say about his present condition, for the skull (as skulls do) seems to be grinning, or whether he is completely down-in-the-mouth (*chap-fallen*), making a joke about the fact that the skull's lower jaw has come loose.
185-8. *Now get . . . at that:* Go and show yourself to a fine lady, who is busy making herself up, and remind her that all her beauty will rot away in time, whatever efforts she makes to preserve it. See if she finds that funny. (In Shakespeare's time, skulls were often used symbolically as reminders of the need to prepare for the life after death, rather than to concentrate all efforts on this one.)
190-1. Hamlet suggests that even Alexander the Great, the splendid prince who conquered a huge empire for himself, would look like this skull when he had been buried for a while.

sore decayer of your whoreson dead body. Here's a
skull now; this skull has lien you i' th' earth three and *165*
twenty years.

Hamlet

Whose was it?

First Clown

A whoreson mad fellow's it was. Whose do you
think it was?

Hamlet

Nay, I know not. *170*

First Clown

A pestilence on him for a mad rogue! 'A poured a
flagon of Rhenish on my head once. This same skull,
sir, was, sir, Yorick's skull, the King's jester.

Hamlet

This?

First Clown

E'en that. *175*

Hamlet

Let me see. [*Takes the skull*] Alas, poor Yorick! I
knew him, Horatio: a fellow of infinite jest, of most
excellent fancy; he hath borne me on his back a
thousand times. And now how abhorred in my
imagination it is! My gorge rises at it. Here hung *180*
those lips that I have kiss'd I know not how oft.
Where be your gibes now, your gambols, your songs,
your flashes of merriment that were wont to set the
table on a roar? Not one now to mock your own
grinning—quite chap-fall'n? Now get you to my *185*
lady's chamber, and tell her, let her paint an inch
thick, to this favour she must come; make her laugh
at that. Prithee, Horatio, tell me one thing.

Horatio

What's that, my lord?

Hamlet

Dost thou think Alexander look'd a this fashion i' *190*
th' earth?

192. *E'en so:* just like that.

193. In spite of his fondness for Yorick, Hamlet brings the conversation down to earth with this unsentimental comment.

195-208. Hamlet returns to the idea he teased Claudius with (Act IV, Scene iii, lines 20-5), that the bodies of the very greatest people can end up in undignified circumstances; so what is the use, he seems to ask, of striving for fame and power? Perhaps Hamlet feels this applies to himself: he too, in his way, has tried to achieve a noble way of life (see Act III, Scene i, line 11 and Act IV, Scene iv, lines 32-66), and also, perhaps, had day-dreamed of being a king.

195. *To what . . . return:* what ignoble things we may end up doing.

196. *dust:* body.

198. As usual, Horatio is cautious and moderate, saying that Hamlet is letting his imagination run away with him.

199-200. *but . . . as thus:* one can prove it quite simply and logically, in this way.

202. *returneth to dust:* rots into the ground.

203. *loam:* a mixture including clay, which used to be used for plastering jobs and, as Hamlet says, for stopping up the bung-holes of casks.

205-8. Far from being depressed by all this consideration of death, Hamlet, perhaps feeling that he has got clear for himself exactly what he feels about it now, lightheartedly breaks into song, this time using a Roman emperor (*imperious:* imperial) as a symbol of power reduced to a lump of clay pushed into a crack in a wall to keep out a cold draught. He stops suddenly, however, when he sees a funeral procession making for the newly-dug grave.

210-13. Rapidly, he deduces that the person being buried must be of high rank, because the king and queen are attending the ceremony, and it must be a suicide because the funeral rites are shortened. He has no idea, as yet, that it is his former sweetheart that is in the coffin, but, wishing to take stock of the situation, tells Horatio to hide with him and watch for a while.

Horatio
E'en so.

Hamlet
And smelt so? Pah!

Throws down the skull

Horatio
E'en so, my lord.

Hamlet
To what base uses we may return, Horatio! Why may   195
not imagination trace the noble dust of Alexander
till 'a find it stopping a bung-hole?

Horatio
'Twere to consider too curiously to consider so.

Hamlet
No, faith, not a jot; but to follow him thither with
modesty enough, and likelihood to lead it, as thus: 200
Alexander died, Alexander was buried, Alexander
returneth to dust; the dust is earth; of earth we make
loam; and why of that loam whereto he was con-
verted might they not stop a beer-barrel?

  Imperious Cæsar, dead and turn'd to clay,   205
  Might stop a hole to keep the wind away.
  O, that that earth which kept the world in awe
  Should patch a wall t' expel the winter's flaw!
But soft! but soft! awhile. Here comes the King.

Enter the KING, QUEEN, LAERTES, *in funeral procession after the coffin, with* PRIEST *and* LORDS
attendant

The Queen, the courtiers. Who is this they follow?   210
And with such maimed rites? This doth betoken
The corse they follow did with desperate hand
Fordo it own life. 'Twas of some estate.
Couch we awhile and mark.

Retiring with HORATIO

215. Laertes angrily asks what has happened to the rest of the funeral service.

216. Hamlet's tribute to Laertes is unconsciously ironical, for the *noble youth* intends to cheat him and poison him!

218-26. Disapprovingly, the priest says that the ritual is as elaborate as the church is authorized to make it. The woman's death occurred in suspicious circumstances, and if the church's practice had not been overruled (by the king) she would have had to be buried in unconsecrated ground till Doomsday. Instead of prayers being offered, broken crockery and stones should be thrown on her (even worse treatment than this was often the custom for the bodies of suicides); yet she is allowed to have the white garlands and flowers customary at the funeral of an unmarried girl, a funeral bell and a proper grave.

227. As the son of someone like Polonius, Laertes, as well as feeling naturally indignant that his innocent sister is treated in this way, seems to feel that he must insist on his family's rights; this shabby funeral damages its reputation.
228. *profane:* make a mockery of.
229-30. *To sing . . . souls:* to sing solemn funeral hymns, saying she has gone to her rest, as though she departed in a state of grace.
232. Why does Laertes think of *violets* in particular?
233-4. Ophelia will be an angel in heaven while the grumpy priest in suffering in hell (probably for being uncharitable). At the words *my sister*, Hamlet realizes with horror that it is Ophelia who has committed suicide. He has no time to work out why she might have chosen to die. (His words are exactly those with which he addressed her in Act III, Scene i, line 89, but now with a very different emphasis.)
235-8. As the coffin is lowered into the grave, the queen comments on how suitable beautiful flowers are as an offering to a lovely girl; she goes on to show how petty Polonius's and Laertes's suspicions were that Hamlet was not likely to be allowed to marry Ophelia.
237. *deck'd:* decorated with flowers (as was the custom).
239-46. *O, treble woe . . . Olympus:* Cursing the man who deprived Ophelia of her reason by his evil deed (killing Polonius), Laertes suddenly leaps into the grave – interrupting the grave-digger, who is about to fill it in – and, embracing her corpse, says he wants to be buried alive with her, with a mountain of earth piled on top of them. *Pelion* and *Olympus* are two famous mountains in Greece. *o'ertop:* rise higher than. *skyish:* high, lofty.

Laertes
  What ceremony else? 215
Hamlet
  That is Laertes, a very noble youth. Mark.
Laertes
  What ceremony else?
Priest
  Her obsequies have been as far enlarg'd
  As we have warrantise. Her death was doubtful;
  And, but that great command o'ersways the order, 220
  She should in ground unsanctified have lodg'd
  Till the last trumpet; for charitable prayers,
  Shards, flints, and pebbles should be thrown on her;
  Yet here she is allow'd her virgin crants,
  Her maiden strewments, and the bringing home 225
  Of bell and burial.
Laertes
  Must there no more be done?
Priest   No more be done.
  We should profane the service of the dead
  To sing sage requiem and such rest to her
  As to peace-parted souls.
Laertes   Lay her i' th' earth; 230
  And from her fair and unpolluted flesh
  May violets spring! I tell thee, churlish priest,
  A minist'ring angel shall my sister be
  When thou liest howling.
Hamlet   What, the fair Ophelia!
Queen
  Sweets to the sweet; farewell! 235

Scattering flowers

  I hop'd thou shouldst have been my Hamlet's wife;
  I thought thy bride-bed to have deck'd, sweet maid,
  And not have strew'd thy grave.
Laertes   O, treble woe
  Fall ten times treble on that cursed head

246-50. Irritated both by Laertes's exaggerated language and his melodramatic behaviour (in public, at any rate, Hamlet was restrained in his grief over his father's death – see Act I, Scene ii, lines 76-86 – for he disliked over-acting) and by Laertes's unspoken assumption that he is the one who suffers most by her death, Hamlet suddenly announces himself royally (*the Dane:* prince – or king – of Denmark) with a contemptuous description of Laertes's speechmaking. He says he shouts about his grief as though he were calling on the stars to stand still and listen to him, wonder-struck.

Stage Direction. To most of those watching the macabre spectacle of two young men struggling in a grave over a flower-strewn corpse, one shock has followed another. What is Hamlet doing here? Why is he angry with Laertes? Is he in one of his mad fits, again? How does Laertes dare to attack the prince, and why does he curse him?

251-5. *Thou . . . hand:* Hamlet at first seems to try to restrain himself from fighting, telling Laertes to let go of him, or he will lose his temper, though he is not normally given to doing so (*not splenitive and rash*); so Laertes would be wise to be cautious.

256. Dismayed that his plan to keep Hamlet and Laertes apart from one another, until the fencing match, has gone wrong, Claudius tries to separate them; why? *Pluck them asunder:* pull them apart. The queen is anxious for quite another reason: her son may get hurt, and anyway should not get involved in a fight with a man whom he has already injured so much.

259. Politely, but with a definite note of reproof in his tone, Horatio adds his quiet voice to the general hubbub. *be quiet:* calm down.

Whose wicked deed thy most ingenious sense   240
Depriv'd thee of! Hold off the earth awhile,
Till I have caught her once more in mine arms.

Leaps into the grave

Now pile your dust upon the quick and dead,
Till of this flat a mountain you have made
T' o'er-top old Pelion or the skyish head   245
Of blue Olympus.
Hamlet [*Advancing*]   What is he whose grief
Bears such an emphasis, whose phrase of sorrow
Conjures the wand'ring stars, and makes them stand
Like wonder-wounded hearers? This is I,
Hamlet the Dane.   250

Leaps into the grave

Laertes
The devil take thy soul!

Grappling with him

Hamlet   Thou pray'st not well.
I prithee take thy fingers from my throat;
For, though I am not splenitive and rash,
Yet have I in me something dangerous,
Which let thy wiseness fear. Hold off thy hand.   255
King
Pluck them asunder.
Queen
Hamlet! Hamlet!
All
Gentlemen!
Horatio
Good my lord, be quiet.

The ATTENDANTS *part them, and they come out of
the grave*

260-1. Now thoroughly roused, Hamlet says he will fight Laertes on this point until he drops. *wag:* move.

262. *what theme?* what about?

263-5. Yet he told Ophelia (Act III, Scene i, line 119) that he didn't love her. Why does he contradict himself? Which is the truth? *Make up my sum:* love her as much as I did. *for her:* to prove your love for her.

266. The king tries to get a warning across to Laertes that this is not the time to fight.

267. *forbear him:* leave him alone.

268. *'Swounds:* God's wounds – a strong oath. *th'owt:* you would. Hamlet's use of the familiar *thou* here indicates contempt. Later on, in a more polite mood (lines 283-4) he calls him *you*.

269-70. *Woo't . . . ?* would you. *eisel:* vinegar. Hamlet scornfully goes through a list of the sort of things romantic lovers might do to prove the strength of their devotion.

272. *outface:* outdo.

273. *quick:* alive.

274. *prate:* hold forth.

274-7. *let them . . . wart:* Hamlet sarcastically parodies Laertes's imagery, saying they can be buried under so much soil that the top of the mountain it forms will be singed by the sun and make *Ossa* (another famous mountain which giants once piled on top of *Pelion* to try to reach the gods) look no bigger than a pimple.

277-8. *Nay . . . thou:* 'I can make fine speeches as well as you.' Contemptuously, Hamlet dismisses all Laertes's bravado – and his own too – for his anger is already beginning to die down.

278-82. Hastily, Hamlet's mother puts in a word, to save her son disgracing himself further, from more attacks by Laertes, and from the king's anger. It is impossible to tell whether she really has decided after all that Hamlet is mad, or whether she uses what she believes to be everyone else's belief that he is, to protect him. The description she gives of the way Hamlet's wild moods (*the fit*) die down suddenly into calm, is, in fact, accurate. *golden couplets are disclos'd:* two yellow nestlings are hatched. *drooping:* with head hanging down.

282-6. At this, Hamlet pulls himself together, and tries to make it up with Laertes, who, however, doesn't deign to reply, so, after what seems to be a brief pause, Hamlet dismisses the whole thing impatiently.

283. *use:* treat. (Why doesn't Hamlet take Polonius's death into account?)

284. *I lov'd you ever:* I have always liked you.

285-6. *Let . . . day:* not even *Hercules* (with whom Hamlet wryly compared himself in Act I, Scene ii, line 153 – see note) could rid the world of every whining, yapping nuisance.

Hamlet

  Why, I will fight with him upon this theme   260
  Until my eyelids will no longer wag.

Queen

  O my son, what theme?

Hamlet

  I lov'd Ophelia: forty thousand brothers
  Could not, with all their quantity of love,
  Make up my sum. What wilt thou do for her?   265

King

  O, he is mad, Laertes.

Queen

  For love of God, forbear him.

Hamlet

  'Swounds, show me what th'owt do:
  Woo't weep, woo't fight, woo't fast, woo't tear thyself,
  Woo't drink up eisel, eat a crocodile?   270
  I'll do't. Dost come here to whine?
  To outface me with leaping in her grave?
  Be buried quick with her, and so will I;
  And, if thou prate of mountains, let them throw
  Millions of acres on us, till our ground,   275
  Singeing his pate against the burning zone,
  Make Ossa like a wart! Nay, an thou'lt mouth,
  I'll rant as well as thou.

Queen   This is mere madness;

  And thus awhile the fit will work on him;
  Anon, as patient as the female dove   280
  When that her golden couplets are disclos'd,
  His silence will sit drooping.

Hamlet   Hear you, sir:

  What is the reason that you use me thus?
  I lov'd you ever. But it is no matter.
  Let Hercules himself do what he may,   285
  The cat will mew, and dog will have his day.

Exit

287. Claudius realizes that in Horatio's company Hamlet will not be likely to get into further trouble with Laertes.

288-93. Leading Laertes to one side, the king tells him to hang on until they are able to carry out the plan they formulated the day before, which they will do immediately. There is an awkward moment when Claudius realizes that his wife may be able to overhear them – he hastily gives her something to do, and then adds, with a double meaning, that Ophelia will have an everlasting memorial (in other words, the tribute of Hamlet's life). Before Laertes can obtain peace of mind they will have to proceed cautiously.

SCENE II

Unaware that a trap is closing around him, Hamlet is in the middle of his account to Horatio of the events that led up to his exile and return. We come upon them in the great hall of the castle – probably the place where once it was he who set a trap for Claudius. The scene begins quietly and casually, making the explosion of violence at its end, to which the whole play has been building up, seem all the more terrible.

1. *see the other:* learn the rest of the story.

2. *circumstance:* details.

3. Horatio's emphatic comment shows how fully, in his quiet way, he is involved in what happens to Hamlet.

4-5. *Sir . . . sleep:* Hamlet was worrying about his failure to take revenge, when we last saw him before his voyage (Act IV, Scene iv), and he mentioned what he called *bad dreams* in Act II, Scene ii, line 256.

5. *Methought:* it seemed to me. *lay:* was in a state.

6. *mutines in the bilboes:* mutineers in fetters.

7. *prais'd . . . for it:* thank God I *was* rash. The adverb *rashly* in the previous line belongs to the verb *grop'd* in line 14, for Hamlet now interrupts his sentence with a philosophical comment.

7-11. *let us know . . . will:* 'let us acknowledge that sometimes acting on impulse is a good idea, while well-laid plans often fail. This should teach us that some power above puts the finishing touches to our destinies, however clumsily we have tried to carve out our own way.' Hamlet shows that he now has faith that life has a pattern, and that he can resign some of the burden of responsibility for what he makes of his life, into the hands of a power greater than himself. This may explain why he seems so much more relaxed since his journey.

11. Horatio has always felt this – see Act I, Scene iv, line 91.

13. *sea-gown:* a short-sleeved garment worn at sea. *scarf'd:* wrapped.

King

I pray thee, good Horatio, wait upon him.

Exit HORATIO

[*To* LAERTES] Strengthen your patience in our last
    night's speech;
We'll put the matter to the present push.—
Good Gertrude, set some watch over your son.—   *290*
This grave shall have a living monument.
An hour of quiet shortly shall we see;
Till then in patience our proceeding be.

Exeunt

SCENE II—*Elsinore. The Castle*

Enter HAMLET *and* HORATIO

Hamlet

So much for this, sir; now shall you see the other.
You do remember all the circumstance?

Horatio

Remember it, my lord!

Hamlet

Sir, in my heart there was a kind of fighting
That would not let me sleep. Methought I lay   *5*
Worse than the mutines in the bilboes. Rashly,
And prais'd be rashness for it—let us know,
Our indiscretion sometime serves us well,
When our deep plots do pall; and that should learn us
There's a divinity that shapes our ends,   *10*
Rough-hew them how we will.

Horatio   That is most certain.

Hamlet

Up from my cabin,
My sea-gown scarf'd about me, in the dark

14. *them:* the sleeping Rosencrantz and Guildenstern.

15. *Finger'd:* stole. *packet:* sealed papers (from Claudius). *in fine:* in short.

17. *My fears . . . manners:* Hamlet's suspicions caused him to ignore the fact that one doesn't normally read other people's letters.

18. *grand commission:* mandate.

19. *royal knavery:* what wickedness in a king. *exact:* firm.

20. *Larded:* decorated. *several:* different, separate.

21. *Importing . . . too:* Saying it was necessary for both Denmark's and England's good.

22. *With . . . life:* adding suggestions that I was capable of such terrible things. *bugs:* bugbears, bogies.

23. *on the supervise:* as soon as it was read. *no leisure bated:* without delay (Claudius did not dare to allow time for Hamlet to explain the situation).

25. Horatio, in spite of his knowledge that Claudius murdered his own brother, can hardly believe this.

26. Hamlet hands him documentary evidence.

27. *how . . . proceed:* what I did next.

28. *I beseech you:* please.

29. *benetted . . . villainies:* caught in the meshes of a wicked trap.

30-1. *Ere . . . play:* my mind began to act even before I had finished describing the situation to it.

32. *Devis'd:* composed. *fair:* neatly, elegantly.

33-6. *I once . . . service:* Hamlet says that once upon a time, like statesmen, he thought it was a clerk's job, not a gentleman's, to be able to write elegantly, and tried to conceal the fact that he could do so, but on this occasion it served him well.

37. *effect:* gist.

38. *conjuration:* request.

39-43. Hamlet makes fun of the pompous style of state documents, and puns about all the conjunctions he used to introduce each reason why the king of England should do what he was asked. *as-es* also means asses, carrying a heavy burden (charge).

39. *tributary.* England, at that period, paid tribute to Denmark (see Act IV, Scene iii, lines 59–66).

40. *As love . . . flourish:* to preserve their friendship. *palm:* a symbol of prosperity.

41-2. These two lines say the same as the one before, on the whole. *comma:* link. *amities:* friendship. Hamlet cleverly includes a veiled threat of further war if the king of England does not obey.

44. *on the view and knowing:* as soon as the letter was read and understood.

Grop'd I to find out them; had my desire;
Finger'd their packet, and in fine withdrew   15
To mine own room again, making so bold,
My fears forgetting manners, to unseal
Their grand commission; where I found, Horatio,
Ah, royal knavery! an exact command,
Larded with many several sorts of reasons,   20
Importing Denmark's health and England's too,
With, ho! such bugs and goblins in my life—
That, on the supervise, no leisure bated,
No, not to stay the grinding of the axe,
My head should be struck off.

Horatio   Is't possible?   25

Hamlet

Here's the commission; read it at more leisure.
But wilt thou hear now how I did proceed?

Horatio

I beseech you.

Hamlet

Being thus benetted round with villainies—
Ere I could make a prologue to my brains,   30
They had begun the play—I sat me down;
Devis'd a new commission; wrote it fair.
I once did hold it, as our statists do,
A baseness to write fair, and labour'd much
How to forget that learning; but sir, now   35
It did me yeoman's service. Wilt thou know
Th' effect of what I wrote?

Horatio   Ay, good my lord.

Hamlet

An earnest conjuration from the King,
As England was his faithful tributary,
As love between them like the palm might flourish,   40
As peace should still her wheaten garland wear
And stand a comma 'tween their amities,
And many such like as-es of great charge,
That, on the view and knowing of these contents,

45. *Without . . . less:* without any hesitation whatever.

46-7. The king of England was to put Rosencrantz and Guildenstern to death without even giving them time to confess their sins (Hamlet had to make sure that they, in their turn, were given no time to communicate with anyone as, for all Hamlet knew at that point, he too would be in England, and they might still contrive to get him into trouble).

47. *How . . . seal'd:* Horatio's practical mind seizes upon the chief difficulty of passing the letter off as genuine, for formerly an official or personal seal was as important as a signature is nowadays.

48. *even . . . ordinant:* heaven arranged even that (see lines 10-11).

49. *signet:* ring containing a personal seal.

50. *the model of:* identical with.

51. *writ:* document. *form of:* same way as.

52. *Subscrib'd: . . . impression:* signed and sealed it. *plac'd it:* put it back among Rosencrantz's and Guildenstern's luggage.

53. *changeling:* changeover.

54. *our sea-fight:* described in Act IV, Scene vi, lines 14-19. *to this was sequent:* followed this.

56. Horatio sounds slightly doubtful as to whether Hamlet was right to send the two men to their death; after all, they probably knew nothing of what was in the letter. *go to't:* are for it, are going to die.

57-62. Hamlet defends his action briskly. They asked for it, he says, by offering their services so whole-heartedly to Claudius, to use as he wished. Hamlet doesn't feel at all uneasy about what he has done, for their downfall is caused by their own meddling: it is unwise for insignificant people to get involved in a fight between powerful antagonists. Hamlet is being prophetic when he describes his conflict with Claudius as a sword-fight (*fell incensed points:* deadly, angry swords).

63. *Does it not . . . stand me now upon:* 'isn't it up to me?' The sentence continues with *To quit him*, line 68, the words between being a description of *him*.

64. Hamlet emphasizes the word *my*, to contrast his father with the present king (just criticized by Horatio). *whor'd:* treated like a whore, or turned her into a whore.

65. *Popp'd in . . . hopes:* 'Nipped on to the throne before I had a chance of being elected king.' This is the first definite evidence that Hamlet resented this. The Danish kings were elected to the throne, as this line indicates, and did not succeed to it automatically (though the vote of a reigning king could go a very long way in securing the crown for his candidate, so Claudius's promise that Hamlet will be his heir means that Hamlet can expect pretty confidently to become king after him). What advantages over Hamlet would Claudius have had?

66. *Thrown . . . life:* 'Tried to take my own life' (like an angler tempting a fish to take his bait – little does Hamlet know that another bait is just about to be dangled in front of him).

67. *coz'nage:* trickery, with a pun meaning 'and such a near relation, too!' *perfect conscience:* perfectly justifiable.

68. *quit:* get rid of him. *to be damn'd:* sinful.

69. With another of the many metaphors of disease used in the play, Hamlet compares his uncle to a cancer spreading through their lives which must be operated on, to prevent it doing more harm.

Without debatement further more or less,   45
He should those bearers put to sudden death,
Not shriving-time allow'd.

Horatio   How was this seal'd?

Hamlet

Why, even in that was heaven ordinant,
I had my father's signet in my purse,
Which was the model of that Danish seal;   50
Folded the writ up in the form of th' other;
Subscrib'd it, gave't th' impression, plac'd it safely,
The changeling never known. Now, the next day
Was our sea-fight; and what to this was sequent
Thou knowest already.   55

Horatio

So Guildenstern and Rosencrantz go to't.

Hamlet

Why, man, they did make love to this employment;
They are not near my conscience; their defeat
Does by their own insinuation grow:
'Tis dangerous when the baser nature comes   60
Between the pass and fell incensed points
Of mighty opposites.

Horatio   Why, what a king is this!

Hamlet

Does it not, think thee, stand me now upon—
He that hath kill'd my king and whor'd my mother;
Popp'd in between th' election and my hopes;   65
Thrown out his angle for my proper life,
And with such coz'nage—is't not perfect conscience
To quit him with this arm? And is't not to be damn'd
To let this canker of our nature come
In further evil?   70

71-2. Horatio hints that Hamlet had better act quickly, before Claudius hears that Rosencrantz and Guildenstern have been put to death and so realizes the game is up (as Hamlet knows about the attempt on his life).

73-4. Hamlet agrees that there is not much time, but he can use what there is, between now and then, and it only takes a moment to kill a man.

75-8. Having justified his other actions and intentions, Hamlet (ironically, in the light of what we know of Laertes's plans) says that he is sorry he lost his temper with him, because, being in a similar situation, and with similar duties, he knows just how he feels. He will try to get on good terms with him.

79. *the bravery of:* the way he showed off about.

80. *Peace:* quiet.

81. Osric, a silly, affected young courtier – the sort of person who makes a point of keeping up with the fashion, however absurd it is – is the latest bait with which Claudius tries to angle for Hamlet's life (Hamlet, in fact, calls him a *water-fly*). He comes to bring the fencing challenge to Hamlet, who is only too ready to take it up, as he has just said he wants to behave in a friendly way to Laertes, to make up for their quarrel.

83. *water-fly:* probably the kind of insect that darts about fussily above the surface of water. Hamlet implies that he is irritated by Osric's mannerisms and superficiality, and wishes he would 'buzz off'. Perhaps his clothes, too, are gaudy, like an angler's artificial fly, or a dragon-fly.

85. *Thy state . . . gracious:* you are lucky.

85-6. *'tis a vice . . . him:* it's the latest bad habit to cultivate him.

86-8. *Let . . . mess:* 'even the lowest of creatures, if he had enough possessions, could eat with the king.' As well as making a general comment on human nature, is Hamlet perhaps criticizing his uncle here?

88. *chough:* a chattering jackdaw.

88-9. *spacious . . . dirt:* 'he owns a lot of land.' Hamlet's contemptuous choice of words recalls his comments about the owner of the second skull (Act V, Scene i, lines 100-8).

90-2. *Sweet lord . . . spirit:* Osric's excessive politeness again receives an elegant reply. *impart a thing:* pass on a message. *with all . . . spirit:* willingly.

92-3. With an abrupt change of tone, Hamlet tells him to stop waving his hat around (with which he is probably assisting his elaborate bows), and put it back on. Elizabethan gentlemen often wore hats indoors – see note on Act II, Scene i, line 80.

94. Osric indicates that he would rather not; he feels more at ease with it in his hand.

Horatio
It must be shortly known to him from England
What is the issue of the business there.

Hamlet
It will be short; the interim is mine.
And a man's life's no more than to say 'one'.
But I am very sorry, good Horatio,   75
That to Laertes I forgot myself;
For by the image of my cause I see
The portraiture of his. I'll court his favours.
But sure the bravery of his grief did put me
Into a tow'ring passion.

Horatio   Peace; who comes here?   80

Enter young OSRIC

Osric
Your lordship is right welcome back to Denmark.

Hamlet
I humbly thank you, sir. [*Aside to* HORATIO] Dost
know this water-fly?

Horatio [*Aside to* HAMLET]
No, my good lord.

Hamlet [*Aside to* HORATIO]
Thy state is the more gracious; for 'tis a vice to know   85
him. He hath much land, and fertile. Let a beast be
lord of beasts, and his crib shall stand at the king's
mess. 'Tis a chough; but, as I say, spacious in the
possession of dirt.

Osric
Sweet lord, if your lordship were at leisure, I should   90
impart a thing to you from his Majesty.

Hamlet
I will receive it, sir, with all diligence of spirit. Put
your bonnet to his right use; 'tis for the head.

Osric
I thank your lordship; it is very hot.

95-100. Hamlet teases Osric, as he did Polonius about the shape of an imaginary cloud (Act III, Scene ii, lines 367-73), and, like Polonius, Osric may remember that he has to humour not just a prince, but a 'madman', especially when Hamlet pointedly mentions his disposition (*complexion*: physical and mental make-up) and a northerly wind (see note on Act II, Scene ii, line 377). *indifferent*: fairly.

99-102. Even Osric realizes that what he has just been made to say is nonsense, and changes the subject with relief, back to his errand. *signify to*: tell. *'a*: he. *the matter*: what it is all about.
Stage Direction: *moves*: motions to, indicates by a gesture.
104. *Nay . . . faith*: No, thank you, I'd rather not. Flustered by Hamlet's teasing, he presses on hurriedly with his message.

104-10. *Sir . . . see*: He begins with a long preamble in praise of Laertes (in order that Hamlet will feel he is a worthy opponent for a prince). Claudius had probably instructed him to praise Laertes's fencing in particular (see Act IV, Scene vii, lines 133-4), but it takes Osric rather a long time to get round to it!
106-7. *full . . . showing*: very distinguished, well-bred and handsome.
107-8. *to speak feelingly of him*: to praise him as he deserves.
108-9. *card or calendar of gentry*: a model gentleman.
109-10. *you shall . . . see*: he sums up all the qualities of a gentleman. (We know, however, that Laertes intends to behave in a most ungentlemanly way.)
111-18. Hamlet goes one better, as he did when talking to Rosencrantz and Guildenstern (Act II, Scene ii, lines 263-5) – in fact, Osric seems to be filling the gap left by those two gentlemen and Polonius, as a butt for Hamlet's wit. Picking up Osric's mixed metaphors – trade (*card and calendar*: catalogue) and exploration (*continent*) he spins them into two complicated sentences which really simply say: 'You describe him well, though I know it would be impossible to list all his good qualities. To speak the truth, I think he is so uniquely perfect that only his mirror could portray him accurately' (*definement*: description; *perdition*: loss; *divide inventorially*: catalogue; *dozy*: baffle; *yet but yaw neither*: just be off-course; *in respect . . . sail*: because he out-distances us; *in the verity of extolment*: to praise him truthfully; *of great article*: possessing a long list of qualities; *infusion*: spirit. *dearth*: rarity; *make true diction*: speak accurately; *semblable*: likeness; *umbrage*: shadow).
119. Has Osric really understood or is he trying to put a good face on it? *infallibly*: accurately.
120-1. Hamlet asks what all this is about, and why they, who are so much less refined, are venturing to talk about Laertes.

Hamlet

No, believe me, 'tis very cold; the wind is northerly. 95

Osric

It is indifferent cold, my lord, indeed.

Hamlet

But yet methinks it is very sultry and hot for my complexion.

Osric

Exceedingly, my lord; it is very sultry, as 'twere—I cannot tell how. But, my lord, his Majesty bade me 100 signify to you that 'a has laid a great wager on your head. Sir, this is the matter—

Hamlet

I beseech you, remember.

       HAMLET *moves him to put on his hat*

Osric

Nay, good my lord; for my ease, in good faith. Sir, here is newly come to court Laertes; believe me, an 105 absolute gentleman, full of most excellent differences, of very soft society and great showing. Indeed, to speak feelingly of him, he is the card or calendar of gentry, for you shall find in him the continent of what part a gentleman would see. 110

Hamlet

Sir, his definement suffers no perdition in you; though, I know, to divide him inventorially would dozy th' arithmetic of memory, and yet but yaw neither in respect of his quick sail. But, in the verity of extolment, I take him to be a soul of great article, and his 115 infusion of such dearth and rareness, as to make true diction of him, his semblable is his mirror, and who else would trace him, his umbrage, nothing more.

Osric

Your lordship speaks most infallibly of him.

Hamlet

The concernancy sir? Why do we wrap the gentleman 120 in our more rawer breath?

122. *Sir?* What do you mean?

123. *Is't not . . . tongue?* Can't you speak plainly?

124. *You will . . . really:* Horatio says that Osric will get there in the end.

125. Hamlet asks, a little more simply, why they are taking Laertes's name in vain.

127-8. Horatio comments with amusement that Osric has used up all his fine words already.

131-2. Quickly, Hamlet picks up Osric on the word *ignorant* (of Laertes's good qualities, he was about to say) and says he wishes he would not treat him like a fool (this irritated him in Rosencrantz, etc., too), but that it would not be much of a compliment to him even if Osric could understand him.

134. *compare:* seem to compete. Hamlet mockingly continues to talk of Laertes as though he were superhuman.

135-6. *to know . . . himself:* if I know anyone well, it is he.

137. *for his weapon:* with his sword.

137-8. *but in . . . unfellowed:* It is not clear whether Osric means 'The reputation his skill with weapons has given him makes him unparalleled in the amount of praise he receives' or 'He is unparalleled even if one just takes into account the reputation he has among those in his service', as *meed* can mean both 'praise' and 'pay'.

140. A form of fencing using a sword and a dagger simultaneously was popular in Shakespeare's day.

142-64. *The King . . . answer:* Osric gives details of the wager he mentioned before. Claudius (according to plan – see Act IV, Scene vii, line 133 – for he wishes to seem on his step-son's side) has bet six horses against Laertes's wager of six fine swords and daggers, with all their accessories, that Laertes will not beat Hamlet by more than two points out of twelve – as opposed to the usual nine. It is probably Laertes who has asked for the three extra rounds, in order to give himself more chance to win by these odds (or rather, as we know, to kill Hamlet). Neither side seems to consider the possibility of Hamlet being a match for Laertes, and that the fight could be a straight one; or perhaps they think that Hamlet will be provoked by their assumption of his inferiority into accepting the challenge.

143. *impon'd:* wagered. *poniards:* daggers.

Osric
  Sir?

Horatio [*Aside to* HAMLET]
  Is't not possible to understand in another tongue?
  You will to't, sir, really.

Hamlet
  What imports the nomination of this gentleman?   125

Osric
  Of Laertes?

Horatio [*Aside*]
  His purse is empty already; all's golden words are
  spent.

Hamlet
  Of him, sir.

Osric
  I know you are not ignorant—   130

Hamlet
  I would you did, sir; yet, in faith, if you did, it would
  not much approve me. Well, sir.

Osric
  You are not ignorant of what excellence Laertes is—

Hamlet
  I dare not confess that, lest I should compare with
  him in excellence; but to know a man well were to 135
  know himself.

Osric
  I mean, sir, for his weapon; but in the imputation
  laid on him by them, in his meed he's unfellowed.

Hamlet
  What's his weapon?

Osric
  Rapier and dagger.   140

Hamlet
  That's two of his weapons—but well.

Osric
  The King, sir, hath wager'd with him six Barbary
  horses; against the which he has impon'd, as I take it,

144. *assigns:* accessories.

145. *hangers:* the straps that attach a sword to its girdle, or belt. Osric insists on calling them carriages.

146. *dear to fancy:* appeal to the imagination. *responsive to:* suited to.

147-8. *of very liberal conceit:* elaborate design.

150-1. Horatio, amused by the fact that even Hamlet is lost now, says that he knew he would have to refer to the notes in the margin before long – i.e. to ask Osric what he means.

153. *germane to the matter:* appropriate. Hamlet is more familiar with the idea of gun-carriages.

162. *laid on:* asked for. *for:* instead of.

162-4. *it would . . . answer:* the match can take place immediately if Hamlet is so kind as to accept the challenge.

165. Hamlet deliberately misunderstands the meaning of *answer*.

166-7. *the opposition . . . trial:* putting you to the test in a duel (i.e. a matter of honour).

168-72. Hamlet sees no reason for refusing the challenge; on the contrary, he accepts it promptly in a sporting spirit, probably glad of a chance to oblige Laertes.

169. *breathing time of day:* time of day for taking exercise.

170. *the gentleman:* Laertes. *hold his purpose:* is still of the same mind.

171. *I will . . . can:* An ironical situation – Hamlet fighting to oblige Claudius! *an:* if.

171-2. *I will gain . . . hits:* I shall just look silly and receive a few hits, i.e. no harm is done.

six French rapiers and poniards, with their assigns,
as girdle, hangers, and so—three of the carriages, in *145*
faith, are very dear to fancy, very responsive to the
hilts, most delicate carriages, and of very liberal
conceit.

Hamlet

What call you the carriages?

Horatio [Aside to HAMLET]

I knew you must be edified by the margent ere you *150*
had done.

Osric

The carriages, sir, are the hangers.

Hamlet

The phrase would be more germane to the matter if
we could carry a cannon by our sides. I would it
might be hangers till then. But on: six Barbary horses *155*
against six French swords, their assigns, and three
liberal conceited carriages; that's the French bet
against the Danish. Why is this all impon'd, as you
call it?

Osric

The King, sir, hath laid, sir, that in a dozen passes *160*
between yourself and him he shall not exceed you
three hits; he hath laid on twelve for nine, and it
would come to immediate trial if your lordship would
vouchsafe the answer.

Hamlet

How if I answer no?   *165*

Osric

I mean, my lord, the opposition of your person in
trial.

Hamlet

Sir, I will walk here in the hall. If it please his Majesty,
it is the breathing time of day with me; let the foils be
brought, the gentleman willing, and the King hold *170*
his purpose, I will win for him an I can; if not, I will
gain nothing but my shame and the odd hits.

173. *redeliver you e'en so:* say this is what you said.

174. *To this effect:* something on these lines.

174-5. *after . . . will:* Hamlet implies that Osric is bound to find it necessary to introduce his answer elaborately.

176. *I commend my duty:* Your humble servant.

177. *Yours, yours:* Rather off-handedly, Hamlet makes a vaguely appropriate reply.

178. *there are . . . turn:* no-one else will speak well of him.

179. Struck by Osric's likeness to a bird as he bows and scrapes away, Horatio compares him to a *lapwing* which is a fussy-seeming bird, and makes bowing movements at times (and whose crest is suggested by Osric's feathered hat). This bird was thought to be a silly creature that, when newly hatched, ran around with its shell on its head for a while. Osric seems 'just out of the egg', immature, and stupid (see Act 1, Scene iii, line 65).

180-6. Hamlet implies that Osric is worse than that, for he, and people like him, have made a fashion of shallowness and insincerity.

180. *'A did . . . it:* He politely asked permission before he sucked his mother's breast. Hamlet is being sarcastic about Osric's exaggerated manners and those of other similarly affected men of the time. *comply:* make complimentary remarks, be ingratiating; *dug:* nipple.

181. *bevy:* flock (of other 'lapwings').

182. *the drossy age dotes on:* are popular in these superficial times (*dross:* scum).

182-3. *only got . . . encounter:* just imitate fashionable ways of speaking and behaving.

183-6. *a kind of . . . are out:* Hamlet compares Osric and his like to the froth on the top of a vat of fermenting beer (*a yesty* (yeasty) *collection*). The barley at the bottom of the vat has been separated from its worthless chaff (*fann'd and winnowed*), and represents sound ideas arrived at with a great deal of trouble, in contrast to the bubbles which rise up through it, making a froth at the top that can easily be blown away; that is, Osric's superficial cleverness disappears as soon as he is put to the test.

187-91. Hardly has Osric gone than another messenger (perhaps Claudius thought Osric took too long over the last errand) is sent to ask if Hamlet is ready to play straight away. Claudius does not dare to give Hamlet too long to think about how strange it is that his uncle is prepared to waste such a large bet on him when they both know that they are bitter enemies, and that a man who feels himself deeply wronged by him is suggesting a friendly game.

192-4. Hamlet replies that he hasn't changed his mind: he goes by what the king wants. If Laertes is ready, so is he; otherwise, any other time that Hamlet can manage will do.

196. *In happy time:* that's fine.

Osric

Shall I redeliver you e'en so?

Hamlet

To this effect, sir, after what flourish your nature
will.   175

Osric

I commend my duty to your lordship.

Hamlet

Yours, yours. [*Exit* OSRIC] He does well to commend
it himself; there are no tongues else for's turn.

Horatio

This lapwing runs away with the shell on his head.

Hamlet

'A did comply, sir, with his dug before 'a suck'd it. 180
Thus has he, and many more of the same bevy, that I
know the drossy age dotes on, only got the tune of the
time and outward habit of encounter—a kind of yesty
collection, which carries them through and through
the most fann'd and winnowed opinions; and do but 185
blow them to their trial, the bubbles are out.

Enter a LORD

Lord

My lord, his Majesty commended him to you by
young Osric, who brings back to him that you attend
him in the hall. He sends to know if your pleasure
hold to play with Laertes, or that you will take longer 190
time.

Hamlet

I am constant to my purposes; they follow the king's
pleasure: if his fitness speaks, mine is ready now—or
whensoever, provided I be so able as now.

Lord

The King and Queen and all are coming down.   195

Hamlet

In happy time.

197-8. *use some gentle entertainment:* say something polite. As well as wishing her son to make up for his quarrelsome behaviour in the grave-yard, the queen is probably also anxious that Hamlet should pacify Laertes. While she probably isn't certain that Claudius has told Laertes who killed Polonius, or that Laertes intends to take revenge some time, she no doubt fears both these possibilities.

198. *fall:* begin.

200. Even Hamlet's best friend does not expect him to do very well in the match, so our misgivings are aroused about the outcome, as even one scratch from Laertes's sword, we know, will kill him.

201-4. Hamlet's attitude, however, is one of quiet confidence about the actual fight, as he has been doing plenty of fencing practice – perhaps to prepare himself to kill Claudius (but why did he say, in Act II, Scene ii, line 289, that he had *forgone all custom of exercises?*). He will win, since Laertes has been given a handicap – he has to get at least three more points than Hamlet. The only trouble is that he feels unaccount-ably uneasy; then he tries to laugh the feeling off.

206. *foolery:* nonsense.

206-7. *such a kind . . . women:* 'the sort of misgiving that only a woman would take notice of' (probably considering it an intuition).

208-9. *forestall . . . hither:* stop them coming here. Is it a surprise to find the sensible Horatio suggesting that Hamlet takes notice of a hunch?

210. *we defy augury:* 'I, the prince will take no notice of presentiments.' He uses the royal *we*.

210-11. *there is . . . sparrow:* Hamlet again expresses his faith in a divine providence watching over everything, referring to a well-known passage in the Bible, *Matthew* 10, 29.

211-13. *If it be now . . . all:* As I have to die some day, I might as well die now, and get it over. The important thing is to be prepared for it.

213-15. *Since . . . be:* 'Since no-one really owns anything on earth, as he has to leave it when he dies, what difference does it make to die earlier rather than later? Leave things as they are.' As he goes to meet what we suspect may be his death, Hamlet shows that all his thoughts about the pointlessness of life in this world have resulted in a calm acceptance of whatever comes his way, even though they began in disillusionment.

While Hamlet is speaking, the whole court ceremoniously assembles, as it did on the night of the play, anticipating, as before, nothing but a little entertainment. We know, however, that again a trap has been set for a probably unsuspecting victim, but this time by Laertes and Claudius. The king perhaps feels that a public occasion like this is a particularly fitting way for him to get his own back on Hamlet, who once made a fool of him in similar circumstances.

216. Claudius makes a show of being a peacemaker.

Lord

The Queen desires you to use some gentle entertainment to Laertes before you fall to play.

Hamlet

She well instructs me.

Exit LORD

Horatio

You will lose this wager, my lord.　　　　　　　　200

Hamlet

I do not think so; since he went into France I have been in continual practice. I shall win at the odds. But thou wouldst not think how ill all's here about my heart; but it is no matter.

Horatio

Nay, good my lord—　　　　　　　　　　　　　205

Hamlet

It is but foolery; but it is such a kind of gain-giving as would perhaps trouble a woman.

Horatio

If your mind dislike anything, obey it. I will forestall their repair hither, and say you are not fit.

Hamlet

Not a whit, we defy augury: there is a special pro- 210
vidence in the fall of a sparrow. If it be now, 'tis not to come; if it be not to come, it will be now; if it be not now, yet it will come—the readiness is all. Since no man owes of aught he leaves, what is't to leave betimes? Let be.　　　　　　　　　　　215

A table prepared. Trumpets, Drums and OFFICERS
with cushions, foils and daggers. Enter KING, QUEEN,
LAERTES *and all the* STATE

King

Come, Hamlet, come, and take this hand from me.

The KING *puts* LAERTES'S *hand into* HAMLET'S

217-35. Obedient to his mother's wish, Hamlet apologizes gracefully to Laertes for the wrong he has done him (he avoids actually mentioning Polonius and Ophelia), saying that he did it accidentally, in a fit of madness. What do you think of the reason he gives?

218. *as you are a gentleman:* Little does Hamlet realize that it is no good appealing to Laertes's gentlemanly instincts, for honour means just one thing to him – revenge.

219. *This presence:* those present.

221. *a sore distraction:* severe mental disturbance.

222. *nature:* feelings. *exception:* resentment.

223. *awake:* provoke.

225-7. *If Hamlet . . . denies it:* If I was not myself when I wronged you, then I was not responsible.

229. *is of the faction . . . wrong'd:* is the one who is ill-treated.

231-5. *in this audience . . . brother:* 'let me say publicly that I did not intend to harm you; please forgive me and see me as someone who has hurt someone dear to him, accidentally' (as with an arrow shot 'blind'). By calling Laertes a *brother*, Hamlet is making an effort to be as friendly as he can – after all, he *would* have been his brother-in-law if he had married Ophelia.

235-41. *I am . . . ungor'd:* Laertes pretends that he is satisfied with this apology for the time being, as far as his feelings are concerned, but at least he is honest enough to say that he reserves his right to keep the matter open, from motives of honour, until he has taken expert advice about what is the 'done thing' in these circumstances.

236. *Whose motive . . . most:* which would be my chief reason for feeling resentment.

237. *in my terms of honour:* as far as my honour is concerned.

238. *will no reconcilement:* don't wish to make things up.

239-41. *Till . . . ungor'd:* Until I have the approval of some of those with experience of questions of honour, and am given an example of someone in the same position who has made peace, so making sure that I am keeping my reputation intact.

241-3. *but till . . . wrong it:* Perhaps catching Claudius's eye, for the king must be becoming uneasy, Laertes finishes his defiant speech on a more friendly note, but one which reminds us that Laertes's idea of honour is a strange one.

243. *embrace it freely:* welcome unreservedly what you say.

244. Hamlet says he will fight Laertes simply as though they were brothers. Thinking he has cleared the air, he feels cheerful.

246-8. With a good-natured compliment, Hamlet puns on two of the meanings of *foil:* a fencing sword, and a setting against which something bright like a jewel shows up. Laertes's talent, he says, will show up all the more because of his own lack of skill, like a star in a dark sky standing out vividly. Laertes's guilty conscience, however, causes him to take it the wrong way. Perhaps not only is he in a touchy mood but he thinks Hamlet may be hinting that he will *foil* Laertes's plans, and show him up for what he is.

Hamlet
   Give me your pardon, sir. I have done you wrong;
   But pardon 't, as you are a gentleman.
   This presence knows,
   And you must needs have heard how I am punish'd 220
   With a sore distraction. What I have done
   That might your nature, honour, and exception,
   Roughly awake, I here proclaim was madness.
   Was 't Hamlet wrong'd Laertes? Never Hamlet.
   If Hamlet from himself be ta'en away, 225
   And when he's not himself does wrong Laertes,
   Then Hamlet does it not, Hamlet denies it.
   Who does it, then? His madness. If 't be so.
   Hamlet is of the faction that is wrong'd;
   His madness is poor Hamlet's enemy. 230
   Sir, in this audience,
   Let my disclaiming from a purpos'd evil
   Free me so far in your most generous thoughts
   That I have shot my arrow o'er the house
   And hurt my brother.

Laertes   I am satisfied in nature, 235
   Whose motive in this case should stir me most
   To my revenge; but in my terms of honour
   I stand aloof, and will no reconcilement
   Till by some elder masters of known honour
   I have a voice and precedent of peace 240
   To keep my name ungor'd—but till that time
   I do receive your offer'd love like love,
   And will not wrong it.

Hamlet   I embrace it freely;
   And will this brother's wager frankly play.
   Give us the foils. Come on.

Laertes   Come, one for me. 245

Hamlet
   I'll be your foil, Laertes; in mine ignorance
   Your skill shall, like a star i' th' darkest night,
   Stick fiery off indeed.

250-1. Before Laertes's barely concealed dislike of Hamlet causes a quarrel which would mean the end of the fencing match, Claudius hastily interrupts, distracting Hamlet's attention to himself by asking him a question, so that Laertes can have an opportunity to pick out the sharp weapon from among the others. Osric, as umpire, had responsibility for the equipment. Do you think Claudius has confided in him, or has he chosen him for the job because he knows Osric is too stupid to notice anything suspicious about one of the foils?

252. Hamlet modestly tells his uncle that he had laid his bet on the losing side.

253-4. Claudius replies that he is not worried, for he has seen them both playing, but Laertes has a handicap because he has had training.

255. Claudius must be on edge while Laertes shuffles through the foils, trying to find the right one, but finally he does.

256. Hamlet, on the contrary, does not bother to examine them all, but takes the first that suits him. *have all a length?* are all the same length? This casual question shows how entirely unsuspicious Hamlet is.

258-70. To distract everyone's attention while Laertes applies poison to his foil (how might he do this?), Claudius makes a speech which also allows him to advertise his good relationship with his nephew, and, drinking a toast to him, promises him the present of a large pearl if he wins the first or second round.

258. *stoups:* drinking vessels.

260. *quit . . . exchange:* score a return hit in the third round.

261. *ordnance:* guns. See Act I, Scene ii, lines 125-8, for this custom of firing guns when the king drank a health.

262. *better breath:* success in the match.

263. *union:* a large pearl. It was a custom to drop a gift, such as a jewel, in the wine of the recipient.

266. *kettle:* kettle-drum. *to the trumpet speak:* signal to the trumpets to sound.

267-8. The sound of the trumpets will be the signal for the guns to go off, whose thunder will re-echo back from the sky.

270. *bear a wary eye:* keep a good look-out.

Laertes   You mock me, sir.

Hamlet

No, by this hand.

King

Give them the foils, young Osric. Cousin Hamlet,   250
You know the wager?

Hamlet   Very well, my lord;
Your Grace has laid the odds a' th' weaker side.

King

I do not fear it: I have seen you both;
But since he's better'd, we have therefore odds.

Laertes

This is too heavy; let me see another.   255

Hamlet

This likes me well. These foils have all a length?

They prepare to play

Osric

Ay, my good lord.

King

Set me the stoups of wine upon that table.
If Hamlet give the first or second hit,
Or quit in answer of the third exchange,   260
Let all the battlements their ordnance fire;
The King shall drink to Hamlet's better breath,
And in the cup an union shall he throw,
Richer than that which four successive kings
In Denmark's crown have worn. Give me the cups;   265
And let the kettle to the trumpet speak,
The trumpet to the cannoneer without,
The cannons to the heavens, the heaven to earth,
'Now the King drinks to Hamlet'. Come, begin—
And you, the judges, bear a wary eye.   270

Hamlet

Come on, sir.

Laertes   Come, my lord.

They play

272. After some fencing, to most people's surprise it is Hamlet, not Laertes, who scores the first hit. Perhaps Laertes, not fancying after all the task ahead of him, is not playing his best. *palpable:* definite.

273-4. Ignoring Laertes's readiness to go on, Claudius, seeing Hamlet may well win the match, and prevent Laertes even scratching him with the poisoned sword, brings the reserve part of his carefully prepared plan into play, drinking a toast, as he had promised, to Hamlet (perhaps from the very cup that he offers Hamlet) and dropping the huge pearl, which we guess contains the poison, into the wine that he offers Hamlet. All this is accompanied by the ceremonious ain of drums, trumpets and cannon. To our relief, and Claudius's disappointment, Hamlet refuses to drink. He goes on to score another hit.

278. *A touch . . . confess't:* I agree you did just touch me.

279. In spite of the fact that all three plans now seem likely to miscarry, Claudius has the presence of mind to play the part of the proud stepfather.

279-80. In the interval before the third round, the queen affectionately offers her handkerchief to her son to wipe his forehead, for the fighting has been brisk – Laertes has been told to keep the pace up, in order to make Hamlet thirsty. *fat:* sweaty, not stout (compare Act I, Scene v, line 32). *scant:* short.

281. From now on, one terrible event follows another, thick and fast, to the bewilderment and consternation of those watching. First, the queen unsuspectingly picks up the poisoned cup to imitate her husband in drinking good luck to Hamlet.

282. Hamlet's reply probably means something like 'thank you'.

282-3. For once, Claudius is not able to think in time of a way of preventing disaster. Desperately he asks his wife not to drink the wine, and helplessly he watches her do so with a playful apology for disobeying him.

285. His mother must have offered Hamlet the cup again, for again he refuses to drink.

286. The queen's last actions and words reconcile us to the weaker side of her nature for they are all full of a tender, motherly concern for her son.

Hamlet   One.

Laertes   No.

Hamlet   Judgment?

Osric

A hit, a very palpable hit.

Laertes

Well, again.

King

Stay, give me drink. Hamlet, this pearl is thine;
Here's to thy health.

Drum, trumpets and shot

                  Give him the cup.   275

Hamlet

I'll play this bout first; set it by awhile.
Come.

They play

Another hit; what say you?

Laertes

A touch, a touch, I do confess't.

King

Our son shall win.

Queen   He's fat, and scant of breath.
Here, Hamlet, take my napkin, rub thy brows.   280
The Queen carouses to thy fortune, Hamlet.

Hamlet

Good madam!

King   Gertrude, do not drink.

Queen

I will, my lord; I pray you pardon me.

King [*Aside*]

It is the poison'd cup; it is too late.

Hamlet

I dare not drink yet, madam; by and by.   285

Queen

Come, let me wipe thy face.

317

287. Meanwhile, forming a contrast with the innocent mother-and-son group, Laertes has a surreptitious word with the king, who replies numbly, as though he is past caring about, or hoping for much from the fight, for in a moment not only will his wife die but his poisoning attempt will be revealed. He hasn't got a story ready for this event.

288-92. For a moment, Laertes wavers about whether he is right or not in attempting to kill Hamlet, but a teasing remark from the prince decides him.

289. *dally:* play around.

290. *pass . . . violence:* fight as hard as you can.

291. *make a wanton of me:* are trifling with me.

293. Now that Laertes is on his mettle, the third round ends in a draw.

294. Suddenly, in desperation, in what should be the interval, Laertes lunges at Hamlet, and manages to wound him. As soon as this happens, Hamlet must realize that all is not above-board, and he manages to obtain Laertes's sharpened sword (not knowing, of course, that it is also poisoned) and wounds him in turn. What methods are there of arranging this exchange convincingly on the stage? As during the fight in the graveyard, Claudius is anxious to separate the two young men, but now for a different reason: who will the furious Hamlet attack next with the deadly sword? *incens'd:* beside themselves with anger.

295. As Hamlet, whose blood is now thoroughly up, tries to attack Laertes again, the queen faints; the poison has begun to work.

296. Horatio, like most of the court, is bewildered about the fact that a fencing foil could cause a wound, and is anxious, as always, about his friend's well-being, for Hamlet is beginning to show the effects of the poison, as is Laertes. The fight is over.

298-9. Laertes repentantly says that he has caught himself like a bird in his own trap; he has been killed by his own wicked plot, and it serves him right

300. Hamlet barely hears what Laertes has said, for all his attention is for his mother.

300-2. Claudius is ready with a lie by now, but his wife foils his attempt to safeguard himself; her last desperate warning to her son, though coming too late to save his life, enables our last impression of her to be of the best side of her nature.

Laertes
  My lord, I'll hit him now.
King   I do not think't.
Laertes [*Aside*]
  And yet it is almost against my conscience.
Hamlet
  Come, for the third. Laertes, you do but dally;
  I pray you pass with your best violence;   290
  I am afeard you make a wanton of me.
Laertes
  Say you so? Come on.

                        They play

Osric
  Nothing, neither way.
Laertes
  Have at you now!

    LAERTES *wounds* HAMLET: *then, in scuffling, they*
      change rapiers, and HAMLET *wounds* LAERTES

King
                    Part them; they are incens'd.
Hamlet
  Nay, come again.

                    The QUEEN *falls*

Osric   Look to the Queen there, ho!   295
Horatio
  They bleed on both sides. How is it, my lord?
Osric
  How is't, Laertes?
Laertes
  Why, as a woodcock, to mine own springe, Osric;
  I am justly kill'd with mine own treachery.
Hamlet
  How does the Queen?
King   She swoons to see them bleed.   300

303-4. In an emergency like this, Hamlet's royal blood shows itself. Taking command of the situation, unaware that he too is doomed to die shortly, he forbids anyone to go until the culprit is found.

305-12. Knowing that he has only a few moments to live, Laertes confesses his guilt, in an attempt to clear his conscience as far as possible before he goes to his death.

305. *slain:* as good as dead.

308. *The treacherous instrument:* the poisoned sword, which Hamlet is still clutching.

309. *Unbated and envenom'd:* not blunted, as a fencing foil should be, sharp, and poisoned. *practice:* trick.

312. *can:* can say.

313-14. There is no need now for Hamlet to wonder about the pros and cons of killing his uncle. In the heat of the moment it is the obvious thing to do (as when he slew the 'rat', Polonius), and in spite of the fact that he, too, is weakened by the poison in his system, he stabs the king violently with the poisoned sword before anyone can interfere, in full view of the panic-stricken courtiers, who have not had time to grasp what Laertes has said about Claudius, but only realize that an assassination is taking place before their very eyes.

316. Unlike the queen and Laertes, Claudius's last words show no concern for anyone else or for the state of his soul, but are just an undignified plea for help. *yet:* still. *but:* only.

317-19. Hamlet, however, forces him to drink up the poison till the hypocritical present of the pearl is revealed at the bottom of the cup. Hamlet makes a bitter joke, punning with the two meanings of *union*, saying that the poison in the pearl will unite Claudius with his wife. Claudius, then, is suitably finished off with all three methods he employed against Hamlet: sword wounds, and two kinds of poison. Hamlet has at last obtained his revenge – but at what a price!

319. *He is justly served:* he has had what he deserves.

320. *temper'd:* prepared.

321-3. Laertes's last words, obtaining forgiveness from Hamlet in return for pardoning him for Polonius's and Ophelia's deaths, allow him to die with a better chance in the afterlife than Claudius. (Why does Hamlet live on for a while after Laertes, though he was poisoned first? How could a stage production make this point convincing?)

Queen
> No, no, the drink, the drink! O my dear Hamlet!
> The drink, the drink! I am poison'd.

Dies

Hamlet
> O, villainy! Ho! let the door be lock'd.
> Treachery! seek it out.

LAERTES *falls*

Laertes
> It is here, Hamlet. Hamlet, thou art slain;   305
> No med'cine in the world can do thee good;
> In thee there is not half an hour's life;
> The treacherous instrument is in thy hand,
> Unbated and envenom'd. The foul practice
> Hath turn'd itself on me; lo, here I lie,   310
> Never to rise again. Thy mother's poison'd.
> I can no more. The King, the King's to blame.

Hamlet
> The point envenom'd too!
> Then, venom, to thy work.

Stabs the KING

All
> Treason! treason!   315

King
> O, yet defend me, friends; I am but hurt.

Hamlet
> Here, thou incestuous, murd'rous, damned Dane,
> Drink off this potion. Is thy union here?
> Follow my mother.

KING *dies*

Laertes   He is justly serv'd:
> It is a poison temper'd by himself.   320
> Exchange forgiveness with me, noble Hamlet.

324. *free:* not guilty. *I follow thee:* After the spurt of energy caused by his anger, Hamlet begins to feel weaker and weaker.

325. *dead:* as good as dead.

326-32. *You that . . . unsatisfied:* Remembering that he has responsibilities towards the country of which, for a few moments, he is king, and also concerned for the reputation he is leaving behind him, Hamlet's dying wish is that Horatio should tell everyone the truth, since he cannot.

326. *chance:* incident.

327. *mutes:* silent actors, 'supers'. Even at this point, Hamlet's wry sense of humour does not desert him, as he puns with *act*, using it in its dramatic sense, as well as its usual meaning; he is irresistibly reminded by the gaping faces of the court of an audience at one of the plays sometimes performed in this hall.

328-9. *this fell sergeant . . . arrest:* Hamlet feels death is seizing him firmly, like a sheriff's officer arresting him. *fell:* deadly.

330. *let it be:* never mind.

331-2. *report . . . unsatisfied:* give a truthful account of me and the motives for which I sought revenge, to those who demand an explanation.

332-4. Horatio, who throughout the play has provided a staunch, almost stolidly sensible contrast to his friend, now shows that his feelings, though so controlled, are strong. He would rather commit suicide, he says, than live on now, and he tries to drink the dregs of the poison from the fatal cup. For the ancient Romans, suicide was an honourable way out of a dead-end situation, such as defeat in battle.

334-41. With a frantic effort, Hamlet manages to grab the cup from Horatio, telling him what a damaged reputation he will leave behind him, if everything is left a mystery. He asks him to forgo the happiness of death for a while, and suffer in this world, while he explains the mysteries of Hamlet's life and death.

341-4. *What warlike noise . . . volley:* The sound of soldiers marching to a drum, and of gun-salutes off-stage, suddenly reminds us of the outside world. It is the almost-forgotten Fortinbras, coming back from his successful campaign in Poland, greeting the English ambassadors who have come with the news that Rosencrantz and Guildenstern have been put to death, according to the forged instructions.

345. *o'ercrows:* triumphs over.

346-50. Concerned about his country's future, Hamlet foretells that Fortinbras will be elected king, and, with his last breath, gives him his support (which would go a long way in influencing the voters). Why does he choose him, when he is not even a Dane?

Mine and my father's death come not upon thee,
Nor thine on me!

Dies

Hamlet
Heaven make thee free of it! I follow thee.
I am dead, Horatio. Wretched queen, adieu!   325
You that look pale and tremble at this chance,
That are but mutes or audience to this act,
Had I but time, as this fell sergeant Death
Is strict in his arrest, O, I could tell you—
But let it be. Horatio, I am dead: 330
Thou livest; report me and my cause aright
To the unsatisfied.
Horatio   Never believe it.
I am more an antique Roman than a Dane;
Here's yet some liquor left.
Hamlet   As th'art a man,
Give me the cup. Let go. By heaven, I'll ha't.   335
O God! Horatio, what a wounded name,
Things standing thus unknown, shall live behind me!
If thou didst ever ·hold me in thy heart,
Absent thee from felicity awhile,
And in this harsh world draw thy breath in pain,   340
To tell my story.

March afar off, and shot within

What warlike noise is this?
Osric
Young Fortinbras, with conquest come from Poland,
To th' ambassadors of England gives
This warlike volley.
Hamlet   O, I die, Horatio!
The potent poison quite o'er-crows my spirit.   345
I cannot hear the news from England,
But I do prophesy th' election lights
On Fortinbras; he has my dying voice.

351-2. *Good night . . . rest:* Horatio's gentle words convey a feeling that death for Hamlet will be a quiet sleep – none of the bad dreams that he feared (Act III, Scene i, lines 65-8) will be there, only the peace of heaven.

353-6. However, it is not the songs of angels but the warlike sound of the drums that breaks in on the moment of silence. Someone has gone to tell Fortinbras what has happened, and he and the English ambassadors now briskly enter the hall, accompanied by the military ceremonial of drums and banners (*colours*) but they pause with horror at the spectacle before them. We suddenly become aware of how it must look to an outsider: the corpses of all three members of the Danish royal family, together with that of another young man, are lying amid blood, scattered swords and spilt wine, signs of a violent struggle are everywhere, and the remaining courtiers are so dazed and horrified that not one of them, except Horatio, seems able to utter a word. The scene looks more like the aftermath of a ruthless day's hunting than anything else (*quarry* and *havoc* are hunting terms for 'heap of carcasses' and 'wholesale slaughter').

355. *If ought . . . search:* If you are looking for something dreadful, here it is.

356-59. With a grim joke, Fortinbras says it looks as if death has planned a banquet. *toward:* in the offing, planned. *thine eternal cell:* death's home, the grave.

358. *at a shot:* at one go.

359-4. *The sight . . . thanks:* The ambassadors seem as much put out as horrified, as now they do not know whom to give their message to; they have probably been hoping for some sort of reward.

360. *affairs:* messages.

361-2. *The ears . . . fulfill'd:* The king, being dead, is not able to receive the news that his orders have been carried out.

364-6. *Not . . . death:* Horatio doesn't waste any sympathy on them, saying that even if Claudius were alive and could speak he wouldn't be grateful to them, as the orders were not his.

367-72. *But since . . . about:* He goes on to say that, since they have arrived so promptly after the bloodshed, Fortinbras and the ambassadors must take charge of the situation, laying the bodies in state on a platform and allowing him to explain in public how it all happened.

So tell him, with th' occurrents, more and less,
Which have solicited—the rest is silence.   350

Dies

Horatio

Now cracks a noble heart. Good night, sweet prince,
And flights of angels sing thee to thy rest!

March within

Why does the drum come hither?

Enter FORTINBRAS *and* ENGLISH AMBASSADORS, *with drum, colours and* ATTENDANTS

Fortinbras

Where is this sight?

Horatio   What is it you would see?
If aught of woe or wonder, cease your search.   355

Fortinbras

This quarry cries on havoc. O proud death,
What feast is toward in thine eternal cell
That thou so many princes at a shot
So bloodily hast struck?

First Ambassador   The sight is dismal;
And our affairs from England come too late: 360
The ears are senseless that should give us hearing
To tell him his commandment is fulfill'd,
That Rosencrantz and Guildenstern are dead.
Where should we have our thanks?

Horatio   Not from his mouth,
Had it th' ability of life to thank you: 365
He never gave commandment for their death.
But since, so jump upon this bloody question,
You from the Polack wars, and you from England,
Are here arrived, give order that these bodies
High on a stage be placed to the view;   370
And let me speak to th' yet unknowing world
How these things came about. So shall you hear

373. *carnal:* lewd (referring to Claudius's 'incestuous' marriage with Gertrude). *unnatural:* contrary to the bonds of family affection (like Claudius's murder of his brother).

374. *accidental judgments:* mistakes. *casual:* accidental (like the killing of Polonius).

375. *put on:* caused. *forc'd cause:* violence.

376. *in this upshot:* finally. *purposes mistook:* plots that have gone wrong.

377. *Fall'n . . . heads:* recoiling on those who planned them.

378. *deliver:* report.

379. *the noblest:* the most important people in the country. *audience:* the hearing of Horatio's report.

380-2. Without seeming either reluctant or over-eager, Fortinbras says that, though it is in unhappy circumstances, he accepts what Fate has brought him: he has some claim to the throne which has not been forgotten, and which this opportunity encourages him to assert.

383. *Of that:* of Fortinbras's claim to the throne.

384. *And from . . . more:* Horatio refers to the fact that Hamlet voted for Fortinbras. He thinks this will encourage others to do the same.

385-7. *But let . . . happen:* 'Let's get the matter settled immediately, before everyone recovers from the shock, so that we don't have more trouble on top of all the plots and mistakes we have already.' Horatio fears that the country will fall into a state of confusion if the new king is not elected promptly.

387-95. The play ends with Fortinbras in charge: Denmark's future seems assured in his capable hands. He says that Hamlet would probably have made an excellent king, if he had had in fact the opportunity of coming to the throne. He gives him the highest honour he can imagine: a soldier's burial, with full honours. As the other bodies are carried away from what to Fortinbras looks like a battlefield, leaving an empty stage, the sombre sound of the guns paying a last tribute to Hamlet gives a dignified ending to the play and to his story: we feel that this is how he would like to be thought of – as someone who died honourably, having fought for a cause and achieved his aim.

Of carnal, bloody, and unnatural acts;
Of accidental judgments, casual slaughters;
Of deaths put on by cunning and forc'd cause;   375
And, in this upshot, purposes mistook
Fall'n on th' inventors' heads—all this can I
Truly deliver.
Fortinbras   Let us haste to hear it,
And call the noblest to the audience.
For me, with sorrow I embrace my fortune;   380
I have some rights of memory in this kingdom,
Which now to claim my vantage doth invite me.
Horatio
Of that I shall have also cause to speak,
And from his mouth whose voice will draw on more.
But let this same be presently perform'd,   385
Even while men's minds are wild, lest more mischance
On plots and errors happen.
Fortinbras   Let four captains
Bear Hamlet like a soldier to the stage;
For he was likely, had he been put on,
To have prov'd most royal; and for his passage   390
The soldier's music and the rite of war
Speak loudly for him.
Take up the bodies. Such a sight as this
Becomes the field, but here shows much amiss.
Go, bid the soldiers shoot.   395

Exeunt marching
A peal of ordnance shot off

SUMMING UP

Now that you have read the play, what are your answers to its central mysteries: what sort of person is Hamlet, and what are the reasons for his delay in obtaining revenge for his father's murder?

It is important to remember here that, whereas, nowadays, the most obvious course for someone who suspected that his father had been murdered would be to go to the police, and leave it to the law to find, judge and punish the criminal, in Elizabethan times the idea of obtaining a private revenge, even if it was officially illegal, was looked upon with more sympathy than it would be now. In fact, if one wished to be respected as a 'gentleman', one had to be careful to avoid any appearance of cowardice, and to take an insult or injury done to oneself or one's family lying down would seem to many not only timid but dishonourable. How important this pride, not only in one's personal reputation but that of one's family, could become is shown by the Polonius family. This 'respectable' elderly counsellor's advice to his son (Act I, Scene iii, lines 55–81) and his daughter (Act I, Scene iii, lines 91–135) is all based on the assumption that one's behaviour should be guided not so much by a sense of right and wrong but by what people around will think of one: Laertes is to get himself respected in Paris as someone who can stand up for himself without showing off, and Ophelia is not to get involved in the sort of love-affair that will get her gossiped about, or give the impression that she is too easy a catch. That Polonius' sense of honour does not go any deeper than this is shown by the fact that he is quite prepared, when it suits him, to read someone else's love-letters, use his daughter's attractions as a decoy when he thinks there is a chance, after all, of bringing off a match for her with Hamlet, send someone to spy on his son, and make a habit of eavesdropping on private conversations. For all his talk of duty and loyalty he makes no attempt to rescue the queen when she thinks she is about to be murdered. It is no wonder, then, that Laertes, when he is faced with a situation requiring a choice between defending his family's 'honour' (though dishonourable means are the only ones open to him of obtaining his revenge on Hamlet) or doing nothing, and keeping his hands clean, decides promptly to safeguard his own and his family's reputation in this world, rather than to bother about what would happen to his soul in the next. He can see no further than his father has taught him to look – than 'what people will say' – until, just in time, before he dies, he suddenly realizes that he has made a mistake. Like Laertes, Fortinbras, too, finds himself in a situation where his honour is at stake – his father killed (but in a fight which he had provoked himself) by Hamlet's father, and his land confiscated – but, unlike Laertes, his methods of going about taking revenge are open and, when he is thwarted in his plan to take back what he considers his rightful inheritance, he cuts his losses and redirects his energies into making a name for himself as a gallant and courageous soldier, instead of continuing to bear a grudge about the past.

We can see, therefore, that Hamlet lives in a society where it is commonly thought better for a gentleman to risk death, or even, according to Laertes, damnation, than the suspicion that he is a coward who lacks a proper sense of honour. Why, then, doesn't he 'sweep' to his revenge as he says he will (Act I, Scene v, line 31)? The answer seems to lie not in the fact that he has a less keen sense of honour than Laertes or Fortinbras – this, like his self-accusations of cowardice, is so obviously untrue – but that, unlike them, he is the sort of person who needs to think out for himself his reasons for what he does. He is, after all, a university man, particularly interested in philosophy, and cannot be content with accepting uncritically a ready-made code of conduct, as they do. He has to decide what 'nobility' and 'honour' really mean, before he can act, and what way of life is the best. On the one hand, he has before him the example of the court he has grown up in, represented by such people as Polonius. This generally respected elder statesman has attained the highest position, apart from the royal family, of any in the court, and he certainly has a high opinion of his own abilities and wisdom – yet he shows himself to be not only foolish but deceitful. Both silliness and hypocrisy are

detestable to Hamlet. The friends, Rosencrantz and
Guildenstern, with whom he once seemed to have everything in common, disillusion him by showing that they are
prepared to go to almost any lengths to make their way in
the world by keeping in with the powers-that-be. Hamlet
longs to be like Horatio, calm and unmoved by both good
and bad circumstances – but even if he could achieve this
state of mind, this is just a passive virtue, and Hamlet is
troubled by the feeling that he ought, perhaps, to be taking
some sort of action. Like many young people, Hamlet seems
to need someone to model himself on and, as he obviously
can't respect Claudius, who has presumed to cast himself in
the role of 'father', Hamlet worships the memory of his real
father as an almost god-like being, and tends to idealize
those of his own age – Fortinbras and, ironically, Laertes –
who, he thinks, possess a clear idea of the gentlemanly
'honour' that he is searching for. It is Hamlet's reading that
finally provides him with the model hero he is looking for:
Alexander the Great, the brilliant prince whose bold con-
quests and personal gallantry created a glamour around his
name that has lasted for centuries. But even Alexander's
splendour and achievements, Hamlet eventually decides,
were cancelled out by death, the absolute conqueror (see
Act V, Scene i, lines 195–204). So, by the time Hamlet meets
his own death at the end of the play, his preoccupation with
choosing the noblest and most honourable way of life, and
his fears of seeming a coward, have paled into insignificance
beside the reality of death. The things that people spend
their time worrying about, even kingship itself, he feels, are
very unimportant really. Since death has to come, the best
thing is to prepare one's mind for that, instead. It is almost
as though this decision has released Hamlet from his doubts
and preoccupations, enabling him to show himself at the
end as the potentially great prince he had once seemed to
be (see Ophelia's description of him, in Act III, Scene i, lines
151–62). It is not just in the minor gentlemanly accomplishment of fencing that he then shows himself superior to the
Laertes he formerly admired but – ironically, only just
before he dies – we see all the best sides of him at once, the
courage, dignity, wit, humility, generosity of mind, warmth
of feeling, and the natural authority which, as Fortinbras

says, would have made him a fine king. Hamlet's last thoughts, in fact, are for the stability of the country of which he is, after all, for a few moments, the acting king.

To someone like Hamlet, therefore, who is still sorting out his values and standards, the encounter with the ghost presents a terrible dilemma that becomes more complicated the more he thinks about it. It might have been easy enough to kill the murderer of his father if that murderer did not also happen to be his uncle and step-father, doubly related to him by blood and by marriage. Killing a member of one's family has always been regarded as a particularly horrible 'unnatural' sin, and the fact that Claudius has already done so does not make it any easier for Hamlet. What is more, the ghost's orders are that Hamlet is not to injure his mother in any way – and wouldn't it be injuring her to kill her husband? The practical difficulties of finding a suitable opportunity and method of obtaining revenge (he is given both in Act III, Scene iii, and declines to use them) are slight, and seem to cause little of the delay, especially as he repeatedly accuses himself of cowardice – which he would not have needed to do if he knew he was just waiting for a convenient moment to take his revenge. But, the time, place and means found, and Claudius killed, how could Hamlet explain the reasons for his action to the world at large, without dishonouring his mother – who would be still alive – by revealing that she had married a man who had killed her first husband, and with whom, Hamlet seems to believe, she had perhaps committed adultery before her first husband's death? As her son, and Claudius' nephew and step-son, perhaps some of Hamlet's hesitation is caused by a reluctance to drag the family name in the mud too publicly. Gertrude's death in the last scene (indeed, the extermination, as far as we can see, of the whole royal family) removes these two obstacles to the full explanation of the situation which Hamlet is then able to ask Horatio to give to the world. For the first half of the play, of course, there is a yet more obvious cause for Hamlet's delay – his reluctance to take the ghost's word on trust (mixed perhaps with a feeling that he needs absolute proof of Claudius' guilt simply because he instinctively dislikes him, and this dislike might cause him to act rashly and unjustly).

Why, in fact, does Hamlet hesitate so long to take the ghost's word as a basis for action? Why do he and Horatio several times speak of it as though it may have come from hell? To understand this, we must bear in mind that, while very few Elizabethans, if any, would go so far as to doubt the existence of spirits, the new Protestant idea that there was no such place as the Roman Catholic purgatory made it difficult to explain the apparitions that for centuries people had regarded as the souls of human beings who, uneasy in the after-life because of something they had on their mind, appeared to people still in this world, usually on the spot where they had lived or died. If the Protestants were right, and the soul, on dying, went straight to Hell – in which it would be imprisoned for good, with no 'leave of absence' – or Heaven – where it would be entirely happy and at rest, and have no reason to bother or frighten those on earth – the only probability left was that 'ghosts' were really devils, masquerading as the departed souls of human beings in order to tempt someone to do something wicked, and so win him for hell. Hamlet, for instance, might have been damned if he had killed an innocent man (and a relative, too) on insufficient evidence that he was a murderer. What does Shakespeare wish us to believe about this? The sensible Horatio is cautious, and refuses to commit himself, but Bernardo and Marcellus, with little knowledge of up-to-date 'philosophy', are convinced the apparition they see is the ghost of the dead king Hamlet. The spirit itself says it comes from purgatory – but then it would claim to do this, too, if it were a devil, to explain its presence. It does tell the truth, as it turns out, about Claudius, but the witches in Shakespeare's *Macbeth* also told the truth in order to tempt their victim into committing murder, and drove him first into sleeplessness, then madness – how similar this is to what happened to Hamlet! It is for us, then, to decide whether we think the ghost is genuine, but not forgetting that Hamlet, who is the only person to whom it speaks, is overwhelmed not just by awe but by intense pity, each time he encounters it, and he doubts the ghost only before it speaks, or when it is not present. It impresses Marcellus and Bernardo, too, with its royal dignity, an effect very different from that created by Macbeth's witches. Finally, if the ghost were really a demon, would it repeatedly warn Hamlet against upsetting his mother?

Apart from the double choice which the encounter with the ghost imposed on Hamlet – whether to believe it, and then, how to obey it – it is, in fact, probably his relationship with his mother that explains much of his disturbed state of mind – for he was disturbed before he ever heard of the ghost. According to psychologists, it is common for a boy to be intensely devoted to his mother, at an early stage in his life, and to resent his father as a rival for her love; sometimes these feelings can continue into adult life. How much more extreme must the emotions be when the 'father-figure' is a step-father who has been foisted on one just a month after one's real father has died, and a step-father like Claudius, at that – a man who is the sort of person Hamlet dislikes anyway. The mixture of disgust and fascination with which Hamlet dwells on the physical side of his mother's re-marriage (see, for instance, Act I, Scene ii, lines 139–57 and Act III, Scene iv, lines 65–95, and lines 183–9) suggest that it is not just the fact that Gertrude and Claudius are tech-nically committing 'incest' (see note on Act I, Scene ii, line 157) that repels and disturbs him – it seems a more personal feeling than this, a feeling that his mother has betrayed not only her first husband's memory, but Hamlet's trust in, and respect for, her. If his mother can behave like this, Hamlet seems to feel, then the whole world must be rotten (see Act I, Scene ii, lines 133–7). Ignoring the fact that his mother's action in remarrying so promptly could be regarded as a sound political move, Hamlet, in his dis-illusionment, exaggerates her lasciviousness until he is telling himself that her only motives had been sexual ones. How right is he? Was she just talked round to agreeing with his point of view in Act III, Scene iv, or did she really think there was some truth in what he said? Certainly, he forces her to respect him as an adult, and not treat him like a little boy, and a closer, more affectionate relationship is restored between them, after this scene. Hamlet makes no more bitter remarks about his mother's character, and Gertrude defends her son, as far as she can, against Claudius (though we also see her defending her husband against Laertes: she has not rejected him entirely). Whether she realized how far

Claudius was prepared to go against her son we cannot know. In the graveyard scene she is still using Hamlet's 'madness' as an excuse for his behaviour – whether she believes in it at this point, we can only guess, but her continuing concern for her son is shown by her anxiety that Hamlet should apologize to Laertes, for she, rightly, expects trouble from that quarter. As Claudius tells Laertes that he has to act behind her back, it is unlikely that she had any idea that the fatal cup of the last scene was poisoned – unless she had a sudden intuition – and, even if she had, she could have warned Hamlet quite effectively without drinking from it herself; yet, the relationship between her and her son at the end of the play, and the manner of her death, leave us with the impression that she redeems herself through her affection for her son, and that this aspect of his troubles, too, has sorted itself out before he dies. On the whole, Hamlet's mother seems a gentle, affectionate woman, most of whose actions and words are concerned with the well-being of others, particularly Hamlet, but she is, perhaps, not very intelligent – at least, she is not given to analysing her own or other people's motives and actions, but generally follows the lead of the men in her life, drifting along quite happily until she finds herself faced with a frightening situation in which an unrecognizable Hamlet, who seems to have gone mad, turns against her, and makes her feel the fault is hers.

As we consider this description of Gertrude, it is suddenly clear that, word for word, it also fits Ophelia. Here is another, though less complicated, trouble that helped to bring about Hamlet's 'distraction'. Perhaps the similarity in the two women's natures explains why the queen is always so gentle to Ophelia (except for a moment of panic at the beginning of Act IV, Scene v), and also why Hamlet was attracted to her, as sons who are close to their mothers are often said to choose wives like them. Perhaps, too, this is the reason why the bitter feelings about women which originated in his mother's behaviour are extended by Hamlet to Ophelia, who has done little to deserve the accusations that he hurls at her when he meets her in the lobby. All women, he seems to feel, at that point, are shallow, vicious creatures, interested in nothing but sex – and this has come to sicken him. After he blows off steam to his mother about the whole

matter, the following night, he never sees Ophelia again,
alive, so we cannot tell for certain whether his relationship
with her, too, would have been restored to what it once was,
if fate had not intervened with the accidental killing of
Polonius; but, at her funeral, he declares emphatically that
he did, after all, love her. By then, Ophelia has shown with
pathetic clarity that she is not the insincere flirt that he
briefly thought her, but it is too late for him to make it up to
her. The gentleness and ease with which Hamlet and his
mother speak to each other in the last scene, however, certainly suggest that Hamlet has learned to trust women
again, perhaps through being convinced of their love for
him.

It is no wonder, then, that under the pressure of these
doubts and suspicions, Hamlet withdraws into himself,
sinks into a deep depression, and, at times, behaves strangely.
It would be odd if he didn't. What we can't be sure of,
however, is how much of his 'mad' behaviour is intent-
ionally exaggerated, and why. We are never really in doubt
of the clarity of Hamlet's mind – at his wildest moments
there is, as even Polonius sees, 'method in his madness'.
Even his most mystifying remarks, such as when he calls
Polonius a fishmonger, all turn out to have perfectly
rational explanations. He never loses contact with reality,
as does Ophelia, who sometimes doesn't know where she is,
or to whom she is speaking. Though Hamlet's mother thinks
he is having a hallucination when he speaks to what looks
to her like empty air, Shakespeare obviously intends us to
believe that the ghost actually appears, as he gives it lines to
speak, and it is seen by three other people, besides Hamlet.
In witty exchanges with Rosencrantz and Guildenstern,
Polonius, Claudius and, in another way, Osric, Hamlet
always gets the better of his opponents (though he meets his
match in the gravedigger!). He gives clear, well-thought-out
advice to the actors, and the apparently crazy letter to
Claudius (Act IV, Scene vii, lines 42–6) is strange only in
phrasing, not in subject-matter, and was written at the same
time as the entirely lucid one to Horatio. But there is no
doubt that though Hamlet's *mind* is, throughout the play,
clear and sharp – perhaps too much so for comfort – his
feelings are very disturbed. He finds himself, to his own

dismay, swinging from depths of apathy and gloom to feverish excitement, both of which contrast with the more conventional behaviour of those around him. Why, he must have asked himself, is he so gloomy after his father's funeral when everyone around him, even his mother, seems quite cheerfully to have forgotten it? He is an outsider in this, as in everything, for not only Claudius and his mother but the whole court, and even his former friends, Rosencrantz and Guildenstern, seem to assume that it is *his* behaviour that is strange, while, to him, it is they who are behaving in an unacceptable way. In his loneliness, and awareness of the intense difference between himself and those around him (both made worse by the fact that he has to conceal a tremendous secret), he may well wonder whether he is indeed 'mad', if madness consists in being different from 'normal' people. Even Horatio is not much help in this respect, for, in spite of his unfailing tact and sympathy, Hamlet must feel that his well-balanced friend cannot really understand the causes of the moods that sweep through him. No doubt, Horatio, in Hamlet's position, would have known exactly what to do, for his principles are clear-cut, and he is the sort of person who always does the right thing without, it seems, a second thought. It is not surprising that he sees himself as more like the ancient Romans (see Act V, Scene ii, line 333), than the Danes, for orderliness and self-restraint are more to his taste than the frivolity and easy living, with an undercurrent of malicious intrigue, that Hamlet, too, dislikes about the Danish court. But Horatio's steady-mindedness, while it is a comfort to Hamlet, in one way, makes him more dissatisfied with himself, in another (see Act III, Scene ii, lines 64–75). His failure to live up to his own standards, and his failure to understand this failure, fill him with a self-distrust and guilt that he expresses over and over again. He must be wicked, or a coward, he thinks, if he cannot cope better than this – cope as his father, or Fortinbras, might have done. The world around seems a bad place to him, and he must be one of its worst inhabitants, since he seems so much more a failure than anyone else (see Act III, Scene i, lines 122–9), even though he despises the corrupt society of which he finds himself unwillingly a part. But when Hamlet finds more and more justification for his feelings (Claudius *is* a murderer, Polonius does prove himself a hypocrite, Gertrude does confess she is in the wrong) and also when he has been able to get away from Elsinore long enough to sort his feelings out, and comes into contact with members of the outside world who, though pirates, are *thieves of mercy*, 'good fellows' who show him, perhaps, that there is still some honesty to be found among men outside courts, then he gains confidence at last in himself and his values, winning through to a maturity beyond the understanding of Claudius, whose manoeuvrings to safeguard his throne, his wife and his life have made him an increasingly unhappy and degraded figure.

Behind some of Hamlet's 'mad' behaviour, however, there is obviously something of a 'since they think I'm odd, I'll give them something to chew over' attitude. Teasing Polonius about the shape of a cloud, or Osric about the temperature, Hamlet seems to feel that he might as well amuse himself at other people's expense, since they don't take *him* seriously. Besides, if he encourages the idea that he has gone out of his mind, and puts, as he says, 'an antic disposition on', it will provide a convenient mask behind which he can think his own thoughts, make his own plans, even speak more freely (for instance, to Polonius and Claudius) than he could otherwise. It is interesting that only Polonius, the queen, Ophelia, Rosencrantz and Guildenstern seem to believe all, or some of the time, in his 'madness', and none of them are very perceptive characters. Laertes reserves his judgement on the question (note his response to Hamlet's apology in Act V, Scene ii), Horatio always speaks to his friend as to a perfectly sane man, and Claudius, who is certainly no fool, exaggeratedly describes Hamlet's strangeness as a state of dangerous lunacy, only because he sees that he can use it against him, and just a few moments afterwards he decided that his nephew was sane (see Act III, Scene i, lines 163–5)!

Hamlet's 'madness', in fact, is just one of the double-edged weapons that he and Claudius use against each other in what turns out to be a struggle to the death between them. The other deaths that take place – Polonius's, Ophelia's, those of Rosencrantz and Guildenstern, Laertes', even the queen's – seem, as Hamlet said, just the inevitable results of a clash between two *mighty opposites*. To Hamlet, the fact that Claudius snatched the throne, when he himself could reasonably expect to rule, is only one of the many wrongs he does him – though one that angers him (see Act V, Scene ii, line 65). However, to the court in general, to the average Elizabethan audience, who would be fully alive to the political implications, and probably to Claudius, too, who has no idea, for a long while (if ever) what other reasons his nephew has for looking preoccupied, Hamlet is a frustrated young prince who needs to be kept as happy as possible by the promise of reigning in due course (see Act I, Scene ii, line 109 and Act III, Scene ii, lines 331–5), and prevented from brooding on the situation. Denmark cannot afford rebellion with a restless Fortinbras on its doorstep and Claudius quickly shows himself to be an efficient administrator who knows the art of keeping everyone in a good humour, even while showing them who is master. Claudius's feasts and drinking-parties, too, which Hamlet dislikes so much, no doubt make him popular with the court, which seems quite satisfied with its new king. So the tension between the two opponents builds up, move and counter-move, neither of them, for different reasons, wishing to risk an open clash, until we feel it as a relief when, in the last scene, Claudius' fresh attempt on his life, together with his mother's death, is the last straw, for Hamlet, and the suspense erupts in a storm of violence. In the hush that follows the slaughter, are there any of the characters who have died that we would wish, for their own sakes, still alive, as Fortinbras steps soberly in, and takes charge?

This index is intended to help you to trace passages in the play which have a bearing on certain topics that you are likely to study. It includes some of the more important characters in the play, but is not intended to be comprehensive.

Characters

Hamlet

His mental state

Depression: I ii 66, 68–71; II ii 296–310; III i 12, 165–6 (attributed to his father's death and mother's remarriage I ii 70–108; II ii 7–10, 56–7) alternates with strange excitable behaviour I iv 87; v 116–34; II i 77–101; III ii 265–88, 300–1; V i 278–82; his personality has altered II ii 4–7, 36, 145–50, 294; III i 151–61. Madness threatens him I iv 69–78; v 85, 96–7.

His madness

Assumed according to himself: I v 170–2; III ii 88; iv 139–146, 189–90 (though he contradicts this III i 148; V ii 220–30); but real according to Gertrude III iv 106, 139–41 (by IV i 7–12, 25–7; V i 278 she may just pretend to think so); Ophelia II i 84–5; III i 151–61; Polonius II i 86, 103, 111 ii 49, 92–100; and popular opinion V i 144–55. Claudius speaks of assumed madness III i 1–2 and dangerous lunacy III i 3–4, 189; iii 1–2; IV i 14–19; iii 2; V ii 266, but privately seems to believe him sane III i 163–5. Rosencrantz and Guildenstern echo king III i 5–10. Hamlet teases others with his 'madness' II ii 173–204, 374–5; III ii 313–75; IV ii 9–14; iii 18, 50; V ii 92–9.

Confining madmen

III i 186–8; ii 328–9; iii 25–6; IV i 14, 18–19.

His attitude to people

Claudius: dislike and contempt I ii 139–40, 152–3; v 40–1, 106–10; II ii 574–8; III ii 278; iv 64–8, 97–103, 192; V ii 63–70, 317; provocativeness I ii 65–7; III ii 93–5; IV iii 27–35; vii 43–7.

Gertrude: I ii 120, 142–58; III ii 383–90; III iv.

341

Horatio: I ii 170–3; III ii 52–75; IV vi 29.

Laertes: V i 216, 268–86; ii 75–80, 218–35.

Ophelia: love: II ii 109–24; III i 115–19; V i 263–5; yet distrust: III i 103–50; ii 149.

Polonius: II ii 173–219; 381–2, 391, 493–4; III iv 31–3, 213–15.

Guildenstern and Rosencrantz: III iv 202–3; IV ii 12–22; V ii 57–62.

People like Osric: V ii 82–9, 177–86.

His feelings about death

Desire for it: I ii 129–32; iv 65; II ii 216; III i 56–88.

Detached interest: IV iii 21–5; V i 64–208; ii 74.

Readiness for it: V ii 211–15.

His feelings about his environment

Disillusionment with life and mankind: I ii 133–7; II ii 178–9, 236–8, 298–310, 522–7; III i 61–3, 70–6, 111–15, 117–40; iv 154–7; V ii 340.

His feelings about revenge

Eagerness: I v 29–31, 95–112; III iii 73–96; V ii 63–70, 313–19; alternating with reluctance: I v 188–90; and guilt over his delay: II ii 545–86; III iv 107–9; IV iv 32–66. (For the reason for his delay compare II ii 594–602 with IV iv 39–46.)

His feelings about women

I ii 146; III i 107–8, 135–150; ii 149, 247; V i 185–8.

His personality and character (see III i 151–5)

Gentlemanly accomplishments and tastes: interest in the arts: II ii 320–51, 419–62; III ii 1–48; literature: I v 100 (an author himself in various styles: II ii 109–24, 536–8; IV vi 12–29; vii 43–7; V ii 33–47); music: III ii 341–63; and 'philosophy': I v 166–7; II ii 366–7.

Soldier, swordsman and man of action: I iv 82–6; III iv 24–5; IV vii 103–5; V ii 201–2, 272–314.

Wit: I ii 65, 67, 180–1; iv 85; II ii 194, 207, 215–16, 262–4, 410–18; III ii 91–104, 294–312; iv 213–16; IV iii 18–21, 49–54; V i 118–24; ii 111–18, 131–2.

Courtesy and generosity: I ii 163; v 182–7; II ii 419–27, 519–29; IV vii 134–6; V ii 217–35, 243–9.

Dislike of affectation: III ii 1–36; V i 246–50, 268–78; ii 79–80, 92–3, 111–18; 153–9, 177, 180–6; flattery: III ii 54–63; and hypocrisy: I ii 76, 147–56; II ii 278 (preference

of simplicity and sincerity: II ii 284–9, 427–46).
Distaste for 'the sins of the flesh': drunkenness, gluttony:
I iv 14–22; III ii 91–5, 294; iii 89; iv 184; and sex: I ii
143–5; III i 111–15; iii 90; iv 40–52, 66–94, 159–67, 181–8.
Modesty: I ii 153; II ii 435–7; V ii 246–8, 252.
Self-distrust: II ii 546–86; III i 83, 117–29; IV iv 39–66; but,
at other times, self-respect and confidence: III ii 354–63;
V i 253–5; ii 131–2, 334–41.
His political standing and attitudes
I ii 108–9, 122; iii 17–24; II ii 240–69, 272; III ii 94–5, 331–
335; V ii 64–5, 389–90.
His youthfulness
I i 170; iii 7, 124; v 101; III i 160 (but his age is thirty at the
end of the play: V i 141–55).

Claudius

The king
Authoritative manner: IV v 122–5; vii 30–3.
Diplomacy abroad: I ii 17–39; at home: I ii 121–4; IV iii
7–9; v 120–52.
Efficiency: III i 167–70; IV iii 56–8; vii 148–62.
Flattery: I ii 42–50, 87–8; II ii 1–4; IV v 147–8; vii 71–6,
95–105; and ruthlessness: IV ii 15–20.
The man
Adultery (according to the ghost): I v 42.
Feasting and drinking: I ii 125–8, 175; iv 8–12; II ii 84; III
ii 294; iii 89.
Guilt: II i 49–54; iii 36–69; and insecurity: IV i 45; iii 67–8.
Hypocrisy: I ii 1–2, 87–8; v 106; IV v 200–1; vii 127.
Lechery: I v 42–57; III iv 183–7.
Selfishness: IV i 13; and shrewdness: III i 163–8.
Contrast with his brother: I ii 139–40, 152–3; v 51–2; III iv
53–77.
Attitude to Gertrude: affection: III i 28; iii 53–5; IV vii
12–16.
Attitude to Hamlet: pretended affection: I ii 64, 106–17;
III i 24–5; IV iii 41–3, 51; but really distrust and fear: III i
164–8; IV iii 65–8.
Attitude to Hamlet's 'madness': compare III i 163–5 with
III i 189 and iii 1–2.

Gertrude

Affection and concern for Hamlet: I ii 68–9, 118–19; II ii 35–6, 168; III ii 107, 303–23; iv 3–4, 106, 199–201; IV vii 11–12; V i 278–82; ii 197–8, 279–81, 286, 301–2.

Kindness to Ophelia: III i 38–42; V i 235–8.

Relationship with her first husband: I ii 71, 143–9; v 47–50; and Claudius: I v 42–6; III iv 65–88, 181–6; IV i 5; v 35, 115–22.

Sense of guilt: I v 85–8; II ii 57; III ii 225; iv 89–92; IV v 17–20.

Ophelia

Beauty, grace and virtue: III i 39–42, 103–8; IV v 186–7; vii 26–9; V i 235.

Meekness and obedience: I iii 45–6, 104, 136; II i 109–11.

Piety: III i 134, 142; IV v 197–8.

Attitude to brother: I ii 4, 46–51, 85–6; IV v 68; and to father's death: IV v 66–8, 182–3, 188–97.

Relationship with Hamlet: concern about his 'madness': II i 84–5; III i 134, 142, 151–61; belief in sincerity of love affair: I ii 99–100, 110–14; III i 116, 120 (love affair discouraged by Laertes and Polonius: I iii 90–135; but approved by queen: III i 38–42; V i 236–7).

Association of flowers and music with Ophelia and her love affair with Hamlet: I iii 7, 39–40; III i 157; IV v 36–8, 157, 174–83; vii 166–80; V i 224–38.

Polonius

Boastfulness and vanity: II ii 131–4, 153–9, 164–7; III ii 100.

Bustling manner (fondness for being a busybody and for organizing): II ii 160–70, 385–401; III i 43–4; ii 262, 264; iii 27–35; iv 1–5, 32–4.

Condescension: II ii 464–5.

Flattery: II ii 43–5; III iii 30–3.

Intrigue: II i 3–73; ii 46–8.

Lack of dignity: II i 50–4; III i 132–3, 179–80; longwindedness, pomposity and fondness for puns: I iii 105–9, 127–31; II ii 86–108; III i 46–9; iv 215–17.

Self-importance: II ii 51–2.

Ungenerous: I iii 61–5, 75–7; II ii 525.

Worldly-wise air: I iii 101–2, 115–20; II ii 180–7.

His stupidity is a butt to Hamlet's wit: II ii 171–219, 379–418, 496–8; III ii 96–105, 365–74.

Imagery

Only a few of the more important groups of images are presented here.

Disease needing drastic treatment (used by Hamlet to describe the evils of life and Claudius, and by Claudius to describe Hamlet!)—general ailments: III i 85; ii 193–9; iii 96; iv 73–4, 155; IV i 21–3; iii 9–11, 67–8; vii 55, 117–18; growths and ulcers: III iv 147–51; IV iv 27–9; vii 123; V ii 68–70; diseases of plants (linking with imagery of flowers and weeds—see below): I iii 39–42; III i 159–60; iv 65–6.

Hunting, sports and trapping (used chiefly of the atmosphere of intrigue surrounding Hamlet): I iii 115; II i 62–6; ii 598–602; III ii 233, 337–9; IV v 109–110; V ii 29, 298–9, 256–9.

Warfare and weapons (used to convey an atmosphere of open conflict): III i 57–60; ii 262, 387; iv 96, 208–11; IV i 42–4; v 76–7, 92–4; vii 21–4; V ii 60–2, 234–5, 393–5.

Weeds and rottenness (usually combined, and used to describe a corrupt society): I ii 135–7; v 32–3; III iii 36; iv 153–4.

Fate

Sometimes a blind, haphazard force. Fortune seems to be in control of events: I iv 32; II ii 228–41, 491–5, 504–5; III i 58; ii 66–9, 270; IV iv 52; but Hamlet shows an increasing belief in a purposeful Destiny of Providence: I iv 81; v 188–9; III iv 175–7; V ii 8–11, 48, 210–15.

Man

Potentially the 'paragon of animals': II ii 304–10; for he alone possesses 'reason': I ii 150–1; IV iv 33–9; but one fault can ruin an otherwise noble character: I iv 23–38. People are fickle: II ii 362–5; III ii 127–30, 200–4; IV v 99–108; too easily influenced by their emotions: II ii 574–86; III ii 69–72; and particularly in youth, their appetites: I iii 115–20; II i 22–4.

Contrast of youth and age: II i 114–18; III iv 67–89; IV vii

77–81; V i 61–72.

Honour and Nobility

'Honour' identified with one's public image (so one should cut a good figure, stand up for one's rights, and avoid scandal) according to Polonius: I iii 59–80, 96–7; and Laertes: I iii 29–38; IV v 211–15; V ii 238–43 (both condone immoral behaviour which society either does not know or does not care about: II i 19–35; IV vii 126–48).

Reputation also important to Hamlet: IV iv 56–65; V ii 331–2, 336–41.

Ophelia's idea of honour: III i 100–1.

Revenge a matter of duty and honour: I v 6–7, 29–34; II ii 545–86; III iii 79; IV iv 53–66; V ii 236–42.

Hamlet's search for the most honourable course of action: III i 56–60; II ii 546–602; IV iv 33–56 (esp. 47–56).

Mere titles and riches worthless: IV ii 15–20; beggars can be better off than kings: II ii 263–4; IV iii 21–32; for death shows the foolishness of worldly ambitions: V i 75–113, 190–208.

It is 'reason' that makes man noble: II ii 305; III i 158; IV iv 33–9.

Hamlet himself 'noble': V ii 351.

Virtue and vice

Honesty (i.e. virtue) rare in this world, and Hamlet's time: II ii 174–9, 237–8, 268; III iv 152–4; and weaker than evil: III i 103–15.

Hypocrisy common: I ii 76, 143–51; iii 47–51; v 46; III i 46–54.

Both virtue and vice strengthened by habit: III iv 159–72.

Osric typifies one aspect of the vice of the times: V ii 85–9, 177–86.

Hamlet dissatisfied with his own lack of virtue: III i 117–29.

Religion

(The 'bad' characters as well as Hamlet, accept unquestioningly most of the beliefs of their time, and these form an important background to their actions.) Men often fail to lead a 'Christian' life: I iii 47–51; and distort what God has created: III i 143–7; ii 20–36; yet heaven watches over them;

HAMLET + MOTHER.
- past - close, respect
but now hurt as feels betrayed father.
mother doesn't really try to understand Hamlet
sides with Claudius a lot of the time
mother does not seem much affected by death of father
(eg. p201 refers to Claud. as Ham's father)
expects Hamlet to accept Claud.
   unaware of what she has done (p. 203 + 205)
never enter Queen's psychology as a character (solilig

     POLONIUS' FAMILY
OPHELIA - cares for Ham, Laertes + respect/love for
          father (grief after death)
father dead, Ham mad (+ killed Pol), Laertes away
   pos. of despair, pressures

         _____

honour of family - for Hamlet.
Laertes - revenge father
Hamlet - revenge father.

         _____

p.61 Laertes warns Ophelia.
         _____
        HAM +.

FURTHER READING

Not surprisingly, a great deal has been written about *Hamlet*, and there are almost as many different interpretations of its characters and meaning as there are critics who write about it, each one, it seems, trying to outdo those who have gone before him in the originality of his suggestions. Much of this criticism will mislead the beginner, and it is not a good idea to read any of it until you have studied the play in detail and thought about it for yourself. Then a useful book to begin with is L. L. Shücking's *The Meaning of Hamlet*, which is clear, well-balanced and readable. A. C. Bradley's *Shakespearian Tragedy* and H. Granville-Barker's *Prefaces to Shakespeare* both contain interesting and important commentaries on the play (the latter concentrating on the play's dramatic qualities) but both make some sweeping remarks about the characters. Finally, you should certainly read J. Dover Wilson's stimulating *What Happens in Hamlet* which, approaching the play in a spirit of detection, makes illuminating suggestions about some of its puzzling aspects, and offers useful background information.

NOBLE

Act II, sc II 171.
Act I, sc V 98-105.
Act V, sc I 264-6

"From this time forth
my thoughts be bloody or be nothing worth

V, II 400-5
III, I 151-2
V II 334
II II 92
V II 364-5
II II 303-4
III II 56-60.

| MOTHER |

45 mult affection.
49 -ack mom only
49 - disgust.
53 — marriage.

813
99
169 - offends mum + Oph.
171
173 (148/9)
209
201
205

Finally kills Claud to avenge mum
+ dad.
Ham saves mum.